THE RECEPTION OF JESUS IN THE FIRST THREE CENTURIES

4

Editors
Chris Keith, Helen Bond and Jens Schröter

TELLING THE CHRISTIAN STORY DIFFERENTLY

Counter-Narratives from Nag Hammadi and Beyond

Edited by
Francis Watson and Sarah Parkhouse

LONDON • NEW YORK • OXFORD • NEW DELHI • SYDNEY

T&T CLARK
Bloomsbury Publishing Plc
50 Bedford Square, London, WC1B 3DP, UK
1385 Broadway, New York, NY 10018, USA
29 Earlsfort Terrace, Dublin 2, Ireland

BLOOMSBURY, T&T CLARK and the T&T Clark logo are trademarks of
Bloomsbury Publishing Plc

First published in Great Britain 2020
This paperback edition published in 2022

Copyright © Francis Watson, Sarah Parkhouse and contributors, 2020

Francis Watson and Sarah Parkhouse have asserted their right under the Copyright,
Designs and Patents Act, 1988, to be identified as Editors of this work.

Cover design: Charlotte James
Cover image: The Good Shepherd, fresco (3rd century) in the Catacomb of Priscilla,
Rome, Lazio, Italy (© INTERFOTO / Alamy Stock Photo)

All rights reserved. No part of this publication may be reproduced or transmitted
in any form or by any means, electronic or mechanical, including photocopying,
recording, or any information storage or retrieval system, without prior
permission in writing from the publishers.

Bloomsbury Publishing Plc does not have any control over, or responsibility for, any
third-party websites referred to or in this book. All internet addresses given in this
book were correct at the time of going to press. The author and publisher regret any
inconvenience caused if addresses have changed or sites have ceased to exist,
but can accept no responsibility for any such changes.

A catalogue record for this book is available from the British Library.

Library of Congress Cataloging-in-Publication Data
Names: Parkhouse, Sarah, editor. | Watson, Francis, 1956– editor.
Title: Telling the Christian story differently : counter-narratives from
Nag Hammadi and beyond / edited by Francis Watson and Sarah Parkhouse.
Description: London; New York: T&T Clark, 2020. | Series: The reception
of Jesus in the first three centuries; 4 | Includes bibliographical references and index. |
Summary: "This volume is devoted to the 'counter-readings' of the core Christian story
proposed by texts from Nag Hammadi and elsewhere. Its chapters retrace the major
elements of the Christian story in sequence, showing how and why each of them was
disputed on inner-Christian grounds and reflecting on the different accounts of Christian
identity underlying these disputes. Contributors present material that is often difficult
and little-known to contribute to ongoing efforts to integrate Nag Hammadi and related
literature into the mainstream of New Testament and early Christian studies"– Provided by
publisher. Identifiers: LCCN 2020012531 (print) | LCCN 2020012532 (ebook) |
ISBN 9780567679529 (hb) | ISBN 9780567679536 (epdf) | ISBN 9780567679512 (epub)
Subjects: LCSH: Jesus Christ. | Jesus Christ–History of doctrines–Early
church, ca. 30–600. Classification: LCC BT304.9.T45 2020 (print) |
LCC BT304.9 (ebook) | DDC 230.09/015–dc23
LC record available at https://lccn.loc.gov/2020012531
LC ebook record available at https://lccn.loc.gov/2020012532

ISBN: HB: 978-0-5676-7952-9
PB: 978-0-5676-9697-7
ePDF: 978-0-5676-7953-6
ePUB: 978-0-5676-7951-2

Series: The Reception of Jesus in the First Three Centuries

Typeset by Newgen KnowledgeWorks Pvt. Ltd., Chennai, India

To find out more about our authors and books visit
www.bloomsbury.com and sign up for our newsletters.

CONTENTS

List of Contributors	vii
List of Abbreviations	ix
INTRODUCTION Francis Watson and Sarah Parkhouse	1
Chapter 1 THE CURSE OF THE CREATOR: *GALATIANS* 3.13 AND NEGATIVE DEMIURGY M. David Litwa	13
Chapter 2 THE *HYPOSTASIS OF THE ARCHONS* AND REIMAGINING *GENESIS* Mark Goodacre	31
Chapter 3 JESUS VERSUS THE LAWGIVER: NARRATIVES OF APOSTASY AND CONVERSION Francis Watson	45
Chapter 4 WHY ARE THE DISCIPLES 'LIKE THE ANGELS'? REDEMPTION THROUGH SIN IN THE *GOSPEL OF JUDAS* Jonathan Cahana-Blum	63
Chapter 5 'SURELY THESE ARE HETERODOX TEACHINGS': THE *GOSPEL OF MARY* AND TERTULLIAN IN DIALOGUE Sarah Parkhouse	77
Chapter 6 ATTEMPTING THE IMPOSSIBLE? PTOLEMY'S *LETTER TO FLORA* AS COUNTER-NARRATIVE Joseph Verheyden	95

Chapter 7
COUNTER-NARRATIVES OR COMPETING VOICES? EARLY CHRISTIANS
AND THE RESURRECTION OF THE FLESH   121
    Outi Lehtipuu

Chapter 8
RESURRECTION IN THE *EXEGESIS ON THE SOUL* (NHC II,6)   133
    Kimberley A. Fowler

Chapter 9
LOSING THE PLOT: IRENAEUS, BIBLICAL NARRATIVE, AND THE RULE
OF TRUTH   153
    Devin L. White

Bibliography   169
Author Index   183
Subject Index   187

CONTRIBUTORS

Jonathan Cahana-Blum is a postdoctoral researcher at the Hebrew University of Jerusalem, Israel.

Kimberly A. Fowler is Lecturer in New Testament at Durham University, UK.

Mark Goodacre is the Frances Hill Fox Professor of Religious Studies at Duke University, United States.

Outi Lehtipuu is Senior Lecturer in the Department of Biblical Studies at the University of Helsinki, Finland.

M. David Litwa is a research fellow in the Institute for Religion and Critical Inquiry at Australian Catholic University, Melbourne.

Sarah Parkhouse is a research fellow in the Institute for Religion and Critical Inquiry at Australian Catholic University, Melbourne.

Joseph Verheyden works in the Research Unit of Biblical Studies at Katholieke Universiteit Leuven (KU Leuven), Belgium.

Francis Watson is Professor in the Department of Theology and Religion at Durham University, UK.

Devin L. White is a research fellow in the Institute for Religion and Critical Inquiry at Australian Catholic University, Melbourne.

ABBREVIATIONS

Ancient Sources

Hebrew Bible/Septuagint

Gen	*Genesis*
Ex	*Exodus*
Lev	*Leviticus*
Num	*Numbers*
Deut	*Deuteronomy*
Isa	*Isaiah*
Hos	*Hosea*

Jesus Texts and Related Literature

AcJohn (AcJn)	*Acts of John*
ApocrJas	*Apocryphon of James* (NHC I,2)
ApocrJn	*Apocryphon of John* (NHC II,1; III,1, IV,1; BG,2)
1ApocJas	*First Apocalypse of James* (NHC V,3; CT 2)
ExegSoul	*Exegesis on the Soul* (NHC II,6)
GJudas	*Gospel of Judas* (CT 1)
GJohn (GJn)	*Gospel of John*
GLuke (GLk)	*Gospel of Luke*
GMarcion (GMcn)	*Marcionite Gospel*
GMark (GMk)	*Gospel of Mark*
GMary	*Gospel of Mary* (BG 1)
GMatthew (GMt)	*Gospel of Matthew*
GPhilip (GPhil)	*Gospel of Philip* (NHC II,3)
HypArch	*Hypostasis of the Archons* (NHC II,4)
TriProt	*Trimorphic Protennoia* (NHC XIII,1)
TrRes	*Treatise on the Resurrection* (NHC I,4)

Pauline and Later New Testament Texts

Rom	*Romans*
1, 2 Cor	*1, 2 Corinthians*
Gal	*Galatians*
Eph	*Ephesians*
Col	*Colossians*
1 Thess	*1 Thessalonians*
2 Tim	*2 Timothy*
Heb	*Hebrews*
1 Pet	*1 Peter*

1 Jn   1 John
Rev   Revelation

Patristic Texts

1 Apol.   Justin, *First Apology*
Adv. Haer.   Irenaeus, *Adversus Haereses*
Adv. Marc.   Tertullian, *Adversus Marcionem*
c. Cels.   Origen, *Contra Celsum*
Dial.   Justin, *Dialogue with Trypho*
Pan.   Epiphanius, *Panarion*
Prescr.   Tertullian, *Prescription against Heretics*
Ref.   *Refutatio omnium haeresium (Philosophoumena)*
Res.   Tertullian, *On the Resurrection*

Coptic Codices

BG   Berlin Codex
CT   Codex Tchacos
NHC   Nag Hammadi Codex

Modern Sources

ACW   Ancient Christian Writers
ATR   *Anglican Theological Review*
BZNW   Beihefte zur Zeitschrift für die neutestamentliche Wissenschaft
CCSA   Corpus Christianorum: Series Apocryphorum
CCSL   Corpus Christianorum: Series Latina
CSCO   Corpus Scriptorum Christianorum Orientalium
ÉPRO   Études préliminaires aux religions orientales dans l'Empire romain
GCS   Die griechischen christlichen Schriftsteller der ersten Jahrhunderte
GCS NF   Die griechischen christlichen Schriftsteller der ersten Jahrhunderte. Neue Folge.
GRBS   *Greek, Roman, and Byzantine Studies*
HTR   *Harvard Theological Review*
HTS   Hervormde Teologiese Studies
JbAC   Jahrbuch für Antike und Christentum
JBL   *Journal of Biblical Literature*
JECS   *Journal of Early Christian Studies*
JSNT   *Journal for the Study of the New Testament*
JTI   *Journal for Theological Interpretation*
JTS   *Journal of Theological Studies*
LCL   Loeb Classical Library
NHC   Nag Hammadi Codices
NHMS   Nag Hammadi and Manichaean Studies

NHS	Nag Hammadi Studies
NIGTC	The New International Greek Testament Commentary
NovT	*Novum Testamentum*
NovTSupp	Supplements to Novum Testamentum
NPNF	Nicene and Post-Nicene Fathers
NTS	*New Testament Studies*
NTTSD	New Testament Tools, Studies and Documents
ProEccl	*Pro Ecclesia*
PTS	Patristische Texte und Studien
ResQ	*Restoration Quarterly*
RHPhR	*Revue d'histoire et de philosophie religieuses*
SBR	Studies of the Bible and Its Reception
SC	Sources Chrétiennes
SNTSMS	Society for New Testament Studies Monograph Series
ST	*Studia Theologica*
STAC	Studien und Texte zu Antike und Christentum
TU	Text und Untersuchungen zur Geschichte der altchristlichen Literatur
VC	*Vigiliae Christianae*
VCSupp	Supplements to Vigiliae Christianae
WBC	Word Biblical Commentary
WGRW	Writings from the Greco-Roman World
WUNT I	Wissenschaftliche Untersuchungen zum Neuen Testament I
WUNT II	Wissenschaftliche Untersuchungen zum Neuen Testament II
ZAC	*Zeitschrift für Antikes Christentum*
ZNW	*Zeitschrift für die neutestamentliche Wissenschaft und die Kunde der älteren Kirche*
ZPE	*Zeitschrift für Papyrologie und Epigraphik*

INTRODUCTION

Francis Watson and Sarah Parkhouse

In its most familiar form, the Christian story is synonymous with the story of the Christian Bible, or at least with the key moments of the biblical narrative as identified by creeds, liturgies, hymns, theologies and artworks. In the ancient creeds, the Christian story is compressed into a list of discrete items distributed between three divine persons: 'God the Father', who creates the universe; 'his son Jesus Christ', who becomes human by way of a miraculous birth and who suffers, dies, is raised and returns to heaven; and 'the Holy Spirit', who is associated with the ongoing life of the Christian community and its future destiny. This credal list is heavily weighted towards the second of the three persons and especially towards the unique beginning and end of his earthly existence, viewed in largely passive terms as events he experienced rather than actions he performed.

Creeds identify certain highlights of the Christian story, but they do not attempt to demonstrate its coherence or narrative logic. The individual items become a coherent story only when the divine persons are viewed as agents cooperating to provide a solution to a problem – specifically, the problem of human 'sin', disobedience to the command of the divine creator and overlord, along with the mortality with which that sin was punished. The unique events that bookend Jesus's earthly career comprise a singular divine act of 'salvation' that opens the way for sin to be removed through 'forgiveness' and death to be overcome by 'eternal life'. The site of this drama of sin and salvation is a world created 'in the beginning' by God, and it is the primal relationship of creator to human creature that underlies the narrative sequence of command, disobedience, disaster and restoration.

This story is familiar to anyone acquainted with the ongoing life of Christian churches, whether as participant or observer. It is foundational to that ongoing life, an ever-present presupposition even when not explicitly articulated, and it is foundational because it is taken to be true: not *a* but *the* true story of the world from beginning to end, the universal metanarrative, a theory of everything. When a congregation recites a creed it does not simply remind itself of key elements in the story, it commits itself to the truth of the story: 'I believe …'. Individual reservations are normally kept private. The story may be overlaid by discourses around contemporary issues of personal spirituality, social justice or environmental concern, but it is too deeply embedded in churches' historic legacy to be easily displaced.

The basic plotline of this drama of sin and salvation is present already in the Pauline Adam/Christ contrast: 'As in Adam all die, so in Christ will all be made alive' (*1 Cor* 15.22). In Christ a universal human problem finds a universal solution. Yet that plotline could be developed in various directions. It might suggest a confrontation between two opposed divine powers, one malevolent, the other beneficent. For a classic account of the Christian story in its familiar 'canonical' form, we may turn not to Paul but to Athanasius – also a key figure in the construction of a two-testament Christian Bible designed to keep rival accounts of Christian truth at bay.

Several pages into his treatise *On the Incarnation*, Athanasius anticipates his readers' surprise that he has not so far said anything about the incarnation, which is supposed to be his topic.[1] Instead, he has spoken about the creation of the world out of nothing, an expression of pure divine generosity, and of the privileged status of the human being, made in the divine image and so eligible for eternal life in spite of its creaturely frailty. God put this creature into a garden and subjected it to a law, threatening it with death if it transgressed – which, almost immediately, it did. In response to the imagined reader impatient to hear his thoughts on the incarnation, Athanasius insists that the incarnation can only be understood in the context of the dilemma posed by human transgression – a habitual practice that began in the garden but increased exponentially as the human race became fruitful and multiplied. Sinful humans are exposed to the death decreed by God's law; created out of nothing, they inevitably revert to that original nothingness when deprived of the promise of immortality. God cannot simply cancel that outcome, for an arbitrary intervention of that kind would compromise both his own integrity and the orderly nature of his creation. Equally, however, God cannot allow that outcome to have the final word. He cares about the human creature, which he created in his own image, and he cannot simply acquiesce in its loss. And so, in the person of his own Word or Son, God assumes human flesh in a virginal womb and is born as a human child in order to take upon himself the death decreed by the law. In that death all humans die, and they participate likewise

---

1. English translations in *St. Athanasius: Select Works and Letters*, NPNF 4, ed. Henry Wace (repr. Grand Rapids, MI: Eerdmans, 1975), 36–67; *Christology of the Later Fathers*, Library of Christian Classics 3, ed. Edward Rochie Hardy (London: SCM Press, 1954), 55–110; Greek text with English translation, R. W. Thomson, *Athanasius, Contra Gentes and De Incarnatione*, Oxford Early Christian Texts (Oxford: Oxford University Press, 1971). The summary here is based on *De Inc.* 1–10. The *De Incarnatione* is the second of a pair of treatises regarded by Jerome as a single work ('Adversus Gentes libri duo', *De Viris Illustribus* 87). This work has been widely regarded as early, predating the Council of Nicaea, but its date is disputed; see Khaled Anatolios, *Athanasius: The Coherence of His Thought* (London: Routledge, 1998), 26–30, arguing for a date in the early years of Athanasius's episcopate, 328–35.

in the rising from death that follows it. As in Adam all die, so in Christ will all be made alive: Athanasius attempts to develop the Pauline antithesis into a well-organized and coherent story, which as such can and should be accepted as true.

Athanasius's retelling of the standard Christian story is one among many and is in no sense definitive. While each retelling may have its own distinctive emphases and nuances, however, there is overall a high degree of stability – which is why we can still describe this story as 'familiar'. Themes of creation, fall, incarnation, atonement and resurrection are still in wide circulation, in defiance of their anomalous status within dominant contemporary worldviews.

This stability is dependent in part on the concept of a fixed canonical boundary, another area in which Athanasius played an important role. In his Easter letter of 367, Athanasius lists the contents of both the Old and the New Testaments, twenty-two books like the letters of the Hebrew alphabet in the one case, twenty-seven often shorter books on the other.[2] In listing the contents of these two collections in sequence, Athanasius underlines their coherence. The divine agent who appears on the scene at the beginning of one collection – creating the world, requiring obedience, punishing transgression – is also the one everywhere presupposed in the four parallel texts that open the other collection: the God who sends his son into the world and acknowledges him in speech at his baptism and transfiguration and in act at his resurrection. Athanasius's emergent Christian Bible is a greatly extended and enhanced version of the standard Christian story. The two are conjoined. Each gives rise to the other and each reinforces the other.

The story as promoted by Athanasius has been retold ever since, supported not least by Bibles that correspond closely to his list of approved texts. It is, then, easy to overlook the polemical purpose of the letter of 367, sent out to churches and monasteries throughout Egypt to announce the dates of the Lenten fast and its Paschal conclusion but also to communicate whatever else was on the formidable patriarch's mind. The approved texts are listed in order to curb the promiscuous reading habits of those who read 'apocrypha' – popular texts featuring prestigious canonical figures as authors or protagonists yet (in Athanasius's view) spurious, dangerous and most probably heretical. Etymologically 'apocryphal' texts are secret texts, hidden from the eyes of the majority and reserved for the privileged

---

2. See David Brakke, 'A New Fragment of Athanasius's Thirty-Ninth Festal Letter: Heresy, Apocrypha, and the Canon', *HTR* 103 (2010), 47–66 (including a full English translation and the Coptic text of a new fragment). For the Greek fragment of paragraphs 15–20 with English translation, and extensive commentary, see Edmon L. Gallagher and John D. Meade, *The Biblical Canon Lists from Early Christianity: Texts and Analysis* (Oxford: Oxford University Press, 2017), 118–29. The more extensive Coptic manuscript fragments are published in *S. Athanase Lettres Festale et Pastorales en Copte*, ed. L.-Th. Lefort, CSCO 150 (Louvain: L. Durbecq, 1955; Coptic, 16–22, 58–62) and CSCO 151 (Louvain: L. Durbecq, 1955; French translation and Greek fragment, 31–40); R.-G. Coquin, 'Les lettres festales d'Athanase (CPG 2102). Un nouveau complement: Le manuscrit IFAO, copte 25', *Orientalia Lovaniensia Periodica* 15 (1984), 133–58.

few who are capable of grasping their teaching. In that sense, apocryphal texts hold a higher status than their publicly available canonical counterparts.[3] Athanasius seeks to overturn that evaluation and to consign apocryphal texts to oblivion. His listings of Old and New Testament texts are intended not just to resolve the issue of canonical boundaries but also to prescribe a reading practice that confines itself to forty-nine supposedly genuine prophetic and apostolic writings and rejects other writings that may bear the same authorial names as malicious forgeries, spreading falsehood under the cover of a pretended divine authorization. Athanasius does not explicitly say what should be done with the many books containing apocryphal texts in monastic libraries or in the hands of church officials or lay persons. He does not need to. If a book is no longer to be read, it must be put out of circulation either by physical destruction or at least by ensuring that it is no longer copied.

There is no evidence of a direct connection between Athanasius's letter and the jar containing twelve more or less intact codices and part of a thirteenth, discovered near the modern town of Nag Hammadi in Upper Egypt in 1945 or 1946.[4] In the late fourth century the surrounding area was dominated by a federation of monasteries founded by Pachomius, and it is likely – although this has been disputed – that the producers and users of these codices were Coptic-speaking monks,[5] who may also have been responsible for translations from Greek originals. What is clear is that many if not all of the works distributed across these volumes would be potential victims of Athanasius's ban. Two of them flaunt their apocryphal status by employing the word 'Apocryphon', alleging the authorship of the apostles John and James respectively (NHC II,1, III,1, IV,1: *Apocryphon of*

---

3. See *4 Ezra* 14.44–47, where Ezra is commanded to make public twenty-four of the books he has had rewritten, to be read by both the worthy and the unworthy, but to restrict a further seventy books to the wise – 'for in them is the spring of understanding, the fountain of wisdom, and the river of knowledge' (v. 47).

4. James M. Robinson suggests that, in the aftermath of Athanasius's letter, the Nag Hammadi codices were 'hidden' or 'buried' in a jar to save them from heresy-hunting authorities and to preserve them 'perhaps for posterity' ('Introduction', in *The Nag Hammadi Library*, ed. James M. Robinson, Leiden: Brill, 1984², 1–25, 19–20). The theory that the codices were concealed reflects Robinson's conviction that the site of the 'burial' of the jar was correctly identified by his local informant, in spite of the absence of the expected corpse that would have identified the codices as grave goods. For Robinson's version of events, see 'The Discovery of the Nag Hammadi Codices' (*Journal of Coptic Studies* 11 [2009], 1–21, partly based on an article published in 1979), and for critiques see Mark Goodacre, 'How Reliable Is the Story of the Nag Hammadi Discovery?' *JSNT* 35 (2013), 303–22; and Nicola Denzey Lewis and Justine Ariel Blount, 'Rethinking the Origins of the Nag Hammadi Codices', *JBL* 133 (2014), 399–419). The implausibility of Robinson's discovery story would not rule out a Pachomian provenance for the codices.

5. See Hugo Lundhaug and Lance Jenott, *The Monastic Origins of the Nag Hammadi Codices*, STAC 97 (Tübingen: Mohr Siebeck, 2015).

John × 3; NHC I,2: *Apocryphon of James*).⁶ Two gospel-like texts attributed to the apostle Thomas both open with an assertion of their 'secret', apocryphal status (II,2: *Gospel of Thomas*; II,7: *Book of Thomas*). Among the apostles, Paul, Peter and Philip are also represented as authors or protagonists. In two codices with content overlapping with those found at Nag Hammadi, secrecy is fundamental to the provocatively named *Gospel of Judas* (Codex Tchacos, 3), whereas the *Gospel of Mary* explicitly thematizes its own heterodoxy in relation to apostolic norms (Berlin Codex, 1).⁷ Back at Nag Hammadi, four Old Testament figures employed for authorship purposes can claim the prestige of an antiquity that long predates Moses, let alone the subsequent prophets: Melchizedek (IX,1: *Melchizedek*), Shem (VII,1: *Paraphrase of Shem*), Seth (III,2, IV,2: *Gospel of the Egyptians*;⁸ VII,2: *Second Treatise of the Great Seth*; VII,5: *Three Steles of Seth*) and Adam (V,5: *Apocalypse of Adam*). From an Athanasian standpoint such titles are already enough to condemn these works. Worse still, if possible, was the content of these texts, which in many cases seems to subvert the orderly and coherent Christian narrative as retold by Athanasius and his Bible and even to take delight in doing so. In relation to that narrative they are *counter-narratives*, deploying familiar characters, events and contexts to radically different ends. The chapters that follow present examples of such counter-narratives.

The term 'counter-narrative' can be understood in a number of different ways, and this volume is not intended to present a unified definition. Some of our contributors take a straightforward approach to the counter-narrative designation, understanding that any text that counters another might fall under this rubric. In early Christian studies, a counter-narrative might present the voice of the underdog, the voices of those who were later deemed heterodox. The *Gospel of Judas*, for example, which ridicules the apostolic tradition, or the writings of Marcion, who fought against the identification of the Father of Jesus with the God who created the world, are clear examples of narratives that intend to contradict the Christian narrative that became the mainstream. Other contributors question whether early Christian texts can be considered to be counter-narratives, and for what purposes we might use this label. If a narrative can only be classified as a counter-narrative within a milieu that had an unequivocal master narrative, then certain early Christian texts might only be understood as counter-narratives within a particular time and place. With the exception of Irenaeus's rule of faith (itself a counter-narrative in its own context), each text discussed in this volume represents a challenge to the narrative told by Athanasius, at least in retrospect.

The challenges to the Athanasian account include exposing the God of *Genesis* to be a malevolent and vindictive character, as in the *Hypostasis of the Archons*,

---

6. Codex I does not provide a title for the *Apocryphon of James*, but this text claims the term 'apocryphon' for itself (1,8–12) and names James as its author (1,35).

7. As argued by Sarah Parkhouse in this volume.

8. Or *Holy Book of the Great Invisible Spirit*. For the alternative titles, see the colophon at NHC III 69,6–17. The translation of the first as 'the Egyptian Gospel' is questionable.

the *Apocryphon of John* and in Marcionite theology. This God created the world, humans and the law. On the status of the law, the *Apocryphon of John*, the *Acts of John* and the *Letter to Flora* offer an alternative narrative to Athanasius. We also encounter early Christian texts that present a drastically different narrative to the one that runs through the New Testament as conventionally understood: the doctrine of Jesus's miraculous conception is rejected (*Gospel of Philip*), the apostolic collective is marginalized as true understanding is ascribed to a single privileged figure (*Gospel of Mary*, *Gospel of Judas*) and an eschatology of individual post-mortem ascent replaces the concept of a universal bodily resurrection at the end times (*Exegesis on the Soul*, *Treatise on the Resurrection*).

The volume has been organized loosely to follow the chronology of the standard Christian story. The first eight chapters examine texts that offer a counter-narrative to the aforementioned Athanasian account. The first two chapters deal with texts that challenge the doctrine that the world was created by the true God; Chapters 3 and 4 present texts that question the relationship of the Law of Moses and the role of Jesus; Chapters 5 and 6 present two quite different gospel texts, both of which undermine the concept of apostolic tradition; and Chapters 7 and 8 present texts that question the doctrine of a future resurrection. The final chapter presents Irenaeus's rule of faith as itself containing a counter-narrative and demonstrates that an early Christian counter-narrative is not just a story that conflicts with the account that became orthodox.

The Bible begins with God's creation of the earth and life upon it. A well-known Christian counter-narrative to the biblical story explains that the creator God was a malevolent or ignorant deity and quite separate from the true God. David Litwa asks where this counter-narrative originated. How did early Christians come to understand the creator God as a hostile or evil being? Litwa argues that a key source for this 'negative demiurgy' is the Pauline claim that the creator cursed the crucified Christ. In *Galatians* 3.13, Paul states that Jesus, when crucified, 'became a curse for us'. Paul refers here to *Deuteronomy* 21.23, in which it is God who curses the one who is crucified. How did early Christian authors react to this? Marcion considered it impossible that a benign God would curse Christ, and so the God of *Deuteronomy* could not be the true God. Two Nag Hammadi texts (the *Second Treatise of the Great Seth* and the *Apocalypse of Peter*) deal with this problem by separating the real Jesus, his spiritual essence, from the man who hung cursed on a cross. Other Nag Hammadi texts apply this separation model to Adam and Eve: the *Apocryphon of John* and *On the Origin of the World* present the first humans as cursed by the creator, but the curse does not harm their spiritual essence. Litwa argues that the idea that the curse was inflicted by a malevolent creator was a Christian counter-narrative that generated a hermeneutical framework that was applied to the crucified Christ but extended to wider humanity.

The *Hypostasis of the Archons* also retells the early chapters of humanity: the creation, Adam and Eve, Cain and Abel, and Noah's Ark. Mark Goodacre takes *Hypostasis of the Archons* to be a counter-narrative as it subverts and rewrites the early chapters of *Genesis*. In this text, the characters familiar from *Genesis* take on new roles: they become the characters 'below' and a new cast of characters 'above' are introduced. The God of *Genesis* becomes Samael, 'the god of the blind', who attempts to usurp the power of the new character, the higher and true God. The base narrative of *Genesis* legitimizes the reimagined story. As Goodacre points out, in both *Hypostasis of the Archons* and *Genesis*, the action that is played out in Eden will look very similar. It is the off-stage action that looks completely different.

The next two chapters continue to ask how some early Christians came to separate the Father of Jesus Christ and the God of Moses. Francis Watson and Jos Verheyden turn our attention to Christian attitudes towards the lawgiver and the law. Watson notes the distance created between Jesus and Moses in the Johannine prologue: 'The law was given through Moses, grace and truth came through Jesus Christ' (*GJn* 1.17). He focuses on four early gospel-like texts that exploit this potential opposition between the law of Moses and the grace and truth of Jesus: the *Apocryphon of John*, the *Acts of John*, the *First Apocalypse of James* and (so far as they can be reconstructed) Marcion's *Antitheses* and *Euangelion*. Watson argues that these texts contain exemplary conversion narratives that serve to demonstrate the incompatibility of venerating both the God of Jesus and the God of the law. On coming to understand the incompatibility of following Jesus alongside the Jewish God, John turns away from the temple (*ApocrJn*) while James abandons the practice of prayer (*1ApocJas*). Marcion, on the other hand, provides a scripturally based demonstration of the difference between the two divine beings. These conversion narratives counter the idea that the Father of Jesus prescribed the Jewish law, while also calling for a radical conversion in the reader.

Verheyden offers the fullest analysis of the term 'counter-narrative' in the volume and examines Ptolemy's *Letter to Flora* under this lens. Counter-narratives may originate in subcultures or from the masses; they are identity-forming and inherently political, claiming to offer liberation and emancipation. Verheyden argues that we can read the *Letter to Flora* as a counter-narrative in that it assumes the existence of a master narrative and challenges it; a counter-narrative must explicitly present itself as such. Indeed, Ptolemy assumes the existence of not one but two master narratives, both of which he deems to be false. The first features a perfect God who has produced an imperfect law and the second presents the law as the work of the devil. Ptolemy strategically dismantles both narratives and offers a third view as a counter-narrative. In this third option, the law can be divided into a part that needs to be fulfilled by Jesus, a part that has been abolished and a part that must be transformed by being read spiritually rather than literally. The format of Ptolemy's treatise as a letter exemplifies a communal identity-forming agenda, although its parameters are unclear. The fact that the *Letter* is only known to us from Epiphanius's *Panarion*, in which Epiphanius admits that it has a certain appeal, indicates that it is still regarded as dangerous.

The next two chapters take rather different approaches to two gospel texts: the *Gospel of Mary* and the *Gospel of Judas*. Sarah Parkhouse takes the concept of counter-narrative not as an external parameter but as embedded within the *Gospel of Mary*. Within this gospel-text we meet disciples who quarrel over the right interpretation of Jesus's message, and Peter and Andrew finally deem Mary's teaching and person to be 'heterodox'. Parkhouse argues that the use of this language shows that *GMary* is explicitly reacting against the mainstream or orthodox church as represented by the apostolic figures of Peter and Andrew, asserting itself as both heterodox and the truth. Parkhouse uses Tertullian's *Prescription against the Heretics* to exemplify the orthodox stance that *GMary* opposes, examining the contrasting ways in which these texts engage with apostolic authority, scripture and the body/soul relationship. By situating *GMary* as a self-proclaimed heterodox challenge to an emerging mainstream Christianity as early as the third century, Parkhouse attempts to change the way we see orthodoxy, heterodoxy and heresiological rhetoric in the early church.

Jonathan Cahana-Blum examines the *Gospel of Judas*, a text that is antagonistic to the narrative of the canonical gospels and offers a completely different picture of Jesus and the apostles. In *GJudas*, Jesus is a nihilistic and alien character who wants nothing to do with the world. He laughs at the stupidity of the twelve disciples who are collaborating with the evil God; Judas himself is either saved or damned, depending on the reading of the single manuscript in which this text is preserved. However, Cahana-Blum nuances the sharp distinction between *GJudas* and the New Testament gospels. The former does not portray the disciples as evil; rather, they are unaware that their actions are wrong and they have good intentions, which in the end have positive consequences. Thus, although *GJudas* is a counter-narrative, it does not have to counter its opponents at every single point. In all these texts, Jesus's crucifixion is an essential element in the plan of salvation, but they disagree on the how and why. In the New Testament gospels, the crucifixion leads to the resurrection and mission; in *GJudas*, it is the culmination of the salvific dissolution of the world which exposes the lie of the archons and the evil God. Although unknowingly evil in themselves, the actions of Judas and the other disciples help to ensure the salvific dissolution of the present corrupt world, and thus *GJudas* is a counter-narrative not only to the New Testament gospels but also to the entire world order.

Outi Lehtipuu offers a contrast to the chapters of Parkhouse and Cahana-Blum, who both see their texts as unambiguously counter-narratives. Like Verheyden, Lehtipuu analyses the concept of a counter-narrative. If counter-narratives are a reaction to a metanarrative or master narrative, then we must be particularly vigilant to remember the diversity of belief in early Christianity. Any dominant narrative is in a constant state of negotiation.

Under this premise, Lehtipuu examines the understanding of the resurrection in two texts found at Nag Hammadi, the *Gospel of Philip* and the *Treatise on the Resurrection*. *GPhilip* is a treatise comprising loosely connected sayings of Jesus, without a linear or coherent narrative. A main theme is the importance of transformation through ritual practice, and *GPhilip* treats resurrection as something attainable prior to one's physical death. *TrRes* offers an exposition on the resurrection in the form of a letter addressed to a certain Rheginos by its anonymous author, who was perhaps associated with the Valentinian school. As in *GPhilip*, *TrRes* understands the believer to be already resurrected in this life, and it insists that the resurrection must not be doubted. At the same time, *TrRes* presents resurrection as coinciding with the moment of death. Both texts speak about resurrection of the *flesh* – but that does not mean the salvation of the earthly body. As Lehtipuu argues, the inner logic of both *GPhilip* and *TrRes* is that they represent mainstream beliefs. Neither text was written to act as a counter-narrative as they were not intended to resist hegemonic, dominant or normative discourses.

Yet the wide variety of literature that we find in the Nag Hammadi codices continued to be read after a dominant orthodox discourse emerged. If these Valentinian, Hermetic and Sethian tractates were inscribed by Pachomian monks, the new, stricter boundaries of orthodoxy were likely to lead to the marginalization and loss of these texts. The act of *becoming* a counter-narrative may be applicable to many of the texts dealt with in this volume. We see this approach in Kimberley Fowler's chapter on another Nag Hammadi text – the *Exegesis on the Soul*. *ExegSoul* is an allegorical narrative of the fallen soul, personified as a woman, finding redemption through repentance. Fowler examines the text's use of *GJohn* 6.44, a rare Johannine example of future eschatological language: 'No one can come to me unless my Father draws him *and brings him to me*; and I will raise him up on the last day' (*ExegSoul* 135,1–4). In spite of the 'last day' language employed here, Fowler argues that *ExegSoul* shares *GJohn*'s predominant emphasis on realized eschatology. *ExegSoul* presents a soteriological process that occurs during the believer's earthly life. *GJohn* 6.44, she argues, is a metaphor for the soul redeemed through repentance and ritual practices; the expanded first part of the citation focuses our attention on the role of the Father rather than an expected future eschaton. In *ExegSoul*, the Father is instrumental at every stage of the soul's redemption.

ExegSoul fits within the stream of early Christian thought also represented by *TrRes* and *GPhilip*. As seen in Lehtipuu's chapter, these texts understand resurrection as something that can already be achieved in the body and they downplay the idea that Christians could look forward to some sort of eschatological resurrection at Christ's return. They may not have started out as counter-narratives, but the Coptic manuscripts were inscribed, read and used in a context that would have felt increasing hostility to them. In the anti-Origenist context of late-fourth- to fifth-century Egypt and a probable monastic milieu, their emphasis on realized eschatology would have been viewed as a counter-narrative to Alexandrian orthodoxy.

The final chapter in the volume reframes the concept of a counter-narrative entirely. Counter-narratives do not exist only within the environment that opposes what became the dominant orthodox movement. They do not just exist within lost texts or in quotations from their opponents. Within the battlefield of early Christian theologies, counter-narratives may be found anywhere and everywhere. Devin White argues that in the time of Irenaeus there is no binary opposition between an established master narrative and counter-narrative, original and response, but only competing narratives countering each other. Irenaeus's 'rule of truth' (*regula veritatis*) comprises a narrative or, more precisely, a grammatically sound summary of scripture's plot that emphasizes the singularity and continuity of the divine agency operative in creation and salvation. This plot summary counters the (post-)Valentinian focus on previously unknown events and characters that precede, transcend and reframe the 'beginning' spoken of in *Genesis*. The rule itself is wielded as an anti-Valentinian cudgel, and White shows that the quarrel between Irenaeus and the Valentinians stems from their irreconcilable accounts of scripture's plot. In arguing for the superiority of his own narrative over its competitor, Irenaeus accuses his opponents of failing to follow basic grammatical rules for construing textual meaning.

It is easy to group together many of the texts discussed under the 'Nag-Hammadi-and-related-codices' or 'gnostic' labels, and this has been done time and time again. However, the chapters in the present collection highlight how these texts demonstrate quite different understandings of the dynamics of early Christianities. Counter-narratives to an Athanasian-style master narrative may differentiate an inferior deity who creates and legislates from the supreme God now revealed in Jesus, but no such differentiation is stated or implied in (for example) *GMary*, *TrRes* or *ExegSoul*. Even those texts that do make this differentiation differ sharply among themselves. They may characterize the creator as malevolent (*ApocrJn*), but equally they may repudiate this functional equivalence of the creator and the devil (*Letter to Flora*). For Irenaeus, these are just more or less extreme versions of the fundamental error of denying the divine unity, but Ptolemy is able to present his well-argued case as the *via media* between two equally crass misstatements of the relationship of deity to the law and the gospel.

There is, then, no definitive counter-narrative to the Athanasian master narrative and its embodiment in the Athanasian scriptural canon. Indeed, within a fourth-century context the Athanasian version of the core Christian narrative was itself subjected to prolonged criticism from anti-Nicene theologians who insisted that divine singularity was logically incompatible with a plurality of coequal divine persons. Only with the benefit of hindsight can we speak of an 'Athanasian master narrative'. This point must be further qualified by the fact that the Christian story can be told differently even within the bounds of what is normally regarded as 'orthodoxy'. In the extended retelling of the biblical narrative in Augustine's *City of God*, a pre-mundane fall within the heavenly world is as fundamental to everything that follows as in post-Valentinian theologies or the *Apocryphon of John*.[9] Differences and convergences do not map neatly onto the conventional distinction between the virtuous orthodoxy of the 'church fathers' and the malign distortions of heretics.

Our use of the concept of 'counter-narrative' is not intended to reinscribe the outmoded binary distinction between orthodoxy and heresy, with or without accompanying value judgements. The initial point is to highlight versions of the Christian story that more or less explicitly challenge key features of the standard

---

9. Augustine notes that in *Genesis* 1.3 God declares the light to be good but not the darkness. God 'divided the light from the darkness', and the sacred text hints here at the expulsion of the rebel angels into the realm of darkness (*De Civ. Dei* 11.9, 19, 33). Thus there came into being two opposed angelic communities, the heavenly archetype of the two 'cities' or communities founded respectively by Cain and Seth.

account as attested in credal summaries and in the Christian Bible construed as a coherent whole. Yet the picture that emerges is more nuanced. On the one hand, there is sheer diversity, impossible to map. On the other hand, there is a common concern with two overarching themes: the problematic nature of human existence and the reality of a divine intervention opening the way to its intended fulfilment. The Christian story is told differently, but in its varied retellings it remains recognizably the Christian story.

1

THE CURSE OF THE CREATOR: *GALATIANS* 3.13 AND NEGATIVE DEMIURGY

M. David Litwa

Of the many counter-narratives in early Christianity, one of the most scandalous is the various presentations of the creator as a hostile or evil being. For short, I will refer to these presentations by the term 'negative demiurgy'.[1] My proposal is that some early Christians arrived at negative demiurgy in part because they believed that the creator cursed the crucified Christ. In *Galatians* 3.13, Paul confessed that Jesus, when crucified, became a curse. The text he cited (*Deut* 21.23 LXX) says that the curse was effected 'by god' (ὑπὸ θεοῦ).[2] Early reception history indicates that Marcion and his communities used *Galatians* 3.13 to show that Christ belonged to a different god, a solely good deity who did not – and could not – curse. Patristic writers tried to mitigate the curse or even deny it outright. In texts from Nag Hammadi, the curse against Jesus is acknowledged, but in several cases it applies only to his mortal part. His spiritual core escapes the curse. This pattern reflects a Christian hermeneutical framework which was applied to the early chapters of *Genesis* in which Adam, Eve and sometimes the serpent are said to be cursed, though their spiritual essence remains untouched.

History of research

There have been many theories about how negative demiurgy arose. Gilles Quispel traced the idea back to a Jewish group called the Magherians. But his source for

---

1. As opposed to Michael Williams's 'biblical demiurgy', which is too broad (*Rethinking 'Gnosticism': An Argument for Dismantling a Dubious Category* [Princeton, NJ: Princeton University Press, 1996], 218).

2. In this chapter, I do not capitalize the 'g' in 'god' (unless when quoting modern authors) so as not to prejudge an issue hotly debated by early Christians as to the nature and identity of true divinity.

their views was a tenth-century CE summary, and it is not clear from this document that the Magherians maintained a distinctly negative demiurgy.[3]

Elaine Pagels argued that negative demiurgy emerged out of hostility towards early Catholic authorities.[4] Her argument may, however, reverse result for the cause. It is just as – if not more – likely that negative demiurgy ignited hostile attitudes towards ecclesiastical leaders.

Ugo Bianchi and Ingvild Saelid Gilhus attempted to explain negative demiurgy by the anthropological model of the trickster.[5] The typical trickster, however, is ambiguous and playful, whereas the Sethian and Marcionite creator – as opposed to the Valentinian – is consistently hostile; malicious, not mischievous.

Jarl Fossum proposed that the demiurge originated in Samaritan theology. But his dependence on late Samaritan sources (from the fourth to the fourteenth century CE) resulted in strained and speculative interpretations of earlier texts. And once again it is not clear that his sources propound a distinctly negative demiurgy.[6]

Jaap Mansfeld explored demiurgical motifs from the philosophers Parmenides, Empedocles and Plato. But he admitted that philosophical ideas could not explain gnostic innovations.[7] It is difficult to think of Empedocles's Strife as a personal creator, in part because its main pursuit is to separate the elements of reality.[8] Pursuing a similar tack, Einar Thomassen argued that negative demiurgy was not the child of Platonism.[9]

In 1992, Michael Williams urged that negative demiurgy cannot be attributed to a single cause or process of development (such as a sociopolitical crisis in the period of the Jewish uprisings between 66 CE and 135 CE). He emphasized various

---

3. Gilles Quispel, 'The Origins of the Gnostic Demiurge', in *Gnostic Studies*, vol. 1 (Istanbul: Dutch Historical and Archaeological Institute, 1974), 213–20.

4. Elaine Pagels, 'The Demiurge and His Archons: A Gnostic View of the Bishops and Presbyters?' *HTR* 69 (1976), 301–24, esp. 314.

5. Ugo Bianchi, 'Der demiurgische Trickster und die Religionsethnologie', in *Selected Essays on Gnosticism, Dualism, and Mysteriosophy* (Leiden: Brill, 1978), 335–43; Ingvild Sælid Gilhus, 'The Gnostic Demiurge – an Agnostic Trickster', *Religion* 14 (1984), 301–11.

6. Jarl Fossum, 'Origin of the Gnostic Concept of the Demiurge', *Ephemerides Theologicae Lovanienses* 61 (1985), 142–52.

7. Jaap Mansfeld, 'Bad World and Demiurge: A "Gnostic" Motif from Parmenides and Empedocles to Lucretius and Philo', in *Studies in Gnosticism and Hellenistic Religions, Festschrift for Gilles Quispel*, ed. R. van den Broek and M. J. Vermaseren, ÉPRO 91 (Leiden: Brill, 1981), 261–314.

8. The author of the *Refutation of All Heresies* argued that Marcion's evil god derived from Empedocles's Strife (*Ref.* 7.29–31). See the notes and bibliography in M. David Litwa, *Refutation of All Heresies*, WGRW 40 (Atlanta, GA: SBL Press, 2016), 539–63.

9. Einar Thomassen, 'The Platonic and Gnostic "Demiurge"', in *Apocryphon Severini Presented to Søren Giversen*, ed. Per Bilde, Helge Kjaer Nielsen and Jorgen Podemann Sorensen (Aarhus: Aarhus University Press, 1993), 227–44.

'problem passages' in Jewish scripture, passages that seemed problematic in light of earnestly held theological and ascetical beliefs.[10]

In his later monograph, *Rethinking Gnosticism*, Williams showed that those who argued for the Jewish origins of gnostic thought often leaned on the interpretation of what they viewed as solely Jewish texts (mainly the first six chapters of *Genesis*).[11] My twist on this proposal is to say that negative demiurgy was in part catalyzed by what is usually thought of as a Christian storyline (the curse inflicted on the Messiah) interpreted by Paul in *Galatians* 3.13.[12]

A Reading of Galatians *3.13*

I begin by translating the relevant passage using the latest critical edition (the NA[28]):

> As many people as are from works of the Law are under a curse [ὑπὸ κατάραν]. For it has been written that, 'Every person is accursed [ἐπικατάρατος] who does not remain in everything written in this book of the Law to perform them' (*Deut* 27.26). This is because by Law no one is justified before god, for 'the righteous person will live from trust.' But the Law is not based on trust; instead 'the one who performed these things will live by them' (*Lev* 18.5; *Ezek* 20.11). Christ has bought us back from the curse of the Law by becoming a curse on our behalf, for it has been written, 'Accursed is every person hanging upon a tree' [ἐπικατάρατος πᾶς ὁ κρεμάμενος ἐπὶ ξύλου]. (*Gal* 3.10–13)

Paul's source text, *Deuteronomy* 21.23, records that every person hanging on a tree is cursed by god (κεκατηραμένος ὑπὸ θεοῦ πᾶς κρεμάμενος ἐπὶ ξύλου, LXX).[13]

---

10. Michael Allen Williams, 'The Demonizing of the Demiurge: The Innovation of Gnostic Myth', in *Innovations in Religious Traditions*, ed. Michael A. Williams, C. Cox and Martin S. Jaffe (Berlin: de Gruyter, 1992), 73–107, esp. 87–91.

11. Notably Guy Stroumsa, *Another Seed: Studies in Gnostic Mythology* (Leiden: Brill, 1984), critically reviewed by Williams, *Rethinking*, 221–23.

12. In making this argument, I am agreeing with the general observation of Simone Pétrement that negative demiurgy 'was brought about within and by Christianity, the crucifixion of Christ, the Pauline theology of the cross' (*A Separate God: The Christian Origins of Gnosticism*, trans. Carol Harrison [San Francisco, CA: Harper & Row, 1990], 10). Pétrement herself, however, did not exploit the potential of *Gal* 3.13. Judith Lieu realizes the importance of *Gal* 3.13 (*Marcion and the Making of a Heretic: God and Scripture in the Second Century* [Cambridge: Cambridge University Press, 2015], 114, 254, 261, 382, 420), but its reception in Marcionite interpretation has still not been treated sufficiently.

13. Some MSS read 'by god' (τοῦ θεοῦ) with definite article or 'by Lord' (κυρίου), κύριος being the standard substitution for the name of the Jewish deity YHWH (John William Wevers, ed., *Genesis, Septuaginta: Vetus Testamentum Graecum Auctoritate Academiae Scientiarum Gottingensis editum* [Göttingen: Vandenhoeck & Ruprecht, 1974], 249).

The perfect tense of καταράομαι expresses the completeness and continuance of the curse. Paul replaced this word with the adjective ἐπικατάρατος, 'accursed' – perhaps taken from *Deuteronomy* 27.26 LXX.

Paul also omitted the words ὑπὸ θεοῦ ('by god') in *Deuteronomy* 21.23. Possibly this change was unintentional, since *Deuteronomy* 27.26 left the agent of cursing unmentioned. It is conceivable, however, that Paul already wanted to avoid the thought that the Jewish deity cursed his own son on the cross.[14]

Paul's omission of 'by god' is important because a Gentile reader unfamiliar with *Deut* 21.23 would not conclude from *Gal* 3.13 that Christ was *divinely* cursed. Only someone independently familiar with *Deut* 21.23 could arrive at this conclusion. Those independently familiar with the latter verse were the traditional caretakers of the Hebrew Bible, or Jews. Jerome complained that 'the Jews customarily raise the objection that our Lord and Saviour was under god's curse'.[15] This is precisely the charge made by the Jew Trypho in Justin's mid-second century *Dialogue with Trypho*.[16] Some scholars believe that Paul himself, when an anti-Christian Jew, opposed early Christians because they supported a crucified – thus accursed – Messiah.[17] These developments suggest that the creator's curse of Christ was originally – at least perceived to be – a *Jewish* charge deriving from *Deut* 21.23.[18] The *Didascalia* (an early third-century CE document probably originating in Syria)

---

14. So Gert Jeremias, *Der Lehrer der Gerechtigkeit* (Göttingen: Vandenhoeck & Ruprecht, 1963), 133–34; F. F. Bruce, *The Epistle to the Galatians: A Commentary on the Greek Text* (Grand Rapids, MI: Eerdmans, 1982),165; C. Marvin Pate, *Reverse of the Curse: Paul, Wisdom, and the Law* (Tübingen: Mohr Siebeck, 2000), 215. In the post-LXX Greek translations of the Hebrew text of *Deut* 21.23, god is also disassociated from the curse. See the versions quoted by Jerome, *Commentary on Galatians* 2 on *Gal* 3.13b (translation by Thomas P. Scheck, *Jerome's Commentaries on Galatians, Titus, and Philemon* [Notre Dame: University of Notre Dame Press, 2010], 137–38).

15. Trans. Scheck, *Jerome's Commentaries on Galatians*, 139.

16. Justin, *Dialogue with Trypho*, 32.1.

17. P. Feine, *Das gesetzesfreie Evangelium des Paulus* (Leipzig: J. C. Hinrichs, 1899), 18. See further A. J. Hultgren, 'Paul's Pre-Christian Persecutions of the Church: Their Purpose, Locale, and Nature', *JBL* 95 (1976), 97–111 at 102–4; Seyoon Kim, *The Origin of Paul's Gospel* (Tübingen: Mohr Siebeck, 1981), 46–48; Mark A. Seifrid, *Justification by Faith: The Origin and Development of a Central Pauline Theme*, NovTSupp 68 (Leiden: Brill, 1992), 164–65; Pate, *Reverse*, 150–52.

18. See Jeremias, *Lehrer* 134–35; Barnabas Lindars, *New Testament Apologetic: The Doctrinal Significance of the Old Testament Quotations* (London: SCM Press, 1973), 232–37; Heinz-Wolfgang Kuhn, 'The Impact of Selected Qumran Texts on the Understanding of Pauline Theology', in *The Bible and the Dead Sea Scrolls Volume Three: The Scrolls and Christian Origins*, ed. James H. Charlesworth (Waco: Baylor University Press, 2006), 153–86 at 173–74; Florentino García Martínez, 'Galatians 3.10–14 in the Light of Qumran', in *The Dead Sea Scrolls and Pauline Literature*, ed. Jean-Sébastien Rey (Leiden: Brill, 2014), 51–67 at 56–60; David W. Chapman, *Ancient Jewish and Christian Perceptions of Crucifixion* (Tübingen: Mohr Siebeck, 2008), 241–52. For a different view, see Kelli S. O'Brien, 'The

even claims that *Deut* 21.23 was added to the Hebrew Bible in a deliberate attempt to blind the Jews by making them believe that their god cursed Christ.[19]

What does it mean to curse? In its most basic sense, to curse means to wish evil or harm on another person or thing. When the agent of a curse is a deity, the harm inflicted is often permanent. In this case, 'to curse' can mean 'to damn'.[20] For the Jewish god in particular, speech results in action (as we learn from the 'Let there be' refrain in *Gen* 1). Thus, when the Jewish deity pronounces his curse over the serpent, the ground and Cain (*Gen* 3.14–19; 4.11), it takes immediate effect – the snake eats dust, the ground bears thorns and Cain trembles upon the earth (*Gen* 4.12 LXX).

Paul spoke of the 'curse of the Torah'. Yet the Torah was given by the Jewish deity, as Paul knew.[21] His comments about the Torah thus raise the question, 'If failure to obey the entire Law brings a curse, what does this say about the lawgiver?'[22] To adapt the question in the *Testimony of Truth* (NHC IX,3), 47,15: 'What kind of god is this?' He curses people in and after a harsh method of execution.[23] He commands that their bodies be taken down before sunset. And he does so not out

---

Curse of the Law (Galatians 3.13): Crucifixion, Persecution, and *Deuteronomy* 21.22-23', *JSNT* 29 (2006), 55–76.

19. R. Hugh Connolly, *Didascalia apostolorum: The Syriac Version Translated and Accompanied by the Verona Latin Fragments* (Oxford: Clarendon Press, 1969), 222, 230, 233 (comments on lx–lxi). It is also significant that in the *Acts of Pilate* 16.7, *Deut* 21.23, is put in the mouth of the Jewish teachers (J. K. Elliott, *The Apocryphal New Testament* [Oxford: Clarendon Press, 1993], 184). Herod the Jew is also the one who quotes *Deut* 21.23 in the *Gospel of Peter* 2.5 (Elliott, *Apocryphal*, 154).

20. GMatthew 25.41 (κατηραμένοι, spoken of the damned on the day of judgement); *Job* 3.5 (καταραθείη, Job curses – wishing to annihilate – the day of his birth); 4 *Kgdms* 9.34 (κατηραμένην, of the dead Jezebel eaten by dogs); *Num* 22.6 (ἄρασαί, Balak's intended curse of annihilation against Israel). Cf. Origen, *On Numbers*, Homily 17 (PG 12.711d, *qui maledicit Christo ... perpetua maledictione damnatus est*); Augustine, *Ennarations on Psalms* 108.20 (*maledictionem, hoc est poenam aeternam* in D. Eligius Dekkers and Iohannes Fraipont, ed., *Sancti Aurelii Augustini Enarrationes in Psalmos CI-CL*, CCL 40 [Turnhout: Brepols, 1956], 1596, lines 19–20).

21. *Rom* 7.22; 8:7; *1 Cor* 9.9, 21; *Gal* 3.21.

22. Richard N. Longenecker: '[O]f course, "the curse of the law" is another way of saying "cursed by God"' (*Galatians*, WBC 41 [Columbia: Word, 1990], 122). Similarly, Mark A. Seifrid: 'Paul's citation of Deut 21.23 ... carries the implication that God himself – not merely the Law – pronounced the curse on the crucified' (*Justification by Faith*: *The Origin and Development of a Central Pauline Theme*, NovTSup 68 [Leiden: Brill, 1992], 168).

23. The Jewish god directly curses Cain (καὶ νῦν ἐπικατάρατος σύ, *Gen* 4.11). Canaan is also cursed (ἐπικατάρατος, *Gen* 9.25), if indirectly, by god. Origen conceded that the biblical god threatens and speaks abusively (ἀπειλεῖ ... ὁ θεὸς καὶ λοιδορεῖ) in the Law and the Prophets, and that 'abundant curses' (ἀραὶ πλεῖσται) are recorded in *Leviticus* (26.14-46) and *Deuteronomy* (28) (*c. Cels.* 2.76).

of mercy, but because the land would otherwise be defiled (οὐ μιανεῖτε τὴν γῆν, *Deut* 21.23).[24]

In 1995, Jack Miles published a book called, *God: A Biography*. In this volume, he performed a character analysis on the deity of the Hebrew Bible. He pointed out significant character development in this figure and was not afraid to hide his destructive side. In the fifth century BCE, the playwright Aeschylus – or an imitator – performed another kind of character analysis. He focused on Zeus, who chained Prometheus, benefactor of humanity, to a cliff. In the Roman era, this punishment was understood to be a form of crucifixion.[25] Witnessing the punishment of Prometheus, the characters in Aeschylus's play do not hesitate to call Zeus a tyrant.[26]

Evidently, some early Christians performed a similar character analysis on the Jewish creator – not out of literary interest but from theological concern. Based on biblical stories, they pointed out flaws in his character (that he was bloodthirsty or showed favouritism, became enraged, changed his mind and so on).[27]

Today it seems strange that some early Christians would read their scriptures without the felt need, in Milton's phrase, 'to justify the ways of God to men'.[28] Yet this assumes that early Christians always presupposed that the Jewish god was the universal god of goodness, and that so-called gnostics, as the heresiologists charged, were responsible for a 'split' in the deity.[29]

---

24. *11QTemple* 64,10–11 is the only Jewish text to interpret *Deut* 21.22–23 to mean that the crucified person is also cursed: 'those hanged on the tree are cursed of god [מקוללי אלוהים] and men.' The apparent meaning of this phrase, according to James L. Kugel, is 'it is [only] the accursed by God who is to be hanged' (*Traditions of the Bible* [Cambridge, MA: Harvard University Press, 1998], 873). See further M. Hengel, *Crucifixion in the Ancient World and the Folly of the Message of the Cross* (Philadelphia, PA: Fortress, 1989), 84–85.

25. Hengel, *Crucifixion*, 11–12. For Prometheus crucified, see Lucian, *Sacrifices* 6 (τοῦτον [Προμηθεύς] ... ὁ Ζεὺς ἀνεσταύρωσεν); *Zeus Catechized* 8 (ὁ Προμηθεὺς δὲ καὶ ἀνεσκολοπίσθη).

26. [Aeschylus], *Prometheus Bound* 222, 310, 736, 761, 942, 957.

27. Documented by Lieu, *Marcion*, 337–49, 357–66. Tertullian indicates that the focus of Marcion's attention in his *Antitheses* was the *ingenium* (character) of the two gods as revealed by their laws (*leges*) and powerful deeds (*virtutes*) (*Against Marcion* 2.29.1). See the comments of Winrich Löhr, 'Did Marcion Distinguish between a Just God and a Good God?' in *Marcion und seine kirchengeschichtliche Wirkung: Marcion and His Impact on Church History, Vorträge der Internationalen Fachkonferenz zu Marcion, gehalten vom 15.-18. August 2001 in Mainz*, ed. Gerhard May and Katharina Greschat (Berlin: de Gruyter, 2002), 131–46 at 145.

28. John Milton, *Paradise Lost* 1.26. For theodicy-oriented readings of scripture, see Williams, 'Demonizing Demiurge', 90–91.

29. For the split theory, see Birger A. Pearson, 'Gnosticism as a Religion', in *Was There a Gnostic Religion?*, ed. Antti Marjanen (Helsinki: Finnish Exegetical Society, 2005), 81–101 at 83. Irenaeus already accused the Marcionites of 'slicing the godhead in two' (*dividens deum in duo*, *Adv. Haer.* 3.25.3 in Adelin Rousseau and Louis Doutreleau, ed., *Irénée de*

But what if this view is false? After all, Gentile Christians had no previous bonds of loyalty to the Jewish deity, and they lived in a culture in which widespread social antagonism towards Jewish customs was already fused with theological criticism.[30] In this environment, is it not equally possible that many Gentiles who became Christians considered the local god of Judea to be 'other', warlike and misanthropic when they compared him with the god Jesus revealed in the gospels?[31]

What, at any rate, might lead a Christian to this conclusion? The Jewish deity's belligerence might be forgiven if it occurred under a different dispensation for pedagogical purposes against people who deserved it (*Gal* 3.24). But what would happen if the Jewish god inflicted a curse against the sinless Christian Saviour (*Heb* 4.15; *1 Pet* 2.22)? Perhaps, as Paul concluded, Christ took on the curse for Christians as an act of interchange.[32] Yet the positive result of the curse did not entirely exculpate the one who inflicted it. The curse stands, and Paul never denied its reality. The Jewish deity's act of cursing Jesus – whatever its results – communicates something about his character.

So what does it say about the Jewish god when he curses the sinless Jesus? Consider the popular Platonic presupposition that a god can only do good and not evil (*Republic* 379b-c). According to Philo of Alexandria (20 BCE–50 CE), for instance, the supreme deity cannot even create a being who can do evil.[33] The passages where the deity inflicts a curse, Philo passed over or transformed by allegorical interpretation.[34] What would a Gentile Christian deduce, armed with

---

Lyon, *Contre les hérésies, Livre III, Tome II, texte et traduction*, SC 211 [Paris: Cerf, 1974]); Cf. Origen's 'they slice the godhead' (διακόπτουσι τὴν θεότητα, *On Prayer* 29.12 in P. Koetschau, ed., *Origenes Werke 2*, GCS 3 [Leipzig: Hinrichs, 1899], 297–403).

30. Peter Schäfer, *Judeophobia: Attitudes toward the Jews in the Ancient World* (Cambridge, MA: Harvard University Press, 1997), 34–196.

31. Hostility towards Judaism and the Jewish deity may have increased across the empire after the Jewish uprisings of 66–71, 115–17, and 132–35 CE. For a particular example (the Jewish god as an ass), see John M. G. Barclay, *Against Apion: Translation and Commentary* (Leiden: Brill, 2007), 350–52, Appendix 4 ('The Judeans and the Ass'); Bezalel Bar-Kochva, *The Image of the Jews in Greek Literature: The Hellenistic Period* (Berkeley: University of California Press, 2010), 206–52.

32. For interchange, see Morna Hooker, *From Adam to Christ: Essays on Paul* (Cambridge: Cambridge University Press, 1990).

33. Thus, Philo assigned delegate creators the task of making humanity's lower soul (*Opif.* 74–75). See further David Runia, *Creation of the Cosmos According to Moses* (Atlanta, GA: SBL Press, 2005), 236–44.

34. For instance, Philo quotes *Deut* 21.23 in *De Posteritate Caini* 26 (including the ὑπὸ θεοῦ phrase), but interprets it to mean that the life of the evildoer 'hangs' on the body (cf. *De Posteritate Caini* 61; *De Somniis* 2.213). Philo exposits *Deut* 21.23 in *De Specialibus Legibus* 3.151–52 but does not mention the curse. See further, Chapman, *Crucifixion*, 133–35, 186–88.

Philo's theology (that god cannot do evil) but not his allegorical impulse? If the creator had cursed Jesus, then he could not be good; and if he was not good, then he could not be the true god.

Marcion

This I believe is what Marcion of Pontus concluded early in the second century CE.[35] Admittedly, we do not know exactly how Marcion arrived at this conclusion. But *Galatians* 3.13 – or more broadly the story that the Jewish deity cursed Jesus – could have played a key role. Adolf von Harnack thought that *Gal* 3.13 was one of the texts showcased in Marcion's lost *Antitheses* (a kind of preface to his gospel).[36] Given its importance in ancient heresiographical reports, the proposal remains plausible.

We know for certain that *Galatians* 3.13 was featured in Marcion's version of the Pauline letters (the *Apostolikon*). Since other material from *Galatians* 3 was apparently omitted, verse 13 was brought into relief. To quote the reconstructed passage (3.10–14):

> For as many as are under Law are under a curse … 'The righteous person will live from trust' (but) 'the one who does them (the commandments of the Law) shall live by them' (*Lev* 18.5). Christ has purchased us from the curse of the Law by becoming a curse on our behalf: 'Accursed is everyone hanged upon a tree'. (*Deut* 21.23)[37]

---

35. For up-to-date treatments of Marcion, see Gerhard May, 'Marcion in Contemporary Views', in *Markion: Gesammelte Aufsätze*, ed. Katharina Greschat and Martin Meiser (Mainz: Philipp von Zabern, 2005), 13–34; Jason D. BeDuhn, *The First New Testament: Marcion's Scriptural Canon* (Salem, OR: Polebridge, 2013), 11–24; Lieu, *Marcion* (entire).

36. Adolf von Harnack, *Marcion: The Gospel of the Alien God*, trans. John E. Steely and Lyle D. Bierma (Durham, NC: Labyrinth, 1990), 61–62. Cf. the reconstruction in the German edition: *Marcion: Das Evangelium vom fremden Gott*, 2nd edn (Leipzig: Hinrichs, 1924), 288*, 307*. For recent discussions of the *Antitheses*, see Eric W. Scherbenske, 'Marcion's *Antitheses* and the Isagogic Genre', *VC* 64 (2010), 255–79, esp. 258; Lieu, *Marcion*; Dieter Roth, 'Evil in Marcion's Conception of the Old Testament God', in *Evil in Second Temple Judaism and Early Christianity*, ed. Chris Keith and Loren T. Stuckenbruck, WUNT II 417 (Tübingen: Mohr Siebeck, 2016), 340–56 at 352–53.

37. Translation made from the text of Ulrich Schmid, *Marcion und sein Apostolos: Rekonstruktion und historische Einordnung der Marcionitischen Paulusbriefausgabe* (Berlin: de Gruyter, 1995), 316: ὅσοι γὰρ ὑπὸ νόμον, ὑπὸ κατάραν εἰσίν.... ὅτι ὁ δίκαιος ἐκ πίστεως ζήσεται (ἀλλὰ) ὁ ποιήσας αὐτὰ ζήσεται ἐν αὐτοῖς. Χριστὸς ... γενόμενος ὑπὲρ ἡμῶν κατάρα, ἐπικατάρατος πᾶς ὁ κρεμάμενος ἐπὶ ξύλου. Words in parentheses are filled in to facilitate understanding. See the comments of BeDuhn, *First New Testament*, 264–65.

Tertullian reports Marcion's view that Christ 'received in himself the creator's curse (*maledictum ... creatoris*) by being hung from a tree'.³⁸ Here it is specifically the *creator's* curse.³⁹ The curse of the crucified was inflicted by the Jewish creator, for it is his Law that announces the curse (*Deut* 21.23). For Marcion, a god who curses is *atrox*, a word that can mean 'savage', 'harsh', 'cruel', 'fierce', 'dreadful', 'shocking', 'heinous', 'ruthless', 'inflexible' or 'unrelenting'.⁴⁰ Jerome specifically says that Marcion, based on *Gal* 3.13, called the creator 'a bloodthirsty, cruel judge'.⁴¹ A god with such character could not be the god of Jesus Christ.⁴² The fact that Jesus was cursed by the creator indicated that the Law was opposed to the character of Jesus, and that he belonged to a higher and wholly benevolent deity incapable of cursing.⁴³

The views of Marcion as they appear in later patristic reports cannot be neatly distinguished from Marcion's various followers. But whether it was Marcion, his followers or both does not much matter for my purposes. The data indicates that

---

38. Tertullian, *Against Marcion* 1.11.8. This text was composed shortly after 207 CE.

39. Cf. Lieu, describing Marcion's views: 'The character of that Law and the character of the Demiurge are inseparable from each other, and ... the contradictions of the Law expose the inconsistency and even deliberate deceit exercised by the Demiurge over those under his sway' (*Marcion*, 356).

40. *Oxford Latin Dictionary, s.v. atrox*.

41. Jerome, *Commentary on Galatians* 2 at 3.13. Jerome's witness is important because it selectively reproduces Origen's commentary on *Galatians* which Jerome often copied without attribution. Adolf von Harnack (*Der kirchengeschichtliche Ertrag der exegetischen Arbeiten des Origenes*, 2 vols. [Leipzig, 1918-19], 2.149) identified this passage as certainly deriving from Origen. What interested Marcion was not only the idea that the creator cursed Christ but that Christ also purchased (ἐξηγόρασεν) believers from the curse of the Law. One cannot purchase what is one's own. Believers were formerly the property of the creator. Jesus bought them from the creator. This act of redemption shows that the god of Jesus and the creator are not the same being. Attacking this view was a major concern of Epiphanius, *Pan.* 42.8.1. Further texts are cited by Harnack, *Marcion*, 288*; BeDuhn, *First New Testament*, 267.

42. Tertullian, *Against Marcion* 5.3.9-10. Marcion, according to his opponents, defined goodness by the qualifiers 'mild', 'peaceful', 'compassionate', identifying its expression in the supreme god's salvific action on behalf of what was not his own, and in his refusal to judge (*Against Marcion* 1.17.1, 22-26). Philosophically speaking, gods only bless whereas demons curse (Origen, *Homilies on Numbers* 13.4.6).

43. Tertullian, *Against Marcion* 5.3.9-10, cf. 3.18.1. A later Marcionite report in the *Dialogue of Adamantius* indicates that the creator plotted against Christ and legislated his crucifixion (ὁ δὲ δημιουργὸς ἠθέλησεν αὐτῷ ἐπιβουλεῦσαι, ὅθεν καὶ ἐνόμισεν αὐτὸν σταυροῦν = 74.23-24 in the edition of W. H. van de Sande Bakhuyzen, *Der Dialog des Adamantius*, GCS 4 [Leipzig: Hinrichs, 1901]). Translation in Robert A. Pretty, *Adamantius: Dialogue on the True Faith in God, De Recta in Deum Fide*, ed. Garry W. Trompf (Leuven: Peeters, 1997), 86.

from the mid-second to the mid-fourth century, Marcionites read *Gal* 3.13 as indicating (1) that the Jewish creator is savage in character, (2) therefore not good, and (3) therefore not the god of Jesus Christ.

Marcion's criticisms are distinguished from prior Jewish criticisms in at least two respects. First, they were based on a reading of *Gal* 3.13 and not independently on *Deut* 21.23. Second, they sought to discredit not the cursed Christ of the Christians but the *author* of the curse – the creator imagined by early Catholic Christians to be the father of Christ. Marcion's criticisms, in other words, represent an intra-Christian debate about the nature and character of god. As such, they have a persuasive purpose: to convince Christians that the true deity was not the cursing creator.

Patristic responses

The earliest critic of Marcion, Justin Martyr, denied that the crucified Jesus was cursed.[44] He presented Trypho, his fictive Jew, as offended because Jesus 'fell headlong under the most extreme curse in the Law of god [τῇ ἐσχάτῃ κατάρᾳ τῇ ἐν τῷ νόμῳ τοῦ θεοῦ περιπεσεῖν], for he was crucified.'[45] Justin waited nearly fifty chapters before he answered this objection; but when he did so, he offered a full defence (89–96).

Justin avoided restating Paul's view that Christ 'became' (γενόμενος) a curse. Only in passing did Justin speak of Jesus 'receiving' a curse (ἀναδέχομαι, 95.2).[46] In the main, Justin dealt with the curse by denying its reality: the curse was only 'seeming' (τὴν δοκοῦσαν κατάραν, 90.3), and Jesus was only 'supposedly cursed' (ὡς κεκατηραμένου, 95.3).

In making these points, Justin was keen to defend the creator's innocence. As in Plato's myth of Er, god is blameless (ἀναίτιος, 94.5). He willed Christ to receive the curses meant for all people (95.2). He prophesied Jesus's death on the cross in symbols (90–95). According to Justin, these prior prophetic signs indicated that Christ was not cursed (94.5). Justin concluded, 'The passage spoken in the Law, "Cursed is every person hanging upon a tree", does not indicate that god cursed this crucified one' (οὐχ ὡς τοῦ θεοῦ καταρωμένου τούτου τοῦ ἐσταυρωμένου, 96.1).[47]

---

44. In his *1 Apol.* 26.5; 58.1–2, Justin argues that Marcion preaches another deity superior to the creator.

45. Justin, *Dial.* 32.1. Trypho is not concerned to distinguish the true deity from the creator. Yet anti-Marcionite polemic plays a role later in the dialogue (89.2; 90.1), and Justin argues directly against Marcionites in 35.2–6.

46. See further Chapman, *Crucifixion*, 247–48.

47. It does not even indicate, according to Justin, that Christ was cursed by the Law (*Dial.* 111.2: Χριστὸς οὐ καθηράθη ὑπὸ τοῦ νόμου).

Justin's quotation from 'the Law' is, however, selective. *Deut* 21.23 (both MT and LXX) says that the crucified is 'cursed by god',[48] and Justin's use of 'god's curse' (τοῦ θεοῦ καταρωμένου) in 96.1 shows that he was aware of this reading.[49] The fact that the Christian Messiah was divinely cursed was not lost upon Trypho who used the passage to say that Christ was god's enemy and accursed (ἐχθρὸν θεοῦ καὶ κατηραμένον, 93.4);[50] nor was it lost upon Marcion who saw implied in it a negative portrayal of the creator.[51]

About fifty years after Justin, Tertullian also denied the curse, offering two reasons. First, Jesus did not die for his own sins; and second, he died to fulfil prophecies (restating Justin's arguments).[52] Yet even a sinless Christ can be cursed, and – generally speaking – a curse can still apply even if predicted. The fact that Jesus was sinless and the Jewish deity planned to curse Jesus ahead of time seems, upon reflection, only to worsen the problem.

Elsewhere Tertullian accepted the reality of the curse but avoided connecting it with the creator. Following Paul's emphasis, he insisted that it applied 'to the Son from the Law [*ex lege in filium competit*]'.[53] In his treatise *On Patience*, Tertullian remarked, 'When you are cursed, rejoice: the Lord himself was cursed in the Law [*maledictus in lege est*]'.[54] 'In saying that Christ is crucified,' Tertullian elsewhere urged, 'we do not curse him [*non maledicimus illum*], but refer to the curse of the Law [*maledictum legis*]'.[55] In short, it is the Law, not the creator, who is blamed for the curse – even though the creator is the (unacknowledged) author of the Law.

48. See Joost Smit Sibinga, *The Old Testament Text of Justin Martyr* (Leiden: Brill, 1963), 96–99.

49. Elsewhere (*Dial.* 91.4), Justin is happy to add that the serpent was cursed 'by God' (ὑπὸ τοῦ θεοῦ) even when these words are lacking in the text of *Gen* 3.14.

50. See further Chapman, *Crucifixion*, 248–51.

51. On Justin, see further Willem Cornelis van Unnik, 'Der Fluch der Gekreuzigten: Deuteronomium 21,23 in der Deutung Justinus des Märtyrers', in *Theologia Crucis, Signum Crucis, FS E. Dinkler*, ed. C. Andresen and G. Klein (Tübingen: Mohr Siebeck, 1979), 483–99.

52. Tertullian, *Against the Jews* 10.3–4 (written between 198 CE and 208 CE), in Hermann Tränkle, ed., *Q.S.F. Tertulliani Adversus Iudaeos mit Einleitung und kritischem Kommentar* (Wiesbaden: Franz Steiner, 1964), 26–27. For the authenticity of this work, see Tränkle, ed., *Q.S.F. Tertulliani Adversus Iudaeos*, XLI–XLIV, LII–LIII; Claudio Moreschini and Enrico Norelli, *Early Christian Greek and Latin Literature: A Literary History*, trans. Matthew J. O'Connell, 2 vols. (Peabody: Hendrickson, 2005), 1.339. Tränkle charts the terminological similarities between *Against the Jews* 10 and *Against Marcion* 3.18 (in *Adversus Iudaeos*, LIV).

53. Tertullian, *Against Praxeas* 29.3, in A. Kroymann and E. Evans, ed., *Quinti Septimi Florentis Tertulliani Opera Pars II Opera Montanistica*, CCSL 2.2 (Turnhout: Brepols, 1954), 1159–205 at 1202.

54. Tertullian, *On Patience* 8.3, in J. G. Ph. Borleffs, ed., in *Tertulliani Opera Pars I*, 299–317 (at 308). In the context, Tertullian is arguing for the joyful acceptance of persecution.

55. In the context, Tertullian is arguing against so-called Patripassians. He states that it is blasphemy if the Father is said to be cursed, but not blasphemy in the case of the Son: 'Just

Late in the fourth century, Epiphanius denied the reality of the curse against his Marcionite opponents. 'The fool [Marcion]', he cried, 'is wholly unaware that Christ has not become a curse either – god forbid!'[56] Like Justin, he appealed to interchange theology and fulfilled prophecy to mitigate the curse.[57]

Taking a different approach, Jerome argued against the Jews that it is only because of his or her *crime* that a crucified person is cursed, not because they are crucified. But the text he dealt with said: 'Cursed by god is everyone who hangs on a tree' (*Deut* 21.23) – *everyone*, whether innocent or guilty (and the innocent Christ was clearly said to be cursed, *Gal* 3.13). Jerome was so disturbed by the curse that he was willing to claim that interpolators added 'cursed *by god*' to *Deut* 21.23 in *both* Christian and Jewish versions of the text. Based on this view, Jerome recklessly – to use his own language – claimed that 'in no place is it written that anyone is cursed by god and wherever a curse is made, the name of god is not added'.[58] But when he quoted the curse against Cain (*Gen* 4.11) he failed to mention that it is *the Jewish god* who spoke the curse; and in the other curse texts Jerome mentioned (notably the curses in *Lev* 26 and *Deut* 28) it is assumed that the Jewish deity brings the curse even if his name is lacking. In fact, Jerome's lengthy discussion of Old Testament curses only reinforces the Marcionite thesis that cursing is part of the character of the creator.

As can be seen from this brief survey, patristic authors took various strategies to confront the creator's curse against Christ. Yet they all agreed that this curse must be somehow dodged or denied, despite the direct language of Paul (Χριστὸς ... γενόμενος ... κατάρα). Early Catholic writers must have had strong motives for overriding the stark language of Paul. One of these motives, it seems, was to protect the goodness of the creator against perceived Marcionite attacks.

Nag Hammadi

When we turn to the Nag Hammadi library, we encounter the diversity we expect from a large anthology. For instance, the figure called Primal Thought, or Protennoia, says at the end of the discourse named after her (100–150 CE):[59] 'I put

---

as concerning a being who is said to have a capacity for something, this is said without blasphemy, so with regard to one who does not have the capacity, to say it is blasphemy' (*sicut autem de quo quid capit dici sine blasphemia dicitur, ita quod non capit, blasphemia est si dicatur*, Against Praxeas 29.3–4).

56. Epiphanius, *Pan.* 42.8 (translation in Frank Williams, *The Panarion of Epiphanius of Salamis* [Leiden: Brill, 2009²], 1.103–4).

57. Epiphanius, *Pan.* 42, 'Elenchus 2' (in Williams, *Panarion* 1.315).

58. Jerome, *Commentary on Galatians* 2 at 3.13: *nullo loco scriptum a deo quemquam esse maledictum et ubicumque maledictio ponitur nunquam dei nomen adiunctum*. Immediately before making this remark, Jerome confessed, 'I proceed to this contest at a reckless pace.'

59. For the dating, see John D. Turner, *Sethian Gnosticism and the Platonic Tradition* (Leuven: Peeters, 2001), 150–55.

on Jesus. I carried him from the cursed wood, and established him in the dwelling places of his Father' (*TriProt* [NHC XIII,1] 50,11–15). Protennoia's appearance as Jesus is part of her third descent in which she reveals herself to her members, and teaches them knowledge and the rite of the Five Seals (47,13–50,4).[60] The 'cursed wood' is metonymic for the whole experience of crucifixion. The author of the curse is not mentioned, and the idea that Jesus himself is cursed is avoided.[61]

In the *Apocryphon of James* (NHC I,2) 13,23–25 (late second or early third century CE), Jesus addresses James and Peter in a secret discourse with a steady stream of paradoxical sayings. Towards the close of the dialogue, Jesus urges them not to take pride in their enlightenment, but to act as he did. Jesus directly put himself 'under a curse' (ϩⲁ ⲡⲥⲁϩⲟⲩⲉ) to save his followers. Although in the immediate context the cross is not mentioned, Jesus earlier notes that he was 'crucified' by the evil one, and strongly urges his disciples: 'Remember my cross and my death, and you will live.'[62] The author of this apocryphon followed Paul in emphasizing the curse's soteriological benefits. He also followed the apostle in not blaming the creator for the curse, since it was self-inflicted.

In other texts, we see the spiritual essence of Jesus disassociated from the 'man of the cross'. This line of approach draws on *1 Cor* 2.8, in which ignorant archons vainly attempt to crucify 'the Lord of Glory'. For instance, in the *Second Treatise of the Great Seth* [NHC VII,2] we read,

> For my death which they think happened, (happened) to them in their error and lack of sight. They nailed their man to their death [ⲉⲁⲩϯ ⲉⲓϥⲧ ⲙ̄ⲡⲉⲩⲣⲱⲙⲉ ⲉϩⲟⲩⲛ ⲉⲡⲉⲩⲙⲟⲩ]. For their minds did not see me, for they were deaf and blind. But in doing these things, they condemn themselves. As for me, they saw me; and they punished me [ⲁⲩⲣ̄ⲕⲟⲗⲁⲍⲉ ⲙ̄ⲙⲟⲉⲓ] ... But I was rejoicing in the height over all the riches of the archons and the offspring of their error and empty glory, and I laughed at their ignorance. (55,30–56,20)

Compare a passage in the following tractate, the *Apocalypse of Peter* (NHC VII,3), where Peter asks Jesus,

> Who is this one above the tree, glad and laughing? And is it another person whose feet and hands they are hammering? The Saviour said to me: 'This one whom you see above the tree, glad and laughing, is the living Jesus [ⲡⲉⲧⲟⲛϩ̄ ⲓ̄ⲥ̄]. But he into whose hands and feet they are driving the nails is his fleshly part

---

60. Cf. *ApocrJn* (NHC II,2) 30,33–31,26.

61. I take exception to the opinion of Turner who understands the cursed cross in *TriProt* as 'not redemptive' (*Sethian Gnosticism*, 147). The whole experience of crucifixion sets in motion a redemptive process, even if that process involves escape from the curse.

62. *ApocrJas* 5,15–20, 33–35. Text edited by Francis E. Williams in *Nag Hammadi Codex I (The Jung Codex), Introductions, Translations, Texts, Indices*, ed. Harold W. Attridge (Leiden: Brill, 1985), 34–36.

[ⲡⲓⲥⲁⲣⲕⲓⲕⲟⲛ], that alternative person [ⲡⲓϣⲉⲃⲓⲱ]. They are putting to shame [ⲛ̄ⲥⲣⲁϩ] that which is in his likeness … the clay vessel in which they dwell, belonging to Elohim, the man of the cross, who is under the law [ⲛ̄ⲧⲉ ⲡⲓⲥ̄ⲣ̄ⲟⲥ ⲉⲧϣⲟⲟⲡ ϩⲁ ⲡⲛⲟⲙⲟⲥ, alluding to *Gal* 4.4]. But he who stands near him is the living Saviour [ⲡⲓⲥⲱⲧⲏ̄ⲣ ⲡⲉ ⲉⲧⲟⲛ̄ϩ], the inner principle which they seized. And he has been released. He stands joyfully looking at those who violated him.' (81,10–82,32)

These authors distinguished the higher and lower platforms of Jesus such that the Jewish creator (Elohim) could curse what belonged to him (Jesus's fleshly and psychic platform), while leaving his spiritual core unharmed.[63]

The paradise story

Some early Christians used this pattern of thinking when interpreting the paradise story (*Gen* 2–3). Adam and Eve are cursed by the creator, but the curse does not and cannot harm their spiritual core.[64]

In *Genesis* 3, only the snake and the soil are expressly cursed, and apologists pointed this out in their attempt to defend the creator.[65] Yet other early Christian texts made the curse against Adam and Eve explicit. In the shorter version of the

---

63. See further *1ApocJas* (NHC V,3) 31,18–26 (parallel text in Codex Tchacos 2, 18,8–15). Jesus says to James, 'Never did I suffer at all, and I was not distressed. These people did not harm me. Rather, this was inflicted upon a figure of the rulers, and it was fitting that this figure should be [destroyed] by them'; *GJudas* 56,19–21 (Jesus speaking to Judas): 'For you will sacrifice the man who bears me.' According to the 'Ophite' report in Irenaeus, *Adv. Haer.* 1.30.13, both Christ and Sophia left Jesus to be crucified on the cross (*ipsum Christum quidem cum Sophia abstitisse in incorruptibilem aeonem dicunt, Iesum autem crucifixum*). Cf. *Adv. Haer.* 1.24.4 (Basilides). See further G. Luttikhuizen, *Gnostic Revisions of Genesis Stories and Early Jesus Traditions* (Leiden: Brill, 2006), 133–36, 145–51.

64. Luttikhuizen observed that there is 'basically the same hermeneutical strategy at work in both the Gnostic rewriting of Genesis stories and the revisionary interpretation of early Christian accounts of Jesus' suffering and death' (*Gnostic Revisions*, 4). He did not, however, expand on this thesis when he came to treat Christ's passion in Nag Hammadi sources (*Gnostic Revisions*, 130–51).

65. Philo argued that Adam could not be cursed because he represents mind (νοῦς), the precipitate of divine breath (*Quaestiones et Solutiones in Genesim* 1.50). Irenaeus denied that the Jewish god cursed Adam, apparently because such a curse implied damnation (*Adv. Haer.* 3.23.3, SC 211:450). Adamantius, the early Catholic exponent in the dialogue named after him, similarly argued that the creator did not curse the first human – only the ground. His Marcionite opponent countered that the creator did curse Adam, for Adam was taken from the ground. This curse, moreover, implied the creator's condemnation (κατάραν αὐτῷ ἔδωκε, πῶς οὖν οὐ κατεδίκασεν; in Kenji Tsutsui, *Die Auseinandersetzung*

Apocryphon of John (170–200 CE), for instance, Yaldabaoth sees Adam and Eve separate from him after eating the fruit, and curses them (ⲥⲁϩⲟⲩ ⲙⲙⲟⲟⲩ).⁶⁶ An expanded set of curses appears in *On the Origin of the World* (NHC II,5) 120,3–11 (third century CE), where blind rulers first curse (ⲁⲩⲥⲟⲩϩⲱⲣϥ) the instructing serpent, then Eve and her children (ⲁⲩⲥⲟⲩϩⲱⲣⲥ̄ ⲙⲛ̄ ⲛⲉⲥϣⲏⲣⲉ) and finally Adam (ⲁⲩⲥϩⲟⲩⲱⲣ), the earth and the fruit because of him: 'Everything they created they cursed. There is no blessing from them. Good cannot be born from evil [ⲙⲛ̄ ϭⲟⲙ ⲛ̄ⲥⲉ ϫⲡⲉ ⲁⲅⲁⲑⲟⲛ ⲉⲃⲟⲗ ϩⲙ̄ ⲡⲡⲟⲛⲏⲣⲟⲛ]' (120,10–12).⁶⁷

The last line may go back to Marcion's adaptation of Jesus's parable that a bad tree does not bear good fruit.⁶⁸ If so, both the Christian and philosophical background of the criticism is revealed. The true god, who is good and can only do good, cannot produce the evil fruit of cursing.

In other Nag Hammadi retellings of *Genesis*, the creator repeatedly tries to harm Adam, Eve and their spiritual descendants. Yet he can only curse their mortal rinds, not their inner spirits. In the case of Adam, he is a psychosomatic organism to which the spiritual core of the true god, metaphorized as breath or light, is infused (a reading of *Gen* 2.7). Although the creator is aware of this spiritual core (since it makes Adam more intelligent), he cannot grasp it, so his various attacks are vain.⁶⁹

For example, in the longer version of the *Apocryphon of John* (around 200 CE), the creator tries to rape Eve ([NHC II,1] 23,35–24,15).⁷⁰ Yet he can only harm Eve's material husk from which the true Eve, called 'Life' or 'Enlightened Insight', has departed. The *Hypostasis of the Archons* (NHC II,4, 185–250 CE) calls this outer

---

mit den Markioniten im Adamantios-Dialog: Ein Kommentar zu den Büchern I-II [Berlin: de Gruyter, 2004]). Tsutsui argues for a dating between 350 CE and 360/378 CE, with Syria or perhaps Asia Minor as the place of composition (Tsutsui, *Die Auseinandersetzung*, 108–9). By contrast, Origen indicates that the curse against 'the earth in your works' was directed 'to Adam' (*Homilies on Numbers* 15.3.1). He also speaks generally of 'the curse of Adam' and the 'curses pronounced against Eve' in *c. Cels.* 4.40.

66. BG 61,7–10 in Bernard Barc and Wolf-Peter Funk, *Le livre des secrets de Jean, Recension brève (NH III,1 et BG,2)* (Leuven: Peeters, 2012). Yaldabaoth immediately makes Adam master of Eve, has his angels chase them from Paradise and clothes them in thick darkness.

67. Cf. *HypArch* 91,6–7: the rulers of this world 'have no blessing, for they are also under a curse' (ⲥⲉϣⲟⲟⲡ ϩⲁ ⲡⲥⲁϩⲟⲩⲉ).

68. See the re-established text in Dieter T. Roth, *The Text of Marcion's Gospel* (Leiden: Brill, 2015), 415 at 6.43. See also Roth, *The Text of Marcion's Gospel*, 4.4.20; 7.4.7; 8.8. Cf. Origen, *Principles* 2.5.4; 3.1.18; *Commentary on John* 13.73; *Ref.* 10.19.2; Pseudo-Tertullian, *Against All Heresies* 6.2. Tertullian suggests that Marcion contrasted *Isaiah* 45.7, 'I am the one who creates evils' with Jesus' parable of the fruits of good and bad trees (*Against Marcion* 1.2.1–2; cf. 4.17.11). See also *Dialogue of Adamantius* 56.14–17 in Tsutsui, *Auseinandersetzung*, 319.

69. *ApocrJn* [NHC II,1] 19,21–20,9. Cf. *HypArch* 87,15–20.

70. For dating *ApocrJn*, see Turner, *Sethian Gnosticism*, 141.

husk a 'a shadow of her likeness' (ⲧⲉⲥϩⲁⲓⲃⲉⲥ ⲉⲥⲉⲓⲛⲉ ⲙ̄ⲙⲟⲥ, 89,26).[71] In the same text, the creator also tries to curse the snake but ends up cursing only its shadow (ⲧⲉϥϩⲁⲓ̈ⲃⲉⲥ, *HypArch* 90,30–33). The attempted curse of the snake lasts 'until the perfect human comes' (ⲡⲧⲉⲗⲉⲓⲟⲥ ⲛ̄ⲣⲱⲙⲉ, 91,2) – evidently a reference to Jesus (cf. ἄνδρα τέλειον, Eph 4.13) who, in the crucifixion, falls under the creator's curse. In both cases, the curse proves ineffective since it only harms the outer husk – the tunic which can, like snake skin, be sloughed off.[72]

In the 'Ophite' report of Irenaeus, Adam and Eve are cursed, but only after Wisdom removes from them the 'moisture of light'. She does so expressly in order to prevent this spiritual essence from falling under the creator's curse.[73]

This protection of the spiritual core, variously expressed, closely parallels what happens to Jesus on the cross in texts like *Second Treatise of Great Seth* and the *Revelation of Peter* (NHC VII,2–3). The closeness of the conceptuality leads me to propose that the minds of these early interpreters of *Genesis* had been conditioned by a central Christian (perhaps specifically Marcionite) counter-narrative. That is to say, some Christians read the curses in Eden in light of the curse inflicted upon the crucified Christ. If so, it was a Christian counter-narrative that generated a hermeneutical framework (the wicked creator cannot curse the spiritual core of the elect) that was then applied to the earliest chapters of Christian scripture (the paradise story and beyond).

---

71. For the dating of *HypArch*, see Ursula Ulrike Kaiser, *Die Hypostase der Archonten (Nag-Hammadi-Codex II,4)* (Berlin: de Gruyter, 2006), 16–18, with earlier sources on 16, n.70. For the rape of Eve, see Stroumsa, *Another Seed*, 42–45; Karen L. King, 'Ridicule and Rape, Rule and Rebellion: The Hypostasis of the Archons', in *Gnosticism and the Early Christian World in Honor of James M. Robinson*, ed. James E. Goehring (Sonoma: Polebridge, 1990), 3–24.

72. It may be significant that in *Hypostasis of the Archons*, the snake and Christ are structurally parallel insofar as the snake is called the 'instructor' (ⲡⲣⲉϥⲧⲁⲙⲟ, 90,6), who leads Adam and Eve into knowledge. As it reveals knowledge, the snake is inhabited by the female instructing principle (ⲧⲣⲉϥⲧⲁⲙⲟ, 90,11). This principle leaves the snake before it falls under the curse. Peratic and Ophite Christians closely associated Christ and the Edenic snake (see *Ref.* 5.16.8, 11–12; 5.17.2). Epiphanius claimed that the Ophites identified Christ and the serpent, counting them both worthy of veneration (*Pan.* 37.1.2, 2.6, 6.5–6, 8.1). See also the 'serpent midrash' in *Testimony of Truth* 45,23–49,10 with Tuomas Rasimus, *Paradise Reconsidered in Gnostic Mythmaking: Rethinking Sethianism in Light of the Ophite Evidence* (Leiden: Brill, 2009), 65–102. Origen even claims that, since the creator cursed the knowledge-giving snake, the Ophites directed their curses against the creator (*c. Cels.* 6.28 [Χριστιανοὶ λέγουσι κατηραμένον θεὸν τὸν δημιουργόν … τοῦ κατηραμένου λέγεσθαι τὸν τῆς κατὰ Μωυσέα κοσμοποιίας θεόν]). Norea also calls the rulers 'accursed' in *HypArch* 92,23.

73. Irenaeus, *Adv. Haer.* 1.30.8: *uti neque maledictionem participaret … is qui esset a Principalitate spiritus.*

Conclusion

The Nag Hammadi authors discussed above were Christian interpreters of Christian texts (including the Septuagint). They read these texts with no love or loyalty to the Jewish creator. Like many Christians, they believed that the Jewish Law had been annulled, wholly or in part, by Christ.[74] Like Marcion, they took this point further by viewing the creator's curse against Christ as incriminating his character.

One reading strategy to protect Christ from the curse was to dissociate Jesus's spiritual core from his mortal platform. This hermeneutical approach gave some early Christians a pattern for understanding the curses unleashed against spirit-endowed humanity in *Genesis* 1–6.

If my hypothesis is correct, then negative demiurgy did not originate with a reading of the first Adam cursed by the creator. It began with an even more central – if problematic – counter-narrative, namely the creator's curse of the crucified Christ. After all, a curse against Adam would not have been enough to lead to negative demiurgy because Adam, the 'man of dust' (*1 Cor* 15.48), could always be blamed for sinning (as happens in *Rom* 5.12). But the creator's curse against the sinless Christ manifested once and for all the creator's hostility and wickedness. Pliny the Younger wrote to Trajan that Christians could never be induced to curse Christ – and yet this is what the Jewish creator does to the one alleged to be his own son.[75]

In short, it was the curse of the last Adam that provided the model for reading the curse against the first. The origins of negative demiurgy were to a great extent hermeneutical, and the inventors of this counter-reading were, in all likelihood, Christians of a Gentile background, with some philosophical acculturation, active in the era of the Jewish rebellions (66–135 CE), who adapted an originally Jewish argument (god cursed the Messiah) to incriminate the character of the creator himself.

---

74. Pate argues that the nullification of the Law was already Paul's position, a position he arrived at by reflecting on the curse of the crucified Jesus (*Reverse*, 212–23).

75. Pliny the Younger, *Letters* 10.36.5.

2

THE *HYPOSTASIS OF THE ARCHONS* AND REIMAGINING *GENESIS*

Mark Goodacre

Obsession with the early chapters of *Genesis* is a major focus in early Christianity, among works later labelled as orthodox as well as works that were ultimately relegated to the margins, lost and only rediscovered in the twentieth century. Among these, the *Hypostasis of the Archons* (*HypArch*) is particularly striking.[1] Like the *Apocryphon of John*, it provides a radical retelling of the early chapters of *Genesis*,[2] but here the retelling is its primary focus, as it moves sequentially through stories of creation, Adam and Eve, Cain and Abel, and Noah's Ark. Anyone who knows *Genesis* is in familiar territory, though that familiarity becomes the basis for something very surprising in which a whole new cast of cosmic characters 'above' shed light on the familiar characters 'below'.

HypArch is a fine example of a new treasure from Nag Hammadi. The work was completely unknown until it emerged among the Nag Hammadi discoveries in 1945. It is the fourth work in Codex II (after *Apocryphon of John*, *Gospel of*

---

1. For an introduction to issues in the interpretation of *HypArch*, see Nicola Denzey Lewis, *Introduction to 'Gnosticism': Ancient Voices, Christian Worlds* (Oxford: Oxford University Press, 2013), 131–49. For a helpful discussion and analysis of *HypArch*, see Ingvild Sælid Gilhus, *The Nature of the Archons: A Study in the Soteriology of a Treatise from Nag Hammadi (CGII, 4)* (Wiesbaden: O. Harrassowitz, 1985).

2. On the use of biblical texts in the *Apocryphon of John*, see David Creech, *The Use of Scripture in the Apocryphon of John: A Diachronic Analysis of the Variant Versions* (WUNT II 441; Tübingen: Mohr Siebeck, 2017).

Thomas and *Gospel of Philip*) and was first published in facsimile form in 1956.³ It is difficult to date with any precision, but the best guess is the first half of the third century.⁴ Its original language must have been Greek,⁵ but scholars can only guess at its place of composition. Along with the *Apocryphon of John*, the *Gospel of the Egyptians* and several other Nag Hammadi works, Hans-Martin Schenke identified *HypArch* as an example of Sethian gnostic literature,⁶ with its interest in the descendants of Seth, a focus on the character of Norea, the idea of the four 'light givers', one of whom is Eleleth, and the chief Ruler Yaldabaoth and his attempts at creation and then corruption.

While some might wish to caricature the work as a gnostic polytheistic distortion of an orthodox monotheistic view of the origins of the world, *HypArch* grounds itself confidently, even nonchalantly, as an exposition of Paul's teaching in *Col* 1.13 and especially *Eph* 6.12. The work begins in the following way:

---

3. Pahor Labib, *Coptic Gnostic Papyri in the Coptic Museum at Cairo* (Cairo: Government Press, 1956). Peter Nagel, *Das Wesen der Archonten aus Codex II der gnostischen Bibliothek von Nag Hammadi* (Wissenschafliche Beiträge, Halle-Wittenberg: Martin-Luther-Universität, 1970) and Roger Aubrey Bullard, *The Hypostasis of the Archons: The Coptic Text with Translation and Commentary* (Berlin: de Gruyter, 1970) subsequently provided editions. See also James M. Robinson, *The Facsimile Edition of the Nag Hammadi Codices: Codex II* (Leiden: Brill, 1974), 152–60; and Bernard Barc and Michel Roberge, *L'Hypostase des archontes: Traité gnostique sur l'origine de l'homme, du monde et des archontes (NH II,4), suivi de Noréa (NH IX,27,11–29,5)* (Bibliothèque copte de Nag Hammadi, Textes, 5; Leuven: Peeters, 1980). For details about the manuscript, see Robinson, *Facsimile Edition*, vii–xix; Bentley Layton, 'The Hypostasis of the Archons or *The Reality of the Rulers*', *HTR* 67 (1974), 351–94, 396–425 (351–62); and Bentley Layton (ed.), *Nag Hammadi Codex II, 2-7, Volume One: Gospel According to Thomas, Gospel According to Philip, Hypostasis of the Archons, and Indexes* (NHS 20, Leiden: Brill, 1989), 220–59.

4. Layton, 'The Hypostasis', 373.

5. See especially Layton, 'The Hypostasis', 373.

6. H.-M. Schenke, 'Das sethianische System nach Nag-Hammadi-Handschriften', in P. Nagel (ed.), *Studia Coptica* (Berlin: Akademie Verlag, 1974), 165–74; H.-M. Schenke, 'The Phenomenon and Significance of Gnostic Sethianism', in Bentley Layton (ed.), *The Rediscovery of Gnosticism: Proceedings of the International Conference on Gnosticism at Yale, New Haven, Connecticut, March 28-31, 1978, vol. 2: Sethian Gnosticism* (Leiden: E. J. Brill, 1981), 588–616. For an introduction to Sethian thought, see Anne McGuire, 'Gnosis and Nag Hammadi', in D. Jeffrey Bingham (ed.), *The Routledge Companion to Early Christian Thought* (London: Routledge, 2010), 204–27 (209–12). It is worth noting, however, that Seth appears only once in *HypArch*, and the attempt to group this work with others like it can be somewhat arbitrary in what it includes and excludes.

HypArch 86,20-30[1]

On account of the reality of the authorities, (inspired) by the spirit of the father of truth,	*Col* 1.13
the great apostle – referring to <u>the authorities of the darkness</u> – (ⲛⲉⲝⲟⲩⲥⲓⲁ ⲙ̄ⲡⲕⲁⲕⲉ) told us that	He has rescued us from <u>the authority of the darkness</u> (τῆς ἐξουσίας τοῦ σκότους) and transferred us into the kingdom of the Son of his love.
	Eph 6.12
<u>our struggle is not against</u> <u>flesh</u> <u>and</u> <u>blood</u>; rather, <u>the authorities</u> of the universe (ⲛⲉⲝⲟⲩⲥⲓⲁ ⲙ̄ⲡⲕⲟⲥ[ⲙⲟⲥ]) and <u>the spiritual forces of evil</u> (ⲙ̄ⲡⲛⲉⲩⲙⲁⲧⲓⲕⲟⲛ ⲛ̄ⲧⲡⲟⲛⲏⲣⲓⲁ).[2]	For <u>our struggle is not against</u> enemies of <u>blood</u> <u>and</u> <u>flesh</u>, but against the Rulers (πρὸς τὰς ἀρχάς), against <u>the authorities</u> (πρὸς τὰς ἐξουσίας), against the cosmic powers of this present darkness, against <u>the spiritual forces of evil</u> (τὰ πνευματικὰ τῆς πονηρίας) in the heavenly places.
I have sent this (to you) because you inquire about the reality of the authorities (ⲑⲩⲡⲟⲥⲧⲁ[ⲥⲓⲥ ⲛ̄]ⲉⲝⲟⲩⲥⲓⲁ).	

[1] Translations of *HypArch* are taken from Layton (ed.), *Nag Hammadi Codex II, 2-7*, except where notified; they are adapted to highlight parallel wording with scriptural texts.
[2] Layton translates this as 'spirits of wickedness'.

This does not appear to be simply some kind of framing device, a proto-orthodox 'hook' to catch the curious reader. The language from *Colossians* and *Ephesians* penetrates the whole work – the 'authorities', 'the Rulers', 'the authorities of the darkness' and ultimately also 'the light', with which the work concludes:

> Then all the children of the light will be truly acquainted with the truth and their root, and the Father of the entirety and the Holy Spirit. They will all say with a single voice, 'The Father's truth is just, and the Son presides over the entirety', and from everyone unto the ages of ages, 'Holy – holy – holy! Amen!' (*HypArch* 97,14-21).

The language of 'the children of light' is probably inspired by *Ephesians* (5.8; cf. *1 Thess* 5.5). As Bentley Layton points out, the author and the audience are Christians, even if the location of the action in the early chapters of *Genesis* precludes a major role for Jesus. And even then, 'the coming True Man (τέλειος ἄνθρωπος) ... is surely meant to be the Christ of the Church'.[7] *HypArch* is, in other words, a reimagining of the primordial story in the light of (deutero-)Paul's language about the Rulers and the authorities.

7. Layton, 'The Hypostasis', 364.

'It is I who am God'!

The altered theology of *HypArch* is clear from the beginning of the work. The Ruler of the archons is introduced with a clear quotation from Isaiah:

> Their chief is blind; because of his power and his ignorance and his arrogance he said, with his power, 'It is I who am God [ⲁⲛⲟⲕ ⲡⲉ ⲡⲛⲟⲩⲧⲉ], there is none apart from me.' When he said this, he sinned against the entirety. And this speech got up to incorruptibility; then there was a voice that came forth from incorruptibility, saying, 'You are mistaken, Samael' – which is, 'god of the blind' (*HypArch* 86,27–87,4).

The quotation is closest to *Isa* 45.5 and 46.9, but statements like it are legion in the Hebrew Bible[8] (*Deut* 32.39; *Hos* 13.4; *Joel* 2.27) and specifically in *Isaiah* (43.10–11; 44.6; 45.6, 18, 22; 47.8, 10), and they all, of course, refer to the God of Israel, often by name. The idea that such speech is characteristic not of YHWH but instead of Samael, 'the god of the blind', is the first of several surprises for the reader familiar with reading the Hebrew Bible.

At the end of *HypArch*, this character's origins are described. Pistis Sophia's attempt at creation results in matter analogous to an aborted foetus that becomes 'an arrogant beast resembling a lion', and he is now revealed by an alternative name. He is Yaldabaoth (or Yaltabaoth), and under this name the chief of the Rulers once again makes the same arrogant claim that is attributed to Israel's God in the Hebrew Bible:

> Opening his eyes, he saw a vast quantity of matter without limit; and he became arrogant, saying, 'It is I who am God and there is none other apart from me.' When he said this, he sinned against the entirety. And a voice came forth from above the realm of absolute power, saying, 'You are mistaken, Samael' – which is, 'god of the blind'. (*HypArch* 94,19–26)

Once again, the author makes clear that the statement is a grave error, a sin 'against the entirety'. He is not the sole God. He is Samael, the 'god of the blind' who is also known as Yaldabaoth and Sakla.

This revelation of the identity of Yaldabaoth, and his arrogant attempt to usurp the true God's power, is the major theological claim of the work. On a third occasion, the chief Ruler again falsely sets out his stall, this time in an announcement to his offspring, and once again, he is contradicted:

> This Ruler, by being androgynous, made himself a vast realm, an extent without limit. And he contemplated creating offspring for himself, and created for

---

8. Although I use the term 'Hebrew Bible', the author is almost certainly dependent on the Septuagint.

himself seven offspring, androgynous just like their parent. And he said to his offspring, 'It is I who am god of the entirety!' And Zoe (Life), the daughter of Pistis Sophia, cried out and said to him, 'You are mistaken, Sakla!' – for which the alternative name is Yaltabaoth. She breathed into his face, and her breath became a fiery angel for her; and that angel bound Yaldabaoth and cast him down into Tartaros below the abyss. (*HypArch* 94,34–95,13)

The theological orientation of *HypArch* is, then, clearly and explicitly at variance with *Genesis*. Language used of YHWH in *Genesis* is clearly transferred to Yaldabaoth. It is worth noting, however, that the work is not simplistically transferring the characteristics of the God of the Hebrew Bible to Yaldabaoth and his fellow Rulers.[9] In spite of the key role now played by the Rulers in its retelling of *Genesis*, it is apparent that 'the Father of the entirety' sees and approves what is happening, illustrated in the occurrence of phrases like 'by the Father's will' (ϩⲙ ⲡⲟⲩⲱϣ ⲙⲡⲉⲓⲱⲧ, *HypArch* 87,22 and 88,34) and 'by the will of the Father of the entirety' (ϩⲙ ⲡⲟⲩⲱϣ` ⲙⲡⲉⲓⲱⲧ` ⲙⲡⲧⲏⲣϥ, *HypArch* 88,11 and 96,12). It is the Father of the entirety who sends the Spirit of truth, whose existence is revealed by the 'the true man' (*HypArch* 96,33–34), and it is the Father of the entirety and the Holy Spirit who are intimately acquainted with the 'children of the light' (*HypArch* 97,13–14).

Reimagining Adam and Eve

HypArch's provocative, subversive recasting of the *Genesis* story is only possible because of the author's intelligent pondering of the problems that the text throws up. As Philip Alexander says, it is 'a highly erudite exegesis of *Genesis* 1–6, albeit from an unusual hermeneutical standpoint'.[10] The point is best illustrated by analysing the most iconic scene in the *Genesis* narrative, which provides the opportunity for the most radical example of *HypArch*'s rewriting, the story of the Garden of Eden. While telling what is clearly the same story, *HypArch* provides new motivations for the characters alongside new cosmic players, but the earthly elements of the story are all present, in the same order, with many of the same details:

---

9. Cf. McGuire, 'Gnosis', 210–11.

10. Philip Alexander, 'Jewish Elements in Gnosticism and Magic c. CE 70–c. 270', in William Horbury, W. D. Davies and John Study (ed.), *The Cambridge History of Judaism*, vol. 3 (Cambridge: Cambridge University Press, 1999), 1052–78 (1058). Bentley Layton also admires the author's skill: 'It is clear that we have here to do with a sophisticated piece of *sectarian and thus esoteric literature*' ('The Hypostasis', 371, italics original); he later adds, 'Although a writer of considerable gifts there is no sign that he is one of the pioneers of gnostic speculation' (372).

Genesis (LXX)	HypArch 88,25-90,31
2.15 The Lord God took the man whom he formed and he put him in the garden, to work it and keep it.	They took Adam and they put him in the garden to work it and keep it.
2.16 And the Lord God commanded Adam saying, 'From every tree of the garden you will eat for food; 2.17 but from the tree of knowing good and evil, you shall not eat from it; so in the day you eat from it, in death you will die.'	And the Rulers commanded him, saying, 'From every tree in the garden you will eat; but from the tree of knowing good and evil, do not eat nor [touch] it; in the day you eat [from] it, in death you will die.'
2.21 And God cast a trance on Adam, and he fell asleep …	The Rulers took counsel with one another and said, 'Come, let us cause a deep sleep to fall upon Adam …'
3.1 Now the serpent was wiser than any other wild animal that the Lord God had made. He said to the woman, 'Did God say, "You shall not eat from every tree in the garden?"'	Then the spiritual female came in the serpent, the instructor; and it taught them, saying, 'What did he say to you? Was it, "From every tree in the garden shall you eat, yet from the tree of the knowledge of good and evil do not eat?"'
3.5 'For God knows that when you eat from it, your eyes will be opened and you will be like gods, knowing good and evil.'	'Rather your eyes will open and you will be like gods, knowing evil and good.'
3.6 … the woman … taking its fruit, she ate …	And the carnal woman took from the tree and ate …
3.7 And the eyes of the two were opened, and they knew that they were naked, and they sewed together leaves of a fig tree and they made themselves loincloths.	… they knew that they were naked of the spiritual element, and they took leaves of a fig tree and bound them upon their loins.
3.10 'I heard your voice walking around in the garden, and I was afraid, for I am naked; and I hid.'	'I heard your voice and I was afraid, for I was naked; and I hid.'
3.12 'The woman whom you gave to be with me, she gave me from the tree, and I ate.'	'The woman whom you gave me, she gave me, and I ate.'
3.13 And the woman said, 'The serpent deceived me, and I ate.'	The woman said, 'The serpent deceived me, and I ate.'

These constant reminders of the base narrative are an effective way of legitimizing the reimagined story. They reassure the reader that this is, in effect, the same story, albeit one in which the reader is given greater and different insights into the actors in the cosmic realm. It is as if the action as it is played out on the stage of Eden will look just the same, whether one views it from the *Genesis* standpoint or the *HypArch* standpoint. What differs is what is happening off-stage, in the heavens, among the Rulers, whose actions and motivations take the reader on a journey that allows a new story to be told.

Thus while the skeleton narrative is the same, the cosmic flesh that the author places on the bones is quite different. The story of humanity's archetypal disobedience becomes a story about the arrogant behaviour of the Rulers, whose bungled attempts at material creation require first the man and subsequently the woman to be endowed with Spirit:

> Afterwards, the Spirit saw the soul-endowed man upon the ground. And the Spirit came forth from the Adamantine Land; it descended and came to dwell within him, and that man became a living soul. It called his name Adam, since he was found moving upon the ground. (*HypArch* 88,11–17)

> They opened his side like a living woman. And they built up his side with some flesh in place of her, and Adam came to be endowed only with soul. And the Spirit-endowed woman came to him and spoke with him, saying, 'Arise, Adam.' And when he saw her, he said, 'It is you who have given me life; you will be called "mother of the living". – For it is she who is my mother. It is she who is the physician, and the woman, and she who has given birth.' (*HypArch* 89,7–17)

It is then the Rulers, and not God, who issue the command not to eat from the tree; and the serpent is now no longer the villain of the piece. Instead, he becomes 'the Instructor' (*HypArch* 89,32) and explains to them that by eating the fruit their eyes would open and they would recognize their true nature. The author's puzzlement with the idea of God refusing knowledge of good and evil (*Gen* 3.5) presumably lies behind this narrative. It is the same logic as that found in the *Testimony of Truth*, from Nag Hammadi Codex IX:

> But what sort is this God? First, he maliciously refused Adam from eating of the tree of knowledge, and, secondly, he said 'Adam, where are you?' God does not have foreknowledge? Would he not know from the beginning? And afterwards, he said, 'Let us cast him out of this place, lest he eat of the tree of life and live forever.' Surely, he has shown himself to be a malicious grudger! And what kind of God is this?[11]

Indeed, the anthropomorphism that has concerned many readers of *Genesis*, when God is heard 'walking in the garden at the time of the evening breeze' (*Gen* 2.8), is like God's apparent lack of foreknowledge, corrected in *HypArch* where the ignorant lack of understanding is just what one expects from the Rulers.

One of the most striking differences between *Genesis* and *HypArch* is the greater terseness of the *HypArch* narrative. In *Genesis*, the curse is narrated over six long verses, detailing the fates of the serpent (3.14–15), the woman (3.16) and the man (3.17–19), with extended direct discourse, followed by the expulsion from the

---

11. For the text (with introduction, English translation and notes), see Birger Pearson and Søren Giverson (ed.), *Nag Hammadi Codices IX and X* (NHS 15; Leiden: E. J. Brill, 1981), 101–202.

garden (3.22–24). In *HypArch*, the rewritten narrative takes a fraction of the time, with no direct discourse, a curse on the snake alone, and a brief and unelaborate expulsion from the garden. Moreover, every piece of geographical detail and narrative colour has gone. There are no rivers or jewels (*Gen* 2.10–14); and there are no cherubim or flaming swords to prevent re-entry to the garden (*Gen* 3.24).

The terseness of the rewritten narrative functions to add to the enigmatic nature of the story. Layton describes this as 'a typical gnostic pose', adding,

> The text itself reminds us of its fundamentally esoteric nature: the terse and sometimes enigmatic narration (some crucial episodes in the recital of Yaldabaoth's creation and demise are mysteriously absent) will have led any ancient reader to conclude that the author knew much more about the matter than he was telling.[12]

But the abbreviation of the *Genesis* account also allows the writer to draw attention to what he has added to the narrative, elements that become all the more prominent in the light of the concise retelling of the familiar story. This is nowhere clearer than in the troubling new story of the rape of the carnal woman:

> Then the authorities came up to their Adam. And when they saw his female counterpart speaking with him, they became agitated with great agitation; and they became enamoured of her. They said to one another, 'Come, let us sow our seed in her', and they pursued her. And she laughed at them for their witlessness and their blindness; and in their clutches she became a tree, and left before them her shadowy reflection resembling herself; and they defiled it foully. – And they defiled the stamp of her voice, so that by the form they had modelled, together with their (own) image, they made themselves liable to condemnation. (*HypArch* 89,17–31)

Given the abbreviation of the *Genesis* narrative, this curious addition stands out as oddly as the tree into which the woman is transformed. The episode reveals a good deal about the work's world view. 'The authorities' behave in a characteristically disgraceful way so that they are roundly mocked by Adam's female counterpoint, and the rape of the carnal woman that she leaves behind provides the prelude to the birth of Cain later in the narrative.[13] This is no longer a narrative about the fall of humankind. It is a narrative that explains the reality of the Rulers, and their condemnation.

---

12. Layton, 'The Hypostasis', 372.
13. The text simply says, 'Now afterwards, she bore Cain, their son . . .' and some speculate that Adam is supposed to be his father, but this element of the parallel in *Gen* 4.1, '*Now the man knew his wife Eve*, and she conceived and bore Cain ...' is here conspicuous by its absence.

Reimagining Noah's Ark

If there is any story in the Hebrew Bible that is as iconic as the story of the Garden of Eden, it is surely the story of Noah's Ark. And if the rewritten narrative of Adam and Eve counters its source in ways fundamental to its theology, similar theological objections appear to be foundational in the work's recasting of Noah:

Genesis 6.1–19 LXX	*HypArch 92,3–14*
And it came to be when humans began to multiply on the earth, and daughters were born to them then the angels of God seeing the daughters of humans that they are beautiful, they took wives for themselves from all that they chose …	Then humans began to multiply and to become beautiful.[1]
… And Lord God seeing that the evil deeds of humans were multiplied on the earth and everyone was pondering in his heart only on evil matters all the days; and God was angry that he made humanity on the earth, and he pondered. And God said, 'I will wipe off humanity that I made from the face of the earth, from human to domesticated animals and from reptiles to birds of the heaven; because I have become angry that I made them.' But Noah found favour before Lord God …	The Rulers took counsel with one another and said, 'Come, let us cause a deluge with our hands and wipe off all flesh, from human to animal.' But when the Ruler of the forces came to know of their decision, he said to Noah,
'… Therefore make for yourself an ark from squared wood … And I will establish my covenant with you; now you shall come into the ark, you, your sons, your wife, and your sons' wives with you. And from all the domesticated animals and from all the reptiles and from all wild animals and from all flesh, two by two from everything you will bring into the ark, to keep them alive with you; they shall be male and female.'	'Make yourself an ark from some wood that does not rot and hide in it – you and your children and the animals and the birds of heaven from small to large – and set it upon Mount Sir.'

[1] Layton has 'Then Mankind began to multiply and improve', but ⲁⲛⲁⲉⲓ here is better translated 'become beautiful' in line with *Gen.* 6.1; cf. Barc and Roberge, *L'Hypostase*, 'Les hommes commencèrent alors à se multiplier et à devenir beaux'. Bullard, *Hypostasis*, 93, considers this possibility but rejects it in favour of 'became better'. I am grateful to Francis Watson and Sarah Parkhouse for this observation.

As with the story of Adam and Eve, the Flood story in *HypArch* is terser than it is in *Genesis*. Indeed, here the abbreviation is dramatic, and the omissions are manifold. We hear nothing of Shem, Ham and Japheth, or of the flood itself, and the animals do not go in two by two (let alone seven by seven!). Moreover, *HypArch* dramatically abbreviates the *Gen* 6.1–5 narrative about the multiplying of the people, the beauty of the women, limited mortality and the Nephilim, in the process effectively eliminating the notion in *Gen* 6.5 that wickedness abounded, and that 'every inclination of the thoughts of their hearts was only evil continually'. Just as the reimagined Eden story writes out the culpability of Adam and Eve, so here the depravity of all humanity is dismissed with a bold abbreviation.

It is a change that is essential given the revised history that the author is writing. Where *Genesis* 2–6 characterizes humankind as going from evil to evil, *HypArch* is revising the story to transfer culpability to the Rulers, and to introduce the non-biblical character of Norea, the virginal daughter of Eve, as a new heroine. Her introduction necessitates a change in the developing story:

> Then Norea came to him, wanting to board the ark. And when he would not let her, she blew upon the ark and caused it to be consumed by fire. Again he made the ark, for a second time. The Rulers went to meet her, intending to lead her astray. Their supreme chief said to her, 'Your mother Eve came to us.' But Norea turned to them and said to them, 'It is you who are the Rulers of the darkness; you are accursed. And you did not know my mother; instead it was your female counterpart that you knew. For I am not your descendant; rather it is from the world above that I am come.' (*HypArch* 92,14–26)

Once Norea appears in the Noah story, all attention is focused on her and the *Genesis* narrative quickly dissolves away. Noah's Ark is a transitional device, allowing the reader to meet Norea and then to move her to the centre of the narrative. What she says here already echoes what the narrator has said ('It is you who are the Rulers of darkness!'), and she does not have anything to do with the Rulers; she is 'from the world above'.

Narrative casualties in rewriting

There is a difficulty with writing counter-narratives. Sometimes the originating narrative is so well-known, so foundational, so pervasive in the thinking of the author, that that narrative bleeds through, as if by fatigue.[14] When the author first tells the story of the prohibition on eating the fruit, he rewrites the *Genesis* story so that the singular 'God' becomes the plural 'Rulers':

---

14. On the concept of editorial fatigue, see my 'Fatigue in the Synoptics', *NTS* 44 (1998), 45–58.

Genesis 2.15–17	*HypArch* 88,24–32
And the Lord God took the man and put him in the garden to till it and keep it. And the Lord God commanded the man, saying, 'From every tree that is in the garden shall you eat; but of the tree of the knowledge of good and evil you shall not eat, for in the day that you eat of it, with death you will die.'	They took Adam and put him in the garden to till it and keep it. And the Rulers commanded him, saying, 'From every tree that is in the garden shall you eat; but of the tree of the knowledge of good and evil you shall not eat nor touch it; for in the day that you eat of it, with death you will die.'

It is no longer the 'Lord God' who puts Adam in Eden as in *Gen* 2.15 but 'they' (88,24), and it is 'the Rulers' who issued a command to him (88,26). The story told in *HypArch* is very close here to *Genesis*; almost the only change here is the theological bombshell of switching the cosmic personnel. But after the creation and pursuit of Eve, the story returns to the command:

Genesis 3.1–5	*HypArch* 89,31–90,10
Now the serpent was wiser than any other wild animal that the Lord God had made. He said to the woman, 'Did God say, "You shall not eat from every tree in the garden?"'	Then the spiritual female came in the serpent, the instructor; and it taught them, saying, 'What did he say to you? Was it, "From every tree in the garden shall you eat, yet from the tree of the knowledge of good and evil do not eat?"'
The woman said to the serpent, 'We may eat of the fruit of the trees in the garden; but God said, "You shall not eat of the fruit of the tree that is in the middle of the garden, nor shall you touch it, or you shall die."' And the serpent said to the woman, 'You will not die; for God knows that when you eat of it your eyes will be opened and you will be like gods, knowing good and evil.'	The carnal woman said, 'Not only did he say "Do not eat", but even "Do not touch it; for in the day you eat of it, with death you will die."' And the serpent, the instructor, said, 'With death you shall not die; for it was out of jealousy that he said this to you. Rather your eyes shall open and you will be like gods, knowing evil and good.'

The story tracks the *Genesis* account quite closely. The major change is of course in the identity of the serpent, now no longer the most crafty of the animals God had created, but the locus of the female principle that departed from Eve, and thus 'the instructor' who speaks wisdom to the carnal woman. Curiously, the account does not follow on coherently from the earlier one, in which it was 'the Rulers' who issued the command. Now the snake asks, 'What did *he say* to you?' The carnal woman says, 'Not only did he say …', and the snake speaks about what 'he said'. The account has inadvertently adjusted to the storyline of the *Genesis* account, with the singular God who has issued the command.[15]

---

15. *On the Origin of the World*, the work that follows on from this in Codex II, does something very similar in the same place, 'Then the seven of them together laid plans. They

The phenomenon is also clear in the recasting of the Cain and Abel story, where *HypArch* temporarily stops talking about the Rulers, or Yaldabaoth, and reverts to the God of *Genesis*.

Genesis 4.1–15	*HypArch* 91,11–30
Now Adam knew his wife Eve, and she conceived and bore Cain, saying, 'I have acquired for myself a human being through God.' Next she bore his brother Abel. Now Abel came to be a shepherd of sheep, and Cain a worker of the ground. And it came to be after some days Cain brought a sacrifice to the Lord of the fruits of the earth, and Abel also brought from the firstborn of his sheep and from their fatty parts. And God looked upon Abel and his offerings, but on Cain and his sacrifices he paid no attention … And Cain said to Abel his brother, 'Let us go over into the field.' And it came to be while they were in the field that Cain rose up against Abel his brother and killed him. And God said to Cain, 'Where is Abel, your brother?' And he said, 'I do not know; am I my brother's keeper?' And God said, 'What did you do? The voice of your brother's blood cries out to me from the earth. And now you are accursed from the earth, which opened its mouth to receive the blood of your brother from your hand … For you will work the earth, and it will not continue to provide its power for you; a groaner and trembler you will be on the earth.' Anyone who kills Cain will release seven vengeances.	Now afterwards, she bore Cain, their son; and Cain worked the ground. Thereupon he knew his wife; again becoming pregnant, she bore Abel; and Abel was a shepherd of the sheepfold. Now Cain brought in from the fruits of his field, and Abel brought in an offering (from) among his lambs. God looked upon the offerings of Abel, but he did not accept the offerings of Cain. And carnal Cain pursued Abel, his brother. And God said to Cain, 'Where is Abel, your brother?' He answered saying, 'Am I my brother's keeper?' God said to Cain, 'Listen! The voice of your brother's blood cries up to me! You have sinned with your mouth. It will return to you: anyone who kills Cain will let loose seven vengeances, and you will exist groaning and trembling upon the earth.'

Somewhat remarkably, the author talks not about Yaldabaoth, or Samael, or the archons. Instead, it is simply 'God'.[16] It is surely no coincidence that *HypArch*

came up to Adam and Eve timidly: they said to him, "The fruit of all the trees created for you in Paradise shall be eaten". … Then came the wisest of all creatures, who was called Beast. And when he saw the likeness of their mother Eve he said to her, "What did God say to you?" Was it "Do not eat from the tree of knowledge?"' She said, 'He said not only, "Do not eat from it", but, "Do not touch it, lest you die."'

16. Curiously, the point is rarely noticed. Gerard P. Luttikhuizen, *Gnostic Revisions of Genesis Stories and Early Jesus Traditions* (Nag Hammadi and Manichean Studies; Leiden: Brill, 2006), 92, speculates that 'the God *Sabaoth*' is meant. Bentley Layton, 'The Hypostasis of the Archons (Conclusion)', *HTR* 69 (1976), 31–101 (61), writes, 'Our author

temporarily reverts to the theology of its source at the same time that it tracks its source most closely. The wording is here closer to *Genesis* than is any other passage in the work, and the secondary nature of *HypArch* is clear in the phenomenon of 'the missing middle',[17] where an author omits the middle part of an account, thereby inadvertently losing some of its narrative logic. So here, *HypArch* 11 follows *Genesis* 4 closely, narrating the births of Cain and Abel, their offerings to God and their contrasting receptions, but the author misses out the ensuing reactions, and Cain's anger, which leads to the murder in *Genesis*. As often in such cases, the missing details go unnoticed because of the reader's familiarity with the source text. The famous line 'Am I my brother's keeper?' is enough to evoke the full story in the reader's mind.

Concluding thoughts

More than many a work that rewrites its source material, *HypArch* provides a fascinating mixture of taking inspiration from *Genesis* while subverting its most fundamental features. The author tells a story that agrees with element after element in *Genesis* 1–6, affirming the human drama that was foundational to the way that Jews and Christians told their stories, but reconceptualizing the cosmology of the piece. The *Genesis* text is a source of inspiration, but the author is fearless in reworking its theology.

Reading *HypArch* as a counter-narrative is both rewarding and challenging. It is rewarding in so far as its author appears to be anxious about so many of the things that have troubled exegetes across the centuries, the God who makes an unreasonable command, who appears to be lacking in foresight, who appears so anthropomorphic, and whose punishments seem so out of proportion with the sins committed. And in a world in which there are still millions who attempt to find 'answers in *Genesis*' to scientific, theological and ethical questions, studying *HypArch* can be stimulating, even liberating.

Nevertheless, it would be easy, in focusing on how this work subverts and rewrites *Genesis*, to explore this exegesis as if it is only of academic interest, a kind of scribal attempt to puzzle out and correct troubling elements. But *HypArch* has attracted scholarly attention because its narrative has such noticeable things to say about women and gender.[18] While other early Christian texts like *I Timothy* 2.11–15 use the *Genesis* narrative to legitimize women's submission to men, *HypArch*

---

or editor abandons the terms of his own narrative in favor of those of the Biblical account, which is summarized here. Quite possibly Sabaoth the *dikaios theos* is meant.'

17. For the concept, and an exposition of how this works in the *Gospel of Thomas*, see my *Thomas and the Gospels: The Making of an Apocryphal Text* (London: SPCK, 2012), 109–27.

18. See especially Anne McGuire, 'Virginity and Subversion: Norea against the Powers in the Hypostasis of the Archons', in Karen L. King (ed.), *Images of the Feminine in Gnosticism* (Pennsylvania: Trinity Press International, 1988), 239–59.

provides a reading (or rereading) of *Genesis* that omits or undermines most of what contemporaries find so disturbing. Although the Rulers' rape of the carnal woman makes for distressing reading, the spiritual Eve plays a major role in the narrative. The Rulers are parodies of a corrupt masculinity, pursuing her to sow their seed, while she laughs at their hubris. Unlike *Genesis*, there is no hint that pain in childbirth is the result of God's curse, or that the husband's authority over his wife is divinely ordained (*Gen* 3.16). And most importantly, the real heroine turns out to be Norea, 'the virgin whom the forces did not defile' who is 'an assistance for many generations of humankind' (*HypArch* 92,1–3).

HypArch, though, remains a difficult work, and one that demands a lot from its readers. Some of the difficulties relate to the fact that we have only one textual witness, and there are points where text is missing or incoherent,[19] but other difficulties emerge from the work itself and its often unexpected changes of gear. What sense does it make for 'the Spirit' to 'come forth from the Adamantine land' when Adam becomes a 'living soul' (*HypArch* 88,13–15)? Is this just obfuscation? And when Eve emerges from Adam, how can she be his mother, or 'She who has given birth' (*HypArch* 88,17)? Similarly, there are places where the allegory is compromised, and the 'meaning' interferes with the storytelling, perhaps most strikingly when the narrator explains that 'the deep sleep that they "caused to fall upon him, and he slept" is Ignorance' (*HypArch* 89,6–7). Moreover, there are positively surreal moments, like when Eve becomes a tree (*HypArch* 89,25) or when Norea blows on Noah's ark and sets it on fire (*HypArch* 92,17). It would, however, be churlish to complain about such elements given that *Genesis* has so many curiosities of its own, like talking serpents and magic trees, and in the end they may serve to remind us of the necessary strangeness of primordial origin narratives. *Genesis* remains as enigmatic to us as it once did to the author of a fascinating counter-narrative that was nearly lost for ever, the *Hypostasis of the Archons*.

---

19. On the textual errors, see Layton, 'The Hypostasis', 359–62.

3

JESUS VERSUS THE LAWGIVER: NARRATIVES OF APOSTASY AND CONVERSION

Francis Watson

'The law was given through Moses, grace and truth came through Jesus Christ' (*GJn* 1.17). This laconic, self-contained statement from the Johannine prologue asserts a fundamental difference between law on the one hand and grace and truth on the other, and in doing so it raises more questions than it answers. What is the nature of that difference, and what are its implications? How can the law be said to be deficient in grace and truth? Why are we told who the two regimes were mediated *through* but not where they originated *from*? Was the law-giving through Moses a preliminary and subordinate work of the deity the Johannine Jesus characterizes as 'the Father who sent me', or does it stem from some other lesser agency?

The Johannine Jesus can claim that Moses 'bore witness to me' (*GJn* 5.39), but he also seems to distance himself from Moses. 'Did not Moses give *you* the law?', he asks on one occasion, and he refers repeatedly to 'your law' or 'their law' as though it had nothing to do with him (*GJn* 7.19; 8.17; 10.34; 15.25). In *GJohn* Jesus's opponents are the accredited leaders of the Jewish community who view themselves as disciples of Moses and are convinced that God truly spoke to him (9.28–29). But which God was that? On a previous occasion Jesus's Jewish audience claims to have 'one father, God', but Jesus retorts that their real father is the devil (8.41–44). Is the deity who gave the law through Moses to be identified with the devil, 'the archon of this world' (cf. 12.31; 14.30; 16.11)? Does Jesus's conflict with the disciples of Moses mirror a metaphysical conflict between the Father of Jesus and the God of Moses?

Such a conclusion is unthinkable if the *Gospel of John* is read within its canonical context, as an integral part of a fourfold gospel within a 'New Testament' coordinated with an 'Old Testament' on the assumption that a single divine identity transcends the differentiation. It is less clear that the Johannine evangelist himself would have been equally resistant to the suggestion that the Law of Moses and the grace and truth of Jesus Christ may stem from different divine origins. At the very least, there seems to be some ambivalence here.[1] Whatever this evangelist's view of the matter, it remains the case that many otherwise diverse early Christians came to believe that the God of Moses and Judaism and the God and Father of Jesus Christ were *not* one and the same, and that conversion to faith in Jesus Christ meant abandoning the service of the God of Israel.

In this chapter, I shall consider four early gospel-like texts that sought to assure their Christian readers that allegiance to Jesus Christ is incompatible with allegiance to the creator-and-lawgiver deity of the Jewish scriptures – a deity worshipped not only by Jews but also by other Christians. The four texts are the *Apocryphon of John*, the *Acts of John*, the *First Apocalypse of James* and (so far as they can be reconstructed) Marcion's *Antitheses* and *Euangelion*.[2] Each of these works seeks to show that Jesus is not the emissary of the deity of Jewish scripture and mainstream Christian tradition but the revealer and embodiment of the previously unknown Father. The reader is assured of this by way of exemplary conversion narratives featuring an individual apostle (John or James) or, in the case of Marcion, a scripturally based demonstration of the difference between the two divine beings, the inferior and the superior.

The Apocryphon of John

In the opening scene of this work, the risen Christ appears to the apostle John and promises to disclose to him 'what is, what was, and what must come to pass'

---

1. As John Ashton notes with reference to *GJohn* 1.17, 'The deliberate replacement of one founder-figure by another … is effectively the proclamation of a new religion' (*Understanding the Fourth Gospel* [Oxford: Clarendon Press, 1991], 473).

2. Two of these texts feature in Coptic codices from Nag Hammadi and elsewhere: *ApocrJn* (NHC II,1; III,1, IV,1; BG 8502,2) and *1ApocJas* (NHC V,3; Codex Tchacos [CT] 2). For a recent English translation of both, see Marvin Meyer (ed.), *The Nag Hammadi Scriptures* (New York: HarperCollins, 2007), 103–32, 321–32, where the translation of *ApocrJn* is based mainly on NHC II while the translation of *1ApocJas* is based on NHC V,3. For a synoptic translation of *ApocrJn* based primarily on NHC II and BG 8502, see Karen L. King, *The Secret Revelation of John* (Cambridge, MA: Harvard University Press, 2006), 26–81. An English translation of *AcJohn* is included in standard New Testament apocrypha collections: e.g. J. K. Elliott, *The Apocryphal New Testament: A Collection of Apocryphal Christian Literature in an English Translation based on M. R. James* (Oxford: Clarendon Press), 303–49. Jason D. BeDuhn has provided a reconstruction of *GMarcion* in English translation, in his *The First New Testament: Marcion's Scriptural Canon* (Salem, OR: Polebridge, 2013), 65–200. Marcion's *Antitheses* were reconstructed a century ago by Adolf von Harnack, but Harnack admits that 'much here may belong to the pupils' and assumes that this 'cannot be separated from the words of the master' (*Marcion: The Gospel of the Alien God*, Eng tr. Eugene, OR: Wipf & Stock, 1990 [German original, 1921], 59, 60–62). For original language critical editions, see below.

(*ApocrJn* 4.8–10).³ There is a parallel, perhaps intended, with the similarly named *Apocalypse of John* (the canonical Book of Revelation), which introduces itself as the 'apocalypse of Jesus Christ, which God gave him to show his servants what must quickly come to pass [ἃ δεῖ γενέσθαι ἐν τάχει]' (*Rev* 1.1). Here, Jesus appears to John – in exile on the island of Patmos – to disclose the mysteries of the future. In the *Apocryphon*, Jesus appears to John – again in a kind of exile, as we shall see, though in the vicinity of Jerusalem – to show how 'what is and what must come to pass' can only be understood in the light of 'what was', in the very beginning, a beginning that precedes and transcends the beginning misidentified as such by Moses at the beginning of the *Book of Genesis*.

The theme of the *Apocryphon* is summed up in the repeated claim that 'it is not as Moses said' (*ApocrJn* 59.13 [BG]).⁴ Moses is an unreliable witness to what happened in the beginning, and he is unreliable because he is the prophet and servant of a deity whose claim to be the one true God is utterly false. In reality, the God he serves is the abortive outcome of his mother Sophia's misguided attempt to produce offspring on her own initiative, without permission from the higher reaches of deity above her and without a male partner (24.1–25.16). Sophia – whose name, 'Wisdom', may hint at a divine providential purpose overruling her folly – names her hideous and embarrassing offspring Yaldabaoth and attempts to conceal him, until he takes himself off to a lowly realm where he establishes the unpleasant regime that Moses identifies as 'heaven and earth' (*ApocrJn* 25.17–34.12). At this point the text makes contact for the first time with the *Book of Genesis*, and the risen Christ proceeds to recount to John the real course of events presented in distorted form in its opening chapters: the creation of Adam (37.6–56.10; cf. *Gen* 1.26–27, 2.7) and of Eve (59.8–62.11; cf. *Gen* 2.18–25), their eating the forbidden fruit at the instigation of the serpent (56.11–59.7; cf. *Gen* 3.1–7), their expulsion from paradise (63.3–14; cf. *Gen* 3.8–24), the begetting of Cain and Abel (63.15–65.3; cf. *Gen* 4.1–2) and of Seth (65.19–67.8; cf. *Gen* 4.25–5.3), the angel marriages and the flood (73.15–79.7; cf. *Gen* 6.1–22).

At each of these points the reader is taken behind Moses's sanitized version of the primeval history, written in the service of Yaldabaoth's false claim to be the only God, in order to learn the true course of events concealed by the ancient scriptural text. The overarching story has to do with the bitter struggle between Sophia and Yaldabaoth for possession of the light power that the estranged son stole from his mother but was tricked into breathing into Adam. The drastic nature of this *Genesis* rewrite is exemplified by the figures known to *Genesis* as Cain and Abel but to the *Apocryphon* as Elohim and Yahweh – demonic figures with animal

---

3. The synoptic reference system used here is that of Michael Waldstein and Frederik Wisse, *The Apocryphon of John: Synopsis of Nag Hammadi Codices II,1: II,1; and IV,1 with BG 8502,2* (NHMS 33, Leiden: Brill, 1995), 11–177.

4. Explicit rejections of Moses's statements occur at *ApocrJn* 35.1–4 (*Gen* 1.2c, the Spirit of God moving over the waters); 59.10–16 (*Gen* 2.21a, Adam's deep sleep); 60.18–61.3 (*Gen* 2.21c, Adam's rib); 76.16–17 (cf. *Gen* 7.7, Noah's entry into the ark).

faces, born to Eve after she had been raped by Yaldabaoth. That is the ugly truth concealed behind the refined falsehood that 'Adam knew Eve his wife, and she conceived' (*Gen* 4.1a). For the Johannine author, the concealment is only partially successful. Moses himself records that Eve's response to the birth of Cain was that 'I have acquired a man *through god* [διὰ τοῦ θεοῦ]' (*Gen* 4.1b). Eve knows exactly who Cain's father was, and it was not Adam (cf. *1 Jn* 3.12).[5]

To a modern reader, this rewriting of the Genesis narrative may seem both disturbing and farcical. That was already the reaction of at least one early reader, Irenaeus, who provides an extensive and disparaging summary of large parts of this text in a form that can date from no later than the mid-second century.[6] Yet there must been many early Christian readers for whom *ApocrJn* was a sacred text – virtually a 'scriptural' text in regard to its status and authority if not in relation to ecclesial usage. Thus in three of the thirteen Nag Hammadi codices it is placed first, providing a *Genesis*-like foundation for the texts that follow. For some who revered this text, it was *Genesis* itself that was disturbing and farcical. That was the view taken by the author of the *Testimony of Truth* (NHC IX,3), who first summarizes the narrative of *Genesis* 2–3 and then lashes out at its deity figure:

> What kind of god is this? First, he was jealous of Adam and forbade him to eat from the Tree of Knowledge. Second, he said, 'Adam, where are you?' So God does not have foreknowledge, as he did not know this in advance! And afterwards he said, 'Let us throw him out of this place, in case he eats from the Tree of Life and lives for ever.' Has he not shown himself to be malevolent and jealous in character? (47,14–30)

In the face of criticism such as this, Irenaeus must labour hard to make the early chapters of *Genesis* credible as the essential backdrop to the gospel story.[7] It is entirely fitting (he claims) that the eternal life that was lost through one tree (the Tree of the Knowledge of Good and Evil) should be recovered through another (Jesus's cross).[8] The question, 'Adam, where are you?' is prophetic of the call to fallen humanity that sounds forth in Jesus's incarnation.[9] Nevertheless, Irenaeus

---

5. This outright hostility to the scriptural deity and to Moses makes it impossible to accept the claim that *ApocrJn* has its origin in intra-Jewish controversy, caused by the rise of a rabbinic orthodoxy in the latter part of the first century and the beginning of the second (so Bernard Barc and Wolf-Peter Funk, *Le Livre des Secrets de Jean, Recension Brève (NH III, 1 et BG, 2)* (BCNH:T 35, Quebec: Les Presses de l'Université Laval; Louvain: Peeters, 2012), 30.

6. Irenaeus, *Adv. Haer.* 1.29.1–4; 30.4–10. Latin text (and Greek where available) in Adelin Rousseau and Louis Doutreleau (ed.), *Irenée de Lyon, Contre les Hérésies*, 10 vols, SC (Paris: Cerf, 1965–92).

7. See Thomas Holsinger Friesen, *Irenaeus and Genesis: A Study in Competition in Early Christian Hermeneutics* (Winona Lake, IN: Eisenbraun, 2009).

8. Irenaeus, *Adv. Haer.* 5.16.2.

9. Irenaeus, *Adv. Haer.* 5.15.4.

knows that the Genesis narrative is vulnerable to criticism and that the claim that 'it is not as Moses said' represents a serious threat.

Irenaeus's summary of an early version of *ApocrJn* does not mention any claim to apostolic authorship, which may suggest that a later author or editor has added the opening and closing narrative in which John is the protagonist.[10] But Irenaeus's summary is selective, and it begins by referring to the supreme deity ('the Father') and the female divinity who proceeds from him ('Barbelo') as though they were independently existing beings: the Father 'wished to reveal himself to Barbelo'.[11] Yet it is not the Father but Barbelo (also known as Ennoia) who now takes the initiative, stepping forward and presenting her request for a companion, Prognosis or Foreknowledge, exactly as in the extant versions of *ApocrJn*.[12] It is likely that Irenaeus has omitted an account of Barbelo's birth from the self-contemplation of the Father, replacing it with an inaccurate and inconsistent statement implying that the two were originally independent of each other. If so, Irenaeus may also have omitted the story of the revelation to John that provides the occasion for this theogony. Authorship claims are often hard to disprove, and Irenaeus may not have wanted to draw attention to this issue. In addition, the claim that the apostolic narrative is a later addition reflects an older and now discredited scholarly assumption that texts originally purely 'Gnostic' were only subsequently 'christianized'.[13] The apostolic narrative should be seen as an integral part of a text that was never anything other than Christian.[14]

The narrative begins as though it were the continuation of a narrative already under way:

> And it came to pass on one of those days that he went up – John the brother of James, who were sons of Zebedee – that he went up into the temple …[15]

Here the author skilfully mimics scriptural terminology to create the pretence of an ongoing narrative with an editorial parenthesis to identify the protagonist.

---

10. For this widely held view, see Michael Waldstein, 'Das Apocryphon des Johannes', in *Nag Hammadi Deutsch, 1. Band*, ed. Hans-Martin Schenke, Hans-Gebhard Bethge and Ursula Ulrike Kaiser (Berlin: de Gruyter, 2001), 95–150, 97; Judith Hartenstein, *Die Zweite Lehre: Erscheinungen des Auferstandenen als Rahmenerzählungen frühchristlicher Dialoge* (TU 146, Berlin: Akademie Verlag, 2000), 70–71.

11. *Adv. Haer.* 1.29.1.

12. *Adv. Haer.* 1.29.1; *ApocrJn* 12.12–14.

13. See Birger A. Pearson, *Gnosticism and Christianity in Roman and Coptic Egypt* (London: T&T Clark International, 2004), 216–18: 'The Urtext behind the christianized text that we now have is testimony to a religiosity that originally had nothing to do with Christianity' (218).

14. Cf. Michael Allen Williams, *Rethinking 'Gnosticism': An Argument for Dismantling a Dubious Category* (Princeton, NJ: Princeton University Press, 1996), 13.

15. *ApocrJn* 1.6–9.

Similar connecting terminology occurs in *GLuke*, which is itself imitating the Septuagint: 'And it came to pass on one of those days that he went up into a boat, with his disciples' (*GLk* 8.22; cf. 2.1, 5.17, 6.12, 20.1). In the Lukan case, there is no need to identify the protagonist, whom the context shows to be Jesus of Nazareth. In *ApocrJn*, the naming of John in relation both to his brother and his father is so full that the narrative has to be restarted with the repetition of '... that he went up ...' The reader is expected to be familiar with this figure from earlier gospel traditions but should also note that the protagonist is John rather than Jesus himself, who is therefore absent. The disciples 'go up' into a boat because Jesus does so, but John 'goes up' to the temple on his own initiative (cf. *Acts* 3.1). The opening of *ApocrJn* places us in an indeterminate narrative context in which time has elapsed since Jesus's departure and John is on his own.

John's isolation is noted by a temple official, Arimanias the Pharisee, who approaches him and asks, 'Where is your teacher, whom you used to follow?' Implicit here is the further question why John is in the temple on his own, when he and other disciples had previously been found there only in the company of Jesus. An earlier encounter with a named Pharisee in the temple is recorded in the gospel fragment known as *POxy* 840 (perhaps an excerpt from the so-called *Gospel of the Egyptians*?),[16] and here the central figure is Jesus himself:

> Then he [Jesus], taking them [the disciples] with him, entered the holy place and walked around in the temple. And a Pharisee who was a high priest, <....> by name, came to meet them and said to the Saviour, 'Who permitted you to set foot in this holy place ...?' (*POxy* 840, ll. 7–13)[17]

It is earlier scenes such as this that are presupposed in Arimanias's question to John about the absent Jesus. John replies that 'he has returned to the place from which he came' (*ApocrJn* 1.15); Jesus's announcement in the temple that 'I am going to the one who sent me' has been fulfilled (*GJn* 7.33, cf. v. 14), and that is the true explanation for his absence.

Arimanias's initial question gives the impression of sincerity, suggesting that he may be a Nicodemus-like figure, a member of the Jerusalem establishment genuinely open to Jesus's claim (cf. *GJn* 3.1–10; 7.50–51; 19.39). Yet early gospel tradition shows that ostensibly friendly approaches to Jesus may mask a deep

---

16. English translations of *POxy* 840 and excerpts from the *Gospel of the Egyptians* preserved in Clement of Alexandria in Elliott, *Apocryphal New Testament*, 16–19, 31–34; Ron Cameron (ed.), *The Other Gospels: Non-Canonical Gospel Texts* (Guildford: Lutterworth Press, 1983), 49–54; Greek text of *POxy* 840 with translation, introduction and commentary in Thomas J. Kraus, Michael J. Kruger and Tobias Nicklas, *Gospel Fragments* (Oxford Early Christian Gospel Texts; Oxford: Oxford University Press), 121–215.

17. While the name of this Pharisee has not been preserved, it cannot have been Arimanias, which is too long for the space available at a missing line end.

hostility (cf. *GMt* 22.15–18), and that is the case here. The mask is removed and Jesus is denounced as a deceiver:

> The Pharisee said, 'This Nazarene utterly deceived you, and filled your ears with lies, and closed your hearts, and turned you away from the traditions of your fathers.' (*ApocrJn* 1.16–2.2)

The Nazarene's lies must relate to the traditions of the fathers, and those traditions are primarily concerned with the God of Israel and his will for his elect people, disclosed through Moses and the prophets. Jesus has led his disciples into apostasy from the deity whose earthly dwelling place is the temple, the setting for this encounter between Apostle and Pharisee. According to the Pharisee, John's presence in the temple is anomalous. He is trying to serve two masters, not realizing that love for the one means hatred for the other (cf. *GMt* 6.24; *GLk* 16.13; *GThos* 47.1–2; *2 Clement* 6.1).

The reader has every right to expect a robust apostolic response, for in other early gospel traditions Jesus's critics are always refuted and rebuked. Yet John has nothing further to say to the Pharisee, whose words have cut him to the quick. He has indeed been serving two masters, failing to realize that following Jesus means withdrawing allegiance from the God of Israel:

> And when I (John) heard these things, I turned away from the temple to a mountain, a desert place, and I grieved greatly in myself saying, 'How was the Saviour appointed, and why was he sent into the world by his Father who sent him, and who is his Father …?' (*ApocrJn* 2.3–10)

This turning away from the temple is symbolically equivalent to turning away from the traditions of the fathers. A gulf has opened up between the service of two radically opposed masters. From the other side of that gulf, the Pharisee has enabled the Apostle to grasp the true reality of his own situation, which is that the God who sent Jesus into the world is not the known God of Israel but an unknown 'Father' whose being and ways are beyond comprehension. John's 'grief' is occasioned by the collapse of his entire belief system, which he had wrongly regarded as compatible with his allegiance to Jesus. Thus the scene is set for the appearance of the exalted Jesus, whose extended retelling and correction of the *Genesis* narrative explains how the incompatibility has come about. The deceiver is not Jesus but Moses, for as Jesus repeatedly tells John, 'It is not as Moses said.' When the revelation is completed, John is commissioned to write it down for the benefit of 'the immovable race' – the true chosen people, the seed not of Abraham but of Seth – and to communicate it to his fellow apostles (*ApocrJn* 82.5–16; 83.4–6). Thus, the apostle John comes to be associated not only with a gospel, open and available to be read by all, but also with a secret and higher revelation which must be confined to the circle of the elect. The apostle is the channel through which the unknown Father becomes known as false deity is unmasked.

The Acts of John

A comparable unmasking of false deity occurs in another Johannine text, the *Acts of John* 87–105.[18] Here too an episode in the life of the apostle John provides the context for a disclosure of the hidden truth that exposes a prior sacred narrative as false testimony to the divine – Moses's narrative of creation and fall in the one case, the gospel passion narrative in the other. In the Johannine *Acts* there is admittedly no equivalent of the explicit rejection of scriptural authority in the Johannine *Apocryphon*, but the outcome is similar: the sacred narrative is radically recontextualized, transforming Jesus into the antagonist of the scriptural deity rather than his agent or obedient servant.

As in the Thecla episode in the *Acts of Paul*, a key theme in *AcJohn* is the renunciation of sexual intercourse. In a farewell discourse immediately before his death, John recalls how Jesus had called him to lifelong virginity and liberated him from sexual desire (*AcJn* 113), and abstention from intercourse within marriage is a theme within his own teaching. In a lost episode that can be reconstructed only in outline, a wealthy Ephesian woman by the name of Drusiana refuses sexual relations with her still pagan husband Andronicus, who confronts her with a stark choice between sex or death. Drusiana unhesitatingly chooses death as the lesser of these two evils, and she is locked in a tomb (cf. *AcJn* 63,6–9). When she is miraculously released, she tells how 'the Lord appeared to me in the tomb in the form of John and of a youth' (*AcJn* 87,2–3). This causes confusion and leads to a long discourse in which John recalls a number of episodes illustrating Jesus's ability to transform himself. When Jesus called John and his brother James to be disciples with the words, 'I have need of you, come to me', he seemed to James to be a child standing on the shore while John saw him as a good-looking and cheerful adult (*AcJn* 88,9–17). A short while later, John sees Jesus as a bald-headed and bearded man while James sees him as an adolescent (89,1–4); other bewildering transformations are also noted (89), including the 'transfiguration' on a mountain top familiar from the synoptic gospels (90,1–4) followed by a second transfiguration in which John approaches the transfigured Lord secretly from behind and has his beard pulled in punishment (90,4–22). Jesus sometimes seems to possess a solid and material body, while at other times he is immaterial (93,1–4). Other unusual characteristics include the fact that Jesus's eyes were never seen to close (89,6–10) and that his feet left no imprint on the ground (93,10–13).

This section of *AcJohn* has been generally regarded as a classic expression of early 'docetic' Christology.[19] Yet it is a mistake to assume a simple binary divide between

---

18. Greek text in Maximilian Bonnet, *Acta Apostolorum Apocrypha* II,1 (repr. Zürich: Hildesheim; New York: Georg Olms, 1990), 193–203; Greek text with French translation in Eric Junod and Jean-Daniel Kaestli (ed.), *Acta Iohannis*, 2 vols, CCSA (Turnhout: Brepols, 1983), 1.188–217. *AcJohn* 87–105 is an incomplete fragment which Junod and Kaestli rightly place between chapters 36 and 37, as there is a backward reference to *AcJohn* 87 in chapter 63. Line numbers in references are taken from the CCSA edition.

19. Junod and Kaestli, *Acta Iohannis*, 2.492n.

'orthodox' Christologies that affirm the full humanity of Jesus and 'heretical' ones that deny it. The difference is one of degree, not of kind. If the Jesus of *AcJohn* walks without making contact with the ground, the canonical Jesus performs a similar feat when he walks on water (*GMt* 14.22–27 + pars.). On Easter Day, the Lukan Jesus disappears like a ghost from the supper at Emmaus but manifests himself in solid bodily form in Jerusalem shortly afterwards (*GLk* 24.31, 39). The pejorative label 'docetic' overlooks the function of these Johannine reminiscences, which is to strengthen faith in Jesus's divinity by showing how it manifested itself in and through his human appearance. That is also the concern of other early Christologies, including the canonical gospels. Jesus's humanity conceals the truth of his identity, which is that he is the divine son of God, but it does so only in part: the divinity makes itself known by shining through its human disguise, as in the synoptic transfiguration story (*GMt* 17.1–8 + pars.) or the Johannine miracle at Cana (*GJn* 2.1–11). In *AcJohn* 87–105, the author deploys a range of motifs to show how Jesus's divinity manifested itself through his human form, and in doing so he follows an authentically Johannine precedent: recounting a selection of the 'signs' or symptoms of the divine identity 'so that you may believe …' (cf. *GJn* 20.30–31). Traditional heresiological categories are inappropriate here. Proposing an aberrant Christology, as if for its own sake, is not at all what is intended.[20]

The 'signs' Christology of *AcJohn* 88–93 is in keeping with the emphasis on Jesus's divinity elsewhere in this text. He is 'Jesus Christ our God' (*AcJn* 84,19, cf. 107,5), and he can be addressed in prayer as 'my Jesus, the only God of truth [ὁ τῆς ἀληθείας μόνος θεός]' (43,2–3), as 'God of the ages Jesus Christ, God of truth' (82,3), and as 'God Jesus, Father of the realms above the heavens [ὁ τῶν ὑπερουρανίων πατήρ]' (112,14–15). Jesus can be identified with the Father because his existence as Jesus is the result of the Father's self-transformation. Thus, the acts of transformation recounted by John have their basis in the ultimate transformative power that enables the Father to be Jesus and Jesus to be the Father. It is by the same power that Jesus appears to Drusiana as John, and she can therefore praise him for manifesting himself 'with your multiformed face [τῇ πολυμόρφῳ σου ὄψει]' (82,6).

This polymorphic Christology may be associated with conventional theological themes.[21] Thus the God who is Jesus has chosen his apostles to preach to the Gentiles, he has spoken through the law and the prophets and he has revealed himself through the natural order (112,1–5). Yet it seems that the God who speaks through the law is not himself the primary author of the law. As John continues the address that follows Drusiana's experience of the polymorphous Christ in

---

20. For a critique of overuse of the concept of 'docetism', see Jean-Daniel Dubois, 'Le docétisme des christologies gnostiques revisité', *NTS* 63 (2017), 279–304.

21. On 'polymorphic' Christology, see Paul Foster, 'Polymorphic Christology: Its Origins and Development in Early Christianity', *JTS* 58 (2007), 66–99, esp. 85–90 (on *AcJohn*). Foster rightly notes that this Christology has its roots in New Testament texts (67–77), although he reserves the term 'docetic' for the non-canonical text (90).

her entombment, he passes from the selection of episodes from Jesus's Galilean ministry to a new version of the passion narrative:

> And before he was apprehended by the lawless Jews who received their law from the lawless serpent [ὑπὸ τῶν ἀνόμων καὶ ὑπὸ ἀνόμου ὄφεως νομοθετουμένων Ἰουδαίων], he gathered us together and said, 'Before I am handed over to them [ἐκείνοις παραδοθῆναι], let us sing a hymn to the Father and in that way go forth to what awaits us.' (AcJn 94,1–4)

The serpent is the serpent from the Garden of Eden, identified elsewhere with Satan but here seen as responsible for inspiring not only the arrest of Jesus by 'the lawless Jews' but also the law that mandates their action. There is already a hint of this in an earlier Johannine passion narrative, where Jesus's accusers (again, 'the Jews') inform Pilate that 'we have a law, and according to the law he ought to die because he claimed to be son of God' (GJn 19.7). This law is on the side of 'the Jews'; it is '*your* law' or '*their* law' (GJn 8.17, 10.34; 15.25). The association between the law and the serpent in the Johannine Acts may also reflect Moses's bronze serpent, displayed on a pole and understood as an object of worship, that is, as representing the God of Israel who is responsible for the Mosaic law (cf. *Num* 21.8–9; GJn 3.14). Thus, Jesus must teach his disciples the crucial difference between himself and the God of Israel who opposes him and is responsible for his crucifixion: 'It is I who am your God, not the God of the betrayer [θεὸς εἰμι σου οὐ τοῦ προδότου]' (AcJn 96,17). This instruction takes place in the unexpected context of a liturgical dance in which the disciples hold hands in a circle around Jesus and respond with an 'Amen' to each line of a hymn as he chants it (AcJn 94,4–95,50).[22] Inspired by *GMatthew* 26.30 ('And after singing a hymn, they went out to the Mount of Olives'), this scene attests a ritual commemoration of Jesus's passion that takes the place of the eucharist.[23]

The 'betrayer' referred to is Judas, though he is not here named, and his God is the God of Israel, who presides over the site of Jesus's crucifixion. What appears to take place at that site is not the reality, which is disclosed to John as he hides in a cave on the Mount of Olives after he and the other disciples have fled in all directions (AcJn 97,2–5; cf. *GMt* 26.56). At the sixth hour, the whole earth is covered with a darkness that signifies the world's ignorance of the mystery that is being enacted:

> And my Lord stood in the middle of the cave and enlightened me [φωτίσας με] saying, 'John, to the crowd below in Jerusalem I am crucified and pierced with

---

22. Parts of this hymn were set to music by Gustav Holst, in his *Hymn of Jesus* (1917). Holst was introduced to this text by G. R. S. Mead, editor of *Pistis Sophia* and other 'gnostic' texts. See Raymond Head, 'The Hymn of Jesus: Holst's Gnostic Exploration of Time and Space', *Tempo* no. 208 (July 1999), 7–13.

23. So Junod and Kaestli, *Acta Iohannis*, 2.595n.

lances and sticks and given gall to drink. But to you I speak …, so that you may hear what a disciple must learn from the teacher and a human from God.' (*AcJn* 97,7–12)

The wooden cross down below in Jerusalem is a mere symbol of the 'cross of light' that John now sees, which represents the redemption of the cosmos from the chaos created by 'powers, principalities, dominions, demons, energies, threats, wraths, devils, Satan, and the lower root [ἡ κατωτικὴ ῥίζα] from which the nature of transient things came forth' (98,17–19). To mistake the symbol for the reality is to fall victim to the error of 'the crowd below in Jerusalem', which is also the error of most hearers of the canonical gospels. Contrary to the general belief, the God who is Jesus suffers not on an instrument of torture devised by humans but insofar as he has not yet been reunited with his 'members':

> You hear that I suffered and I did not suffer, that I did not suffer and I did suffer, that I was pierced yet I was not wounded, hanged and I was not hanged, that blood flowed from me and it did not flow. And in sum, what they say of me did not happen, and what I suffered is what they did not say. (*AcJn* 101,6–11)

Thus, as in the case of the Johannine *Apocryphon*, a canonical story is challenged and corrected as the apostle is enabled by the living Christ to grasp the truth concealed by the appearance – the truth of cosmic redemption.[24] The deity who gave the law and used it to secure Jesus's condemnation is utterly inferior to the true God who is Jesus himself.

The First Apocalypse of James

Later gospels or gospel-like texts invariably take over stories, sayings, events, characters or motifs drawn from earlier ones, adapting them to serve their own distinctive agendas. As we have seen, *AcJohn* develops an elaborate liturgy out of the passing Matthean reference to the hymn sung by Jesus and his disciples as they leave the Upper Room, and finds in the darkness at the crucifixion the occasion for John's enlightenment in his mountain-top retreat. In the *First Apocalypse of James*, the synoptic Jesus's announcement of his passion together with Peter's shocked response provides the template for an analogous scene involving James the Lord's brother, also known as James the Just.[25]

---

24. The polemical character of this passion narrative is noted by Junod and Kaestli: 'L'auteur fait davantage que compléter le récit canonique: il lui substitue un autre évangile' (*Acta Iohannis*, 2.595). The mythologizing of Jesus's cross as the means of cosmic redemption is already evident in *Colossians* 2.14–15.

25. Coptic texts and German translations of the two extant copies of *1ApocJas* in Johanna Brankaer and Hans-Gebhard Bethge, *Codex Tchacos: Texte und Analysen* (TU 161,

> From then on Jesus began to show his disciples that he must go to Jerusalem and suffer many things from the elders and chief priests and scribes, and be killed, and on the third day be raised. And taking him Peter began to rebuke him, saying, 'God forbid, Lord! This shall never happen to you!' (*GMt* 16.21–22)

In *1ApocJas* Jesus's announcement to James occurs shortly before its fulfilment, when he is already in Jerusalem.

> 'Behold, I will reveal to you the mystery. They will seize me after three days, and then the crowd of elders will accuse me and condemn me and curse me. But my redemption is near.' And James answered and said: 'Rabbi, what are you saying? If they seize you, then what am I to do?' (CT 11,8–19 [NHC V 25,5–12])[26]

James here begins to realize that Jesus's condemnation makes him liable to a similar fate, but it is only after Jesus's suffering and return – this text does not speak explicitly of 'resurrection' – that the full reality of his situation becomes clear to him. Up to this point, James has been a zealous servant of the God of Israel and a renowned teacher with his own group of loyal disciples. Jesus's return will compel him to abandon the service of the 'just' deity, exposing himself to his wrath. In this text as in the two Johannine ones already discussed, the disciple receives the crucial revelation that transforms his understanding of deity on a mountain, where Jesus finds him in a state of acute distress and confusion.

In spite of his agitated state of mind, James continues to teach his disciples, who respond to his teaching with enthusiasm and view him as Jesus's successor. James is characterized as a rabbi positioned between a christianized Judaism and the claim of Jesus, not yet fully grasped. He is generally known as 'James the Just' but he is addressed by Jesus as 'James my brother', and so long as he maintains his Jewish identity he is ignorant about himself (cf. CT 10,2–6). The tension generated by this double identity becomes clear during the interval between the departure and the return:

> And Jesus went, he fulfilled what was necessary for him. And James heard of his sufferings and was greatly grieved. And he waited for his coming. (In this alone did he find comfort, in waiting for his coming.) And two days passed, and behold, James was ministering on the mountain called Galgelam, where he remained another day with his disciples, who heard him gladly. And they found comfort in him, for they said, 'This is the Second Teacher.' And behold, they dispersed, and James remained alone and prayed much, as was his custom.

Berlin: de Gruyter), 88–129. My translations follow the CT version, with a few exceptions. Textual variants are listed in the notes.

26. Textual variants: 'I will reveal' (NH) / 'I have revealed' (CT); the mystery (CT) / 'everything of the mystery' (NH); 'after three days' (CT) / 'after tomorrow' (NH); 'and then … curse me' (CT, om. NH).

As he did so, Jesus suddenly appeared to him, and he ceased praying and began to embrace him, saying, 'Rabbi, I was separated from you. I heard what you endured and I grieved greatly – you know my compassion!' (CT 16,26–17, 26 [NHC V 30,11–31, 9])[27]

The author's familiarity with early James traditions is clear.[28] In GThomas 12, Jesus instructs his disciples to regard 'James the Just' as their leader following his own departure, characterizing him in extravagant terms as 'the one for whose sake heaven and earth came into being'. The Second Teacher seems as exalted a figure as the First. James is celebrated for his piety. According to Hegesippus, he lived an ascetic lifestyle, abstaining from alcohol, meat, haircuts, oil and baths. In the temple he enjoyed the high priestly privilege of entry into the holy place [τὰ ἅγια], where 'he was to be found on his knees asking forgiveness for the people, so that his knees became hard like a camel's' (cited by Eusebius, HE 2.23.3). James is remembered as one who acknowledges his brother Jesus's messiahship while remaining deeply embedded in traditional Jewish piety, and his piety is exercised for the well-being of the Jewish people for whom he intercedes as Moses, Daniel and Ezra had done before him. This second-century James-image expresses a Christian desire for participation in and benefit from the cultural capital of Judaism and its prestigious institutions.[29] Thus, James is everywhere known as 'the Just', and his exceptional justice or righteousness is that of a messianic Jew.[30]

This James-image is well known to the author of 1ApocJas, and he is determined to shatter it. When Jesus returns after his passion, James learns that his celebrated justice or righteousness is worthless since it has been exercised in the service of a false deity. He learns this through an interpretation of his seemingly innocent response to Jesus's reappearance, when he stops praying in order to embrace him. This turning from prayer to Jesus represents nothing less than apostasy from the God of Israel. At the very moment of opening himself to the truth, James is exposed to acute danger. Jesus warns him to

---

27. Variants: 'And Jesus went' (CT) / 'And the Lord greeted him' (NH); 'fulfilled' (NH) / 'prepared' (CT); 'for him' (CT, om. NH); 'for his coming' (CT) / 'for the type of his coming' (NH); 'In this … coming' (CT, om. NH); 'And two days passed' (CT) / 'And he came after some days' (NH); 'ministering' (CT) / 'walking' (NH); 'where … day' (CT, om. NH); 'And they found comfort in him' (CT) / 'And he did not know there was a comforter' (NH).

28. For early James traditions, see David R. Nienhuis, *Not by Paul Alone: The Formation of the Catholic Epistles Collection and the Christian Canon* (Waco, TX: Baylor University Press), 121–50.

29. A similar concern might be seen in the temple setting of the early career of the Virgin Mary, as recounted in another James text, the *Protevangelium of James*.

30. James is referred to as 'the Just' in the *Gospel of the Hebrews* (Jerome, *Vir. ill.* 2), Hegesippus (Eusebius, *HE* 2.23.4), Clement of Alexandria (Eusebius, *HE* 2.1.2), Origen (*c. Cel.* 1.47), *Gospel of Thomas* 12, *Second Apocalypse of James* 44,13–14 (cf. 49,9, 59,22, 60,12–14, 61,14: 'the Just One').

'take heed to yourself, for the just god is angry, for you were his servant, which is why you received the name "James the Just". See, already you have been freed! You know me and know yourself, and you abandoned the prayer the just god required, and so you have embraced me and kissed me. Truly I say to you, he has directed his fury against you and his wrath; but this too must take place.' And James was afraid, and he wept and grieved greatly. And the two of them sat down on a rock. (CT 18,16–19,10 [NHC V 31,29–32, 15])[31]

As in *ApocrJn*, the occasion for the sudden breach with the God of Israel seems trivial. John and James both assume that faith in Jesus as the Christ is compatible with loyalty to their Jewish heritage. John visits the temple to worship, James intercedes for his people, but both of them experience a sudden moment of fundamental disruption in which their long established relationship to their God is destroyed, initially plunging them into confusion and despair. In the one case, the agent of that destruction is Arimanias the Pharisee, who enables John to see that faith in Jesus is incompatible with loyalty to the traditions of the fathers. In the other case, it is Jesus who declares that James's turning from his prayer to embrace him is definitive, an act of apostasy that the rejected deity will finally avenge when James is stoned to death (CT 11,20–23; 30,23).

The Marcionite Euangelion

Gospels or gospel-like texts are the work of authors who are also editors: authors when new narratives featuring the earthly or risen Jesus are produced, editors when older narratives are modified and adapted. The two roles are often interwoven. The same evangelist may be the author of some parts of the text, an editor in others. The narratives of apostolic apostasy and conversion discussed so far seem to belong to the authorial end of the spectrum. While they all draw on earlier Christian traditions, there is no evidence in them of substantial editorial activity. In contrast, the gospel handed down in Marcionite communities would seem to be the product of editorial activity – if, as seems likely, the conventional view is correct and this work is an abbreviated and emended version of the text known elsewhere as the *Gospel according to Luke*.[32] In order to create space for themselves

---

31. Variants: 'See … required' (CT) / 'You see how you will be sober on seeing me, and you have abandoned this prayer, since you are a just man of God' (NH); 'so … kissed me' (NH) / 'and I – he received me and greeted me' (CT); 'but … place' (CT) / 'but so that these other things come to pass' (NH).

32. For the minority view that *GLuke* is a later expansion of *GMarcion*, see Markus Vinzent, *Marcion and the Dating of the Synoptic Gospels* (Leuven: Peeters, 2014), 255–80. J. BeDuhn sees the two gospels as alternative, though not ideologically opposed, versions of the same text, one adapted for Gentiles, the other for Jewish readers (*First New Testament*, 78–92). On that view, Marcion inherits 'his' *euangelion* from earlier gospel traditions.

in the marketplace of early Christian literature, the narratives featuring John and James claim to have been transmitted by way of a secret tradition that withholds them from the wider Christian public and reserves them for the few who are able to grasp the higher truths they contain – above all, the truth that the Father of Jesus is not to be identified with the God of Israel. *GMarcion* too seeks to persuade its readers of this non-identity: the gracious and previously unknown deity disclosed in Jesus is someone other than the vengeful tyrant who created this imperfect world and who reveals his true character through the writings of Moses and the prophets. For this text, no new narrative is necessary. The differentiation between the two deities is achieved, economically and with a minimum of effort, by simple editorial activities: erasures, emendations and the provision of a preface.[33]

In Book 4 of his work *Against Marcion*, Tertullian turns his attention to the Marcionite gospel, arguing in exhaustive detail that its account of the ministry of Jesus is entirely compatible with the scriptural portrayal of the God of Israel as a God in whom goodness and retributive justice are combined. Marcionite beliefs are refuted by appeal to the Marcionite gospel. Tertullian also reports that this gospel was provided with an interpretative key (entitled *Antitheses*) which 'seeks to demonstrate that the gospel is incompatible with the law, so as to argue from the difference between the claims of the two documents to a difference between the deities' (*Adv. Marc.* 1.19.4). Tertullian always refers to the *Antitheses* in connection with Marcion's *Euangelion* and not as a free-standing work, and it is best understood as a preface consisting mainly or even exclusively of summaries of passages from the gospel juxtaposed with contrasting passages from the law and the prophets.[34] If Marcion had provided his opposed texts with an extensive commentary, Tertullian would surely have engaged with it directly. Located immediately before the gospel text itself, the function of the *Antitheses* is to warn the reader to avoid the fatal error to which so many Christians fall victim – identifying the infinitely gracious God who freely discloses himself in Jesus Christ with the capricious and vengeful Creator revealed through Moses and the prophets.

Christ in the gospel commands us to love our enemies and to turn the other cheek when assaulted (cf. *GMcn* 6.27–29 [= *GLk* 6.27–29]; Tertullian, *Adv. Marc.* 4.16.1–2). In contrast, the Creator repeatedly insists on a strictly equivalent

---

33. For a reconstruction of the Marcionite gospel text based primarily on Tertullian, Epiphanius and Adamantius, see Dieter Roth, *The Text of Marcion's Gospel* (Leiden: Brill, 2015). The most important sources are Tertullian, *Adv. Marc.* 4, and Epiphanius, *Panarion* 1.42.11, where differences between *GLuke* and *GMarcion* are listed. Texts and translations: Ernest Evans (ed.), *Tertullian Adversus Marcionem*, 2 vols. (Oxford: Oxford University Press, 1972); Karl Holl, *Epiphanius II, Ancoratus und Panarion haer. 34–64*, rev. Jürgen Dummer (GCS, Berlin: Akademie Verlag, 1985); Frank Williams, *The Panarion of Epiphanius of Salamis*, Book I (Sects 1 – 46) (Leiden: Brill, 2009).

34. The view taken here of the *Antitheses* is in broad agreement with Judith Lieu, *Marcion and the Making of a Heretic: God and Scripture in the Second Century* (Cambridge: Cambridge University Press, 2015), 272–89.

retribution in such cases: 'eye for eye, tooth for tooth, hand for hand, foot for foot' (*Ex* 21.24, cf. *Lev* 24.20). This principle of equivalence must be rigidly enforced, even if it means the death penalty; 'your eye shall not pity' (*Deut* 19.21). For Marcion if not for Tertullian, the opposition between Christ and Moses could hardly be clearer, and the only rational explanation is that they speak for different deities.

Christ is touched by a pathologically menstruating woman, who is instantly healed (cf. *GMcn* 8.43–44; *Adv. Marc.* 4.20.9). The Creator decrees that even indirect contact with a menstruating woman renders one unclean, and this includes a case like the one in the gospel, where 'a woman has a discharge of blood for many days, not at the time of her impurity' (*Lev* 15.25). Yet Jesus is unconcerned about his own ritual purity and feels no need to 'wash his clothes and bathe himself in water' (*Lev* 15.27). It seems that he recognizes no obligation to the God who speaks through Moses.

Christ's attitude to children is incompatible with the Creator's, as exemplified by the harsh punishment meted out to boys who jeered at Elisha's baldness (cf. *GMcn* 9.46–47; *4 Kgdms* 2.23–24). Here Tertullian may quote directly from the *Antitheses*:

> Christ loves children, teaching that those who aspire to be greater ought to be like them. But the Creator sent bears against young boys, avenging the prophet Elisha who had been mocked by them. (*Adv. Marc.* 4.23.4)

Instructed by these and other contrasting examples, the reader turns from the gospel preface to the gospel itself, which opens as follows:

> In the fifteenth year of the reign of Tiberius Caesar, in the times of Pontius Pilate, Jesus descended to Capernaum, a city of Galilee. And he was teaching them in the synagogue, and they were all amazed at his teaching, for his word was with authority. (*GMcn* 3.1a+4.31–32)[35]

Here there is none of the elaborate preparation for Jesus's ministry attested in the opening chapters of *GLuke*, with their portrayal of a context shaped by the law (the priest Zechariah, the temple, sacrifices, circumcision) and the prophets (extended citations of Isaianic prophecies fulfilled in John the Baptist and Jesus).[36] In this gospel opening, there is nothing to associate Jesus with the law, the prophets, or the God who speaks in them and of whom they speak. Unlike his Lukan counterpart in the synagogue at Nazareth, the Marcionite Jesus does not attempt to impress his audience by claiming to fulfil scripture (cf. *GLk* 4.16–21). He does not need to

---

35. Roth, *Text*, 412 (with cross-references to detailed discussion).

36. Zechariah's priesthood, *GLk* 1.5–23. The temple, *GLk* 1.9–23; 2.22–38. Sacrifice, *GLk* 1.9–11; 2.24. Circumcision, *GLk* 1.59, 2.21. Isaianic prophecies, *GLk* 3.4–6 (*Is* 40.3–5), *GLk* 4.17–19 (*Is* 61.1–2).

appeal to other established authorities, since his own word is authoritative in itself in spite of its utterly unexpected announcement of the previously unknown God who is pure goodness.

Other smaller-scale differences between *GMarcion* and *GLuke* seem to have been similarly motivated by the need to distance Jesus from the Creator. At *GLuke* 10.21, Jesus addresses God as 'Father, Lord of heaven and earth', whereas at the equivalent point in *GMarcion* this has been reduced to 'Lord of heaven'.[37] The absence of 'Father' is probably not significant, but the reference to 'earth' may have been omitted because it implies a reference to the Creator. The creator-deity is also the lawgiver, and the lawgiver is necessarily also a judge. In *GLuke* 11.42, Jesus criticizes the Pharisees for observing the minutiae of the law – tithing their herbs – while neglecting 'the judgement [κρίσιν] and the love of God'. In *GMarcion* they neglect 'the *calling* [κλῆσιν] and love of God', a reading that avoids attributing punitive justice to the God of love and speaks instead of Jesus's own mission, rejected by the Pharisees because of their stubborn loyalty to the Lawgiver.[38] Positive Lukan references to scriptural figures are omitted or emended. The Lukan Jesus speaks of a time 'when you will see Abraham and Isaac and Jacob and all the prophets in the kingdom of God and yourselves thrown out' (*GLk* 13.28), whereas his Marcionite counterpart warns that 'you will see *all the righteous* in the kingdom of God and yourselves *kept out*'.[39] The righteous are those who respond to Jesus's call to the love of God; the unrighteous cannot be 'thrown out' of a realm that was never theirs in the first place. Differences of this kind are not just random accidents of textual transmission but reflect the theological agenda made explicit in the *Antitheses*.

In *GMarcion* the accusations made against Jesus at his trial are, at least in part, true. Chief priests, scribes and elders inform Pilate that 'we found this man corrupting our nation *and destroying* [καταλύοντα] *the law and the prophets*, and forbidding us to give tribute to Caesar, *and turning away* [ἀποστρέφοντα] *women and children*' (*GMcn* 23.2).[40] Like the Pharisee Arimanias in *ApocrJn*, Jesus's accusers have rightly understood that his opposition to Jewish scripture and tradition is absolute. Destroying the law and the prophets is indeed what Jesus does: the Marcionite Gospel is diametrically opposed to its Matthean counterpart at this point (cf. *GMt* 5.17). Thus, Marcion undertakes to purge the corrupt Lukan text of passages claiming that Jesus is actually dependent on the law and the prophets, and that his mission and call are not sufficiently persuasive in themselves. On Easter Day, the as yet unrecognized Jesus will therefore criticize the two disciples on the Emmaus road for their failure to believe 'all that I have said to you' (*GMcn* 24.25), rather than 'all that the prophets have said' (*GLk* 24.25–27).[41]

37. Roth, *Text*, 420.
38. Roth, *Text*, 422.
39. Roth, *Text*, 425.
40. Roth, *Text*, 433–44.
41. Roth, *Text*, 435. My citation follows Epiphanius and Adamantius (ἐλάλησα πρὸς ὑμᾶς) rather than Tertullian (*locutus est ad vos*).

The narrative texts discussed here do not all oppose Jesus to the creator-lawgiver deity and to Moses his servant in exactly the same way. Moses remains an important figure in *ApocrJn*, and a knowledge of the early chapters of *Genesis* is a prerequisite for understanding the later text as it rewrites and corrects them. Moses is also significant in the *Antitheses* prefaced to *GMarcion*, but his texts are taken at face value even as their normative claim is radically challenged by the gospel. In *AcJohn* and *1ApocJas*, Moses remains unnamed but presupposed as the definitive representative of a deity fundamentally hostile to Jesus and his followers. This opposition may be condensed into a Marcionite antithesis or elaborated in new gospel-like narratives that challenge the assumptions of their precursors, but in each case the attempt is made to make that opposition unambiguously clear. These texts confront their Christian reader with a choice: either to continue in the impossible service of two masters or gratefully to accept the liberation from the one offered by the other.

4

WHY ARE THE DISCIPLES 'LIKE THE ANGELS'? REDEMPTION THROUGH SIN IN THE *GOSPEL OF JUDAS*

Jonathan Cahana-Blum

Irenaeus of Lyon, writing in the late second century, has this much to say regarding the *Gospel of Judas*:

> And they say Judas the betrayer had meticulous knowledge of these things, and since only he among all the other [disciples] knew the truth, he accomplished the mystery of the betrayal: through him all things, both earthly and heavenly, were dissolved, they say. And they adduce a work of fiction to this effect, calling it 'The Gospel of Judas'. ... They also hold, like Carpocrates, that there is no other way to be saved except by having gone through all kinds of experience. An angel, they maintain, attends them in every one of their sinful and abominable actions, and urges them to venture on audacity and bring on impurity. Whatever the nature of the action, they declare that they do it in the name of the angel, saying, 'O angel, I use your deed; O you power, I accomplish your operation!' And they maintain that this is 'perfect knowledge', without shrinking to rush into such actions that are not lawful even to name.[1]

In a very different context, the eminent historian of religion and scholar of Jewish mysticism, Gerschom Scholem, while analysing the 'nihilism' propounded by Sabbatian sects active during the seventeenth and eighteenth centuries, argued,

> The desire for total liberation which played so tragic a role in the development of Sabbatian nihilism was by no means a purely self-destructive force; on the contrary, beneath the surface of lawlessness, antinomianism, and catastrophic

---

1. Irenaeus of Lyon, *Adv. Haer.* 1.31.1–2 (my translation). For the text, see A. Rousseau and L. Doutreleau, ed., *Irénée de Lyon – Contre les hérésies*, livre I, vol. II (Paris: Éditions du Cerf, 1979), 386.

negation, powerful constructive impulses were at work, and these, I maintain, it is the duty of the historian to uncover.[2]

In investigating a text as perplexing as the *Gospel of Judas*, we would do best to keep in mind both arguments, the heresy hunter's and the historian of religion's, in order to be sensitive to the constructive impulses active within this powerful counter-narrative of the canonical Jesus's story.

Whatever position one chooses to adhere to regarding the controversial *Gospel of Judas*, it can easily be demonstrated that the narrative it offers is a thorough counter-narrative to the canonical gospels, both pertaining to the details and to its general framework.[3] Whether Judas is a positive or negative character, the gospel offers us a picture in which the whole group of disciples (none of which, except Judas, is named) are collaborators of the evil God.[4] None of them will be saved, and Jesus continually dissociates himself from their company, declaring 'their God' as completely alien to him. If Judas is a positive character, the gospel at least leaves one disciple to spread the gospel. If indeed he is evil, Jesus leaves no human disciples on earth to spread his word. In that case, Jesus is a thoroughly alien

---

2. Gershom Scholem, 'Redemption through Sin', in *The Messianic Idea in Judaism and Other Essays on Jewish Spirituality* (New York: Schocken Books, 1971), 84.

3. *GJudas* is believed to be a second-century Greek early Christian text, and it has been (badly) preserved in the fourth-century Coptic Tchacos Codex. For the text and the codex, see R. Kasser, G. Wurst, M. Meyer and F. Gaudard, ed., *The Gospel of Judas, together with the Letter from Peter to Philip, James, and a Book of Allogenes from Codex Tchacos: Critical Edition* (Washington, DC: National Geographic, 2007), and the additional fragments published in H. Krosney, M. Meyer and G. Wurst, 'Preliminary Report on New Fragments of Codex Tchacos', *Early Christianity* 1 (2010), 282–94.

4. For a positive Judas, see, in addition to the editors and translators of the text, Elaine H. Pagels and Karen L. King, *Reading Judas: The Gospel of Judas and the Shaping of Christianity* (New York: Viking, 2007); yet, note that King has partly retracted her position in Karen L. King, 'Christians Who Sacrifice and Those Who Do Not?: Discursive Practices, Polemics, and Ritualizing', in *'One Who Sows Bountifully': Essays in Honor of Stanley K. Stowers*, ed. Caroline E. Johnson Hodge, Saul M. Olyan, Daniel C. Ullucci and Emma Wasserman (Providence, RI: Brown University Press, 2013), 307–18. For a negative view, see, for instance, Louis Painchaud, 'Polemical Aspects of the *Gospel of Judas*', in *The Gospel of Judas in Context*, ed. Madeleine Scopello (Leiden: Brill, 2008), 171–86. For the third camp, which appears to be gaining popularity by problematically deciding not to decide, and in the process toning down the ferocity of *GJudas* well into our own comfort zone, see, for instance, Lance Jenott, *The Gospel of Judas: Coptic Text, Translation, and Historical Interpretation of 'The Betrayer's Gospel'* (Tübingen: Mohr Siebeck, 2011), and Deborah Niederer Saxon, *The Care of the Self in Early Christian Texts* (Cham: Palgrave Macmillan, 2017), 92–118. I have provided a complete overview of this discussion in Jonathan Cahana, 'Salvific Dissolution: The Mystery of the Betrayal between the New Testament and the Gospel of Judas', *NTS* 63 (2017), 111–24.

figure, whose gospel was not understood, and perhaps could not be understood, by any of his disciples. It is hard to tell which narrative is more counter to the New Testament gospels, the one which leaves Jesus with no apostles to spread his message or the one in which only Judas is a true disciple and apostle. Perhaps both are equally so.

Judas and salvific dissolution

In a recent article, I have argued that to understand this gospel one must address a thoroughly gnostic idea regarding the meaning of the crucifixion. This concept, which I described as 'salvific dissolution', argues that while Christ could not have been harmed by the crucifixion, the attempt of the archons to crucify him started a process that shook the very basis of their world order, or, to use Irenaeus's terminology, a process that culminated in 'all things, both earthly and heavenly, [being] dissolved'.[5] This understanding is evinced in such gnostic works as *The Concept of Our Great Power*, *The Paraphrase of Shem*, *The Second Treatise of the Great Seth* and the *Gospel of Mary*.[6] I have also argued that salvific dissolution, in turn, is what holds the key to understanding both the purpose and role of Judas in the *Gospel of Judas*. This work was made with the intention to explicate the role of Judas, who enabled the crucifixion and thus opened up the possibility for redemption, within salvation history. It may have been triggered by an enigmatic account such as that preserved in *The Concept of our Great Power*, which describes the salvific dissolution and Judas's role in it in the following way:

> Then a great turmoil arose; the archons roused their wrath against him and wished to deliver him to the ruler of Hades. Then they came to know one of his followers; a fire had seized his soul. He handed him over without anyone's knowledge. They acted and seized him; they themselves brought their judgement upon themselves. And they handed him over [i.e. Christ] to the ruler of Hades but gave him [i.e. Judas] to Sasabek and Berot. He [Christ] had prepared himself

---

5. Jonathan Cahana, 'Salvific Dissolution'. I have argued in detail for the usefulness of the category of Gnosticism as far as it pertains to a specific kind of ancient Christians (cf. Jonathan Cahana-Blum, *Wrestling with Archons: Gnosticism as a Critical Theory of Culture* [Lanham, MD: Lexington Books, 2018]), but here it is enough to admit that GJudas shares, in addition to 'salvific dissolution', much of its imagery, motifs and concepts with the other Nag Hammadi texts mentioned, as well as that they all vociferously argue against the idea that Jesus came from the God of the Hebrew Bible. Far from 'dismissing it as "heretical"' (Saxon, *The Care of the Self*, 118), this means accepting the full and inconvenient force of GJudas's argument, which seems to be a bit more than an issue of 'anger management'.

6. *The Paraphrase of Shem* 39,28–40,1; *The Second Treatise of the Great Seth* 58,13–59,14; and the *Gospel of Mary* 15,16–20. For *The Concept of Our Great Power* 41,13–42,29, see below.

to go down and confound them. Then the ruler of Hades took him, but the manner of his flesh he could not hold, to show it to the archons. But he kept repeating: 'Who is this? What is he? His word has annulled the law of the aeon …' The archons inquired into what had taken place. They did not know that this was the sign of their destruction and the change of the aeon. The sun set in the daytime; the day was darkened. The demons shuddered. And after these things he will appear ascending, and the sign of the aeon will come to appear, and the aeons will melt away. And blessed will be those who will understand … And they will be revealed and be blessed because they will have understood the truth.[7]

According to this account in *The Concept of Our Great Power*, Judas was no more than an unfortunate individual who was being taken advantage of by the archons, and, once he was not useful for them anymore, thrown to the demons. Yet, from a gnostic point of view, his role was crucial for salvation, and whoever wrote the *Gospel of Judas* (or, perhaps as had been correctly suggested by the late Marvin Meyer, the *Gospel for Judas*) found such an enigmatic and laconic description of Judas's role inadequate and perhaps even troubling.[8] This writer came up with a solution that reasoned that since Judas was so crucial to salvation he had to know something of the gnostic mysteries. On the other hand, this same author, probably due to the nihilistic attitude which sought to represent Jesus as thoroughly alien to this world – and even more so, to his Jewish surroundings – was not willing to make him a gnostic disciple, but still reasoned that he was worthy to receive some reward for his service. I would argue that this is the only way in which the following exchange between Jesus and Judas could be explained:

'You will grieve much when you see the kingdom and all its generation.' When Judas heard this he said to him, 'What is the advantage that I have received? For you have set me apart from that generation.' Jesus answered and said, 'You will

---

7. *The Concept of Our Great Power*, 41,13–42,29; translation and emendations according to Francis E. Williams, *Mental Perception: A Commentary on NHC VI.4, The Concept of Our Great Power* (Leiden: Brill, 2001), 8–11, with slight revisions: I have consistently translated παραδιδόναι as 'handed over' (Williams uses 'betrayed' for Judas and 'delivered' for the archons) and have preferred to leave aeon(s) untranslated throughout. For discussion of this scene from the *The Concept of Our Great Power* and its many parallels to *The Second Treatise of the Great Seth*, as well as the identity of the demons Sasabek and Berot, see Williams, *Mental Perception*, 114–33.

8. See Marvin Meyer, 'Interpreting Judas: Ten Passages in the Gospel of Judas', in *The Gospel of Judas in Context*, ed. M. Scopello (Leiden: Brill, 2008), 41–55, who remarks regarding the slightly awkward title ⲡⲉⲩⲁⲅⲅⲉⲗⲓⲟⲛ ⲛ̄ⲓⲟⲩⲇⲁⲥ that 'the common pseudonymous attribution that a gospel is the good news "according to" (ⲕⲁⲧⲁ or ⲡⲕⲁⲧⲁ) a given disciple or apostle is not provided here. Rather, this is the good news of Judas, perhaps about Judas or even for Judas' (42).

become the thirteenth, and you will be cursed by the other generations, and you will come to rule over them.'[9]

Here, Judas complains that, though he received knowledge and he himself will become crucial for salvation, he received no real benefit from either. Jesus acknowledges the problem and promises him the best award he can hope for in the lower world.

Read in such way, the *Gospel of Judas* becomes an interesting specimen of counter-narrative to the New Testament gospels. In both, the crucifixion is crucial for salvation. However, in the New Testament this is mostly because of its expiatory meanings and/or the event of the resurrection, while in the *Gospel of Judas* it is the culmination of a salvific dissolution that exposes the lie of the archontic world. In both, Judas is the one who effects the crucifixion, and thus salvation. Nevertheless, in the New Testament gospels he does so inadvertently, for the wrong reasons and/or out of avarice, and (in some of the accounts) is punished for his deeds. Thus, in the *Gospel of Matthew*, for instance, he receives the infamous thirty pieces of silver and ends up committing suicide out of remorse, while *Luke-Acts* tells us that Judas ended by falling and 'bursting open' in the field he bought with his blood money.[10] The *Gospel of Judas*, on the other hand, is much more coherent in describing Judas as fully aware of what he is doing, and receiving his appropriate reward for his role in salvation.[11]

The (other) disciples and their dreams

It is even more complex to try to analyse how the other disciples – who only act as a group and never individually – are subjected to counter-narrative in this gospel. A crucial passage for understanding its evaluation of their deeds is one of the most hotly debated parts of this gospel:

---

9. GJudas 46,12–23. Text and translation according to R. Kasser et al., *The Gospel of Judas*, and the additional fragments published in H. Krosney et al., 'Preliminary Report'.

10. *GMt* 26.14–15; 27.5; *Acts* 1.18.

11. While the New Testament gospels surely differ from one another in the portrayal of Judas, the other disciples, and the crucifixion event, none of them even comes close to the idea that the disciples worshipped an evil god who is opposed to Jesus, or that Judas was a chosen disciple to receive a special secret revelation, or that the crucifixion started a process that exposed the lie of the creator god. In comparison to *GJudas*, the differences between the New Testament gospels are negligible. At the end of the day, the New Testament gospels offer a powerful combined narrative that is thoroughly countered by *GJudas*, which is probably responding to their general narrative rather than to a specific one of them. For a discussion of the portrayal of Judas and his liability for the crucifixion in the New Testament and early Christian proto-orthodox tradition, see, e.g., Kim Paffenroth, *Judas: Images of the Lost Disciple* (Louisville, KY: Westminster John Knox, 2001), 1–58.

> Truly I say to you, Judas, those [who] offer sacrifices to Saklas … [three lines missing] … everything that is evil. But you will exceed all of them. For you will sacrifice the man who bears me.[12]

According to my reading, if Judas's betrayal is crucial to salvation, and in that respect he exceeds, excels or simply does more than the other disciples, it only follows that their work also contributes to the salvific dissolution, if in a lesser way. Yet what exactly are the disciples doing that contributes to redemption? That is described three times in the surviving text. In the first of these, the disciples have a disturbing dream, which receives an even more disturbing interpretation from Jesus:

> And they [said, 'We have] seen a great house [with a] large altar [in it, and] twelve men – they are the priests, we would say; and a name <--->; and a crowd of people is waiting at the altar [until] the priests [finished presenting] the offering. And we kept waiting.' [Jesus] said, 'What are [—] like?' and they said, '[Some] fast [for] two weeks; others sacrifice their own children, others their wives, in praise and in humility with each other; others sleep with men; others are involved in slaughter. Still others commit a multitude of sins and deeds of lawlessness. [And] the men who stand [before] the altar invoke your [name].'… Jesus said to them, 'It is you who are presenting the offerings on the altar you have seen. That one is the god you serve, and you are the twelve men you have seen. And the cattle that are brought in are the sacrifice you have seen – that is, the many people you lead astray before that altar.'[13]

Then, just after Jesus interprets the disciples' dream for them, he apparently turns to prophesy their role in the end days. After almost two lines missing, we read that they (or, since the subject changes to the third person, perhaps their successors)

> will stand and make use of my name in this way, and <the> generations of the pious will be loyal to him. After him another man will stand there from the [fornicators], and another [will] stand there from the slayers of children, and another from those who sleep with men and those who abstain, and the rest of the people of pollution and lawlessness and error, and those who say, 'We are like angels'; they are the stars that bring everything to completion.[14]

Considerably later in the text, towards the end of Jesus's private revelation to Judas regarding the origin of the created world and its ultimate demise, Jesus once again

---

12. *GJudas* 56,9–20. The Coptic expression p̄ ϩογο ε–, here translated as 'exceed', literally means 'do more than' and parallels Judas's question to Jesus cited above, in which ϩογο is translated as 'advantage'.
13. *GJudas* 38,1–26; 39,18–40,1.
14. *GJudas* 40,3–18.

returns to the same issue, accentuating again how the disciples' – or, again, perhaps their successors' – actions will lead to the dissolution of archontic realm:

> [And] Judas said to Jesus, 'So what will those generations do?' Jesus said, Truly I say to you (pl.), above them all, the stars bring matters to completion. And when Saklas completes the span of time assigned to him, their first star will appear with the generations and they will finish what has been said (above). Then they will fornicate in my name and slay their children and [they will …] evil … the aeons that bring their generation which represent them to Saklas. [And] after that … rael will come bringing the twelve of [Israel] from …, and [the generations] will all serve Saklas, [also] sinning in my name.[15]

Two main solutions have been offered in scholarship to this enigmatic description of the disciples' wrongdoings. The first, which is intimately connected with portraying the *Gospel of Judas* as a document that thoroughly counters a sacrificial understanding of Christianity, stresses mostly the reference to the sacrifice of women and children. This, it is argued, is an oblique reference to the bishops and rest of the clergy who advocate martyrdom to their flock.[16] The second solution notes the general anomistic character of the allegations, and points towards stock allegations against the 'other' in the ancient world, also underlining how such allegations were used in intra-Christian debate, in which the proto-orthodox directed them against the gnostics. Here, it is argued, the gnostics return the favour.[17]

Nevertheless, I would like to suggest that neither solution adequately answers the evidence. The anti-martyrdom reading addresses only a small part of the allegations, and even then we are expected to understand the reference to 'women and children' as referring to members of the congregation over which a certain bishop presides. While this is not impossible, it is still far from being self-evident, and not easy to parallel in other sources. On the other hand, the stock allegations solution has its own problems. First, it is clear that at least in the first instance the disciples are unaware of what they do. They are left dumbfounded when Jesus interprets their dream to mean that they themselves are unwarily committing these atrocities. Second, in each case, the people involved in the rituals are depicted

---

15. *GJudas* 54,13–55,9.

16. This has been argued in most detail in Pagels and King, *Reading Judas*, 59–75, although in that study it is also argued that the sacrifice of Jesus is viewed positively in this gospel. See, however, King's updated views in King, 'Christians who Sacrifice', 307–18.

17. See already Bart D. Ehrman, *The Lost Gospel of Judas Iscariot: A New Look at Betrayer and Betrayed* (Oxford: Oxford University Press, 2006), 136–37. More recently, Ismo Dunderberg has argued that these solutions are not necessarily mutually exclusive, and that the criticism is directed against 'sacramental ideology based upon blood sacrifice' ('The Eucharist in the Gospels of John, Philip, and Judas', *Early Christianity* 7 (2016), 484–507 at 504).

as having some positive characteristics as well. Thus, they act 'in praise and in humility with each other', 'the generations of the pious are loyal' to one of them, and another group collectively argue that they are 'like angels'. Third, and perhaps most importantly, their atrocious actions have an inadvertent positive outcome, as they work against the rule of the archons, and contribute to its dissolution, which culminates in Christ's crucifixion. They are, to use the gospel's own terminology, 'the stars that bring everything to completion'.

'Libertinism' or Redemption through Sin?

I would like here to suggest another solution, which would once again stress the overall motif of the gospel: only the dissolution of the archontic world would allow the truth to shine through the archontic lie and enable the salvation of those gnostic believers who adhered to this work. Regarding gnostic 'libertinism', Hans Jonas argued many years ago that it was meant to counteract a system of laws that kept the cosmos in place. Jonas writes,

> For what is the law – either as revealed through Moses and the prophets or as operating in the actual habits and opinions of men – but the means of regularizing and thus stabilizing the implication of man in the business of the world and worldly concerns; of setting by its rules the seal of seriousness, of praise and blame, reward and punishment, on his utter involvement; of making his very will a compliant party to the compulsory system, which thereby will function all the more smoothly and inextricably?[18]

Gnostic 'libertinism', on the other hand, served

> the double interest in asserting the authentic freedom of the self by daring the Archons and injuring their general cause by individually thwarting their design.[19]

While the historicity of such accounts of subversive gnostic approach to the rules of the cosmos has been doubted by some scholars, I find the evidence quite convincing, as I have argued elsewhere.[20] Yet, something quite different is

---

18. Hans Jonas, *The Gnostic Religion: The Message of the Alien God and the Beginnings of Christianity* (Boston, MA: Beacon, 1963), 272.
19. Jonas, *Gnostic Religion*, 272.
20. I have presented my most complete argument for the historicity of gnostic subversive sexual rituals and their corroboration by different types of evidence in *Wrestling with Archons*, 34–46; 80–98. In Jonathan Cahana, 'Gnosticism and Radical Feminism: From Pathologizing Submersion to Salvaging Re-emergence', in *Submerged Literature in Ancient Greek Culture: The Comparative Perspective*, ed. Andrea Ercolani and Manuela Giordano (Berlin: de Gruyter, 2016), 183–200, I have also argued for its historicity through comparative

happening in the *Gospel of Judas*. On the one hand, the *Gospel of Judas* renders this ordered world, or cosmos, by the word 'corruption'[21] and, as we saw above, stresses how only the dissolution of its laws and very being would lead to salvation. On the other hand, those who actually effect this dissolution are not in the gnostic camp, and, except for Judas, are not even aware of what they are doing. Thus, in the *Gospel of Judas*, we find an interesting specimen of a nihilistic concept that Jonas termed 'freedom by abuse', which should not be brushed away but analysed according to the gospel's internal theology and its own view of salvation history. For that, however, it is highly useful to engage with the work of yet another scholar of religion, Gershom Scholem, who analysed the concept of 'a commandment which is fulfilled by means of a transgression' (*mitzvah ha-ba'ah ba-averah*) or 'redemption through sin'. In analysing this concept, Scholem was specifically referring to the Sabbatian and Frankist sects which stirred the Jewish world in the seventeenth and eighteenth centuries, but was working from a comparative perspective that engaged ancient Gnosticism as well.[22] Scholem sets out to explain how sin could come to be understood as leading to salvation, and comes out with the following prerequisites for such development:

1. The belief in the necessary apostasy of the Messiah and in the sacramental nature of the descent into the realm of the *kelipot* (evil forces).
2. The belief that the 'believer' must not appear as he really is.

---

reasoning. It is important to note that 'libertinism' could be a highly misleading term in this context, since it implies careless license to do whatever one wished. This was certainly not the gnostic viewpoint, nor does it correlate with what Jonas defined as 'freedom by abuse' (Jonas, *Gnostic Religion*, 274–75).

21. GJudas 50,10–14.

22. These sects were formed in response to the apostasy and conversion of Sabbatai Zvi in 1666. Many of these sects' adherents believed in Sabbatai Zvi's messiahship and were struggling to give religious meaning to his apostasy and his apparent failure to redeem the Jewish people, often by developing antinomian concepts such as 'Redemption through Sin'. Jacob Frank (1721–91) was a religious leader who carried such tendency to its extreme logical conclusion, or, as Scholem phrased it, 'a man who was not afraid to push on to the very end, to take the final step into the abyss' (Scholem, 'Redemption through Sin', 128). For a discussion of the historical and scholarly context of Scholem's research on Sabbatianism, as well as more up-to-date bibliography on these groups, see Amir Engel, *Gershom Scholem: An Intellectual Biography* (Chicago, IL: University of Chicago Press, 2017), 124–67. While Scholem's historical reconstructions of Sabbatianism may have been superseded today, in no small part due to the availability of many new sources, his insights into the forces active within the religious development of these sects are still of much use for understanding them and similar phenomena comparatively. *Mutatis mutandis*, the same could be said of Jonas's research into Gnosticism (cf. Cahana-Blum, *Wresting with Archons*, 1–8 and *passim*).

3. The belief that the (true) Torah of *atzilut* must be observed through the violation of the (unredeemed) Torah of the *beriah*.
4. The belief that the first cause and the God of Israel are not the same, the former being the God of rational philosophy, the latter the God of religion.
5. The belief in the three hypostases of the Godhead, all of which have been or will be incarnated in human form.[23]

It is highly illuminating that, *mutatis mutandis*, these concepts could be used for the elucidation of the *Gospel of Judas*. In both cases, the descent of the Messiah and his 'apostasy' is crucial for salvation; in both cases there are two systems of laws or, to use Judas's terminology, 'generations' which are thoroughly opposed to one another, and one of them shines through the dissolution of the other. In both cases, there is a clear differentiation between two gods. And, most intriguingly, in both cases the advent of the redeemer effects a paradoxical relationship between what one does internally and what one does externally, and the equation of both comes in, or even brings on, the apocalyptic future.[24] In other words, if one reads the *Gospel of Judas* as advocating a Redemption-through-Sin theology, Christ arrives and apostatizes from the disciples' God, revealing a deep dualism between two gods and a new law which is opposed to the previous one internally kept by the disciples, while outwardly everything continues 'as is', at least until the salvific dissolution, which is brought to fruition precisely through that paradox.[25] Nevertheless, the *Gospel of Judas* transforms this concept through externalizing the process to the very servants of the wrong God, and thus these latter bring

---

23. Scholem, 'Redemption through Sin', 126. Scholem defines the *kelipot* as 'the hylic forces of evil whose hold in the world is particularly strong among the gentiles' (94), the Torah of *atzilut* as 'the "true" Torah which … has been in concealment for the entire period of the exile', and the Torah of the *beriah* as 'the Torah of the unredeemed world of exile' (112).

24. Scholem details this aspect of redemption through sin (numbered 3 in the paradigm) earlier in his text: 'a "true act" cannot be an act committed publicly, through the eyes of the world. … Prior to the advent of the Redeemer, the inward and the outward were in harmony … Now that the redeemer has arrived, however, the two spheres are in opposition: the inward commandment … has become synonymous with the outward transgression. *Bittulah shel torah zehu kiyyuma*: the violation of the Torah is now its true fulfillment' (Scholem, 'Redemption through Sin', 110). Considering the damaged condition of the text, we cannot say whether *GJudas* also adheres to the idea that the three hypostases of the Godhead must be incarnated, but this concept could easily be paralleled in other gnostic texts. Cf., for instance, *ApocrJn* 4.2–4, where Christ introduces himself to John as father, mother and son.

25. Scholem notes in passing the similarities between the concepts developed by the Sabbatian sects and those of 'such nihilistic gnostics as Carpocrates and his followers', citing Jonas's incisive analysis of such gnostic nihilism (Scholem, 'Redemption through Sin', 132–34). The availability of a text like *GJudas* both confirms and nuances Scholem's intuitive comparativism.

about the dissolution while the true believers ('the great and holy generation') remain innocent.

In view of this internal logic of the *Gospel of Judas*, the historicity of the allegations regarding the sexual and violent subversive rituals must recede into the background, especially since the gospel acknowledges that the practitioners are not aware of what they are actually doing, and the text seems to concede, if grudgingly, that their intentions are good. Yet, the author clearly believes that their nihilistic and anomistic actions have an important salvific function. Moreover, if we go back now to Irenaeus's description of the gospel he knows, we can see he corroborates such a reading. As I argued elsewhere, his specific claims regarding the *Gospel of Judas*, namely that Judas received perfect knowledge and effected the mystery of betrayal leading to a salvific dissolution in which 'all things, both earthly and heavenly, were dissolved', are meticulously paralleled in this gospel.[26] The rest of his account is a little more tricky, but through careful analysis, we can see how it too corroborates the gospel as we have it. Irenaeus apparently misunderstood the gospel as proclaiming that those who adhered to it should practice the actions of the disciples, since, as he understood rightly, they saw Judas's action as positive and were appreciative of his role. He was not exactly wrong, since these atrocious actions do lead to the destruction of the archontic illusion, although adherents of this gospel apparently did not do these things themselves, but, in externalizing the concept of Redemption through Sin, believed in some kind of self-destructive mechanism functioning within the creator's servants, activated through the arrival of the gnostic redeemer. It is especially intriguing that Irenaeus is also aware that these people associate themselves with angels. As we saw above, Irenaeus is careful to note that 'whatever the nature of the action, they declare that they do it in the name of the angel', which seems to be corroborated in the *Gospel of Judas*, in which those who commit these apparently atrocious actions proudly claim that they are 'like angels' (*GJudas* 40,18). Considering that in other gnostic texts, Irenaeus could easily find the gnostics positively associating themselves with angels along with their forefathers the Sodomites, he could easily have reached the conclusion that these gnostics themselves rushed into actions that are 'not lawful even to name'.[27] It seems that the full complexity of the gospel was either lost on Irenaeus, or, if he did understand it, he preferred to falsify his evidence in order to make his point more fiercely. He could have surmised, and more so as this fitted his agenda, that since

26. Cahana, 'Salvific Dissolution', 117–19.

27. Cf. *Apocalypse of Adam* 64,5, in which Adam refers to the state before his separation from Eve by saying that 'we resembled the great eternal angels, for we were higher than the god who created us and the powers with him'. Later in this same work the Sodomites themselves are said to become 'like angels' for 'they work in the imperishable seed' (76, 5–6). This appear to be a specific gnostic strand of interpretation that ultimately goes back to the ungendered nature of these heavenly creatures, hinted at already in the synoptics (*GMt* 22.30 // *GMk* 12.25 // *GLk* 20.36). Irenaeus was well aware that those who read *GJudas* also trace their lineage to the Sodomites (*Adv. Haer.* 1.31.1).

people believed such actions were crucial to salvation, they may have condoned or even participated in them. Since otherwise the gospel would leave Jesus without any real disciples, a position he may have thought nonsensical, he may have used this as another point to strengthen his reading.

Conclusion: Counter-narrative as a mirror image

To conclude, in reading the disciples' actions and depiction in the *Gospel of Judas* in the context of Redemption-through-Sin theology, the same thrust of a counter-narrative that effected the gospel depiction of Judas and the meaning of his actions is carried further into the depiction of Jesus's disciples. These completely misunderstand Jesus and are still thoroughly influenced by 'Jewish opinions', as Irenaeus says elsewhere.[28] Nevertheless, they inadvertently contribute to the dissolution of the archontic world to which they, in contradistinction to Jesus and the unnamed 'great and holy generation', rightly belong. Unbeknownst to themselves, their keeping of the commandments leads to the overflowing of sin, and thus not to the counter-overflowing of grace that Paul postulated in his Epistle to the Romans, but to the dissolution of the archontic world that comes to fruition, without fruit, with Judas's betrayal and Christ's crucifixion.[29] None of the disciples ends up spreading the gospel, but all of them are crucial to salvation, in a way not dissimilar to Judas and his actions in the New Testament gospels. In a way, the *Gospel of Judas* thus presents us with a mirror image of both the disciples and Judas: the New Testament Judas effects salvation inadvertently; in his own gospel, he does so with full understanding. In the New Testament, the disciples are sent to spread the gospel and thus help to effect salvation. In Judas's gospel, the disciples receive no gospel to spread but effect salvation through the atrocious actions they perform *inadvertently*. Perhaps most importantly, Jesus in the New Testament gospels is betrayed by Judas but the rest remain loyal to him and set about to spread his word. Jesus in the *Gospel of Judas* is a totally nihilistic and alien character who seems to have nothing, and even less to wish to have something, to do with anyone or anything in this world of corruption. He taunts and scolds his disciples, including Judas, who receives the revelation, consciously helps him to effect salvation, but will never be able to reach Jesus and his 'great and holy

---

28. Cf. Irenaeus, *Adv. Haer.* 3.2.2, on certain heretical Christians who 'imagined that they have themselves discovered more than the apostles by finding out another God; and that the apostles preached the Gospel still somewhat under the influence of Jewish opinions, but that they themselves are purer and more intelligent than the apostles'.

29. Cf. *Rom* 5.20–6.2: 'Law came in, to increase the trespass; but where sin increased, grace abounded all the more, so that, as sin reigned in death, grace also might reign through righteousness to eternal life through Jesus Christ our Lord. What shall we say then? Are we to continue in sin that grace may abound?' The possible effects of Pauline theology on G*Judas* merit a separate discussion.

generation', nor preach his gospel. Yet the remarkable literary characteristics of this text make us feel that it is the disciples who are lonely and helpless, while Jesus whistles or, more correctly, laughs, past this graveyard.[30]

---

30. Jesus laughs no less than four times in the preserved text of *GJudas*. This in itself posits yet another counter-narrative to the Synoptic Gospels, in which Jesus never laughs. For comparative discussion, see Marius J. Nel, 'He Who Laughs Last: Jesus and Laughter in the Synoptic and Gnostic Traditions', *HTS Teologiese Studies/Theological Studies* 70 (2014), 1–8. As Nel notes, Jesus's laughter in this gospel 'predominantly serves to underline the superiority of Jesus in relation to his disciples and Judas. It is also not playful or innocent as it causes great anxiety and uncertainty amongst his disciples' (6).

5

'SURELY THESE ARE HETERODOX TEACHINGS': THE *GOSPEL OF MARY* AND TERTULLIAN IN DIALOGUE

Sarah Parkhouse

Andrew answered and said to the brothers, 'Say whatever you say about what she (Mary) said. I myself do not believe that the Saviour said such things, for surely these are heterodox teachings (ⲉⲛⲕⲉⲙⲉⲉⲩⲉ // ἑτερογνωμονεῖν).' Peter answered, he spoke about such matters. (BG 17,10–17)

The current trend in scholarship on early Christianity is to highlight the diversity and pluriformity of the second- and third-century church(es). There was no orthodoxy, no mainstream church. Heresiologists do not provide an accurate picture of the Christian landscape and twentieth-century discoveries such as the Nag Hammadi codices demonstrate that there was a fluid and varied model of what it meant to be a Christian. To a large extent, this picture of diversity is accurate. The writers we label as 'orthodox' or 'mainstream', such as Irenaeus and Clement of Alexandria, Ignatius and Tertullian, show great variation in their understanding of their faith and its practices: there is no one, single, unified definition of Christianity in the early period. The texts that we label as 'heterodox' may, at points, have more in common with 'orthodox' texts than the orthodox do with each other.[1] However, this paper asks what happens when we encounter a self-proclaimed 'heterodox' text? And how might this modify our understanding of Christianity in the first three centuries?

The *Gospel of Mary* tells a dramatic story and offers a counter-narrative that challenges the 'orthodox' Christian story. Within the gospel named after Mary, the character of Mary reveals that Jesus appeared to her in a vision and taught her about

---

1. See, e.g., David Brakke, 'Self-Differentiation among Christian Groups: The Gnostics and Their Opponents', in *The Cambridge History of Christianity*, ed. M. Mitchell and F. Young (Cambridge: Cambridge University Press, 2006), 245–60. Elsewhere Brakke writes, 'In several important ways such proto-orthodox teachers as Justin Martyr and Clement of Alexandria had more in common with, say Valentinus than they did with Bishop Irenaeus. There was no single and uniform proto-orthodoxy, but multiple modes of piety, authority, and theology that later orthodoxy represents as its forerunners.... So there was no single proto-orthodox horse in the race... proto-orthodoxy itself was highly diverse and, in many respects, not very orthodox'; David Brakke, *The Gnostics: Myth, Ritual, and Diversity in Early Christianity* (Cambridge, MA: Harvard University Press, 2010), 10.

the ascent of the disembodied soul. Mary is then confronted by Peter and Andrew who deem her teachings 'heterodox'. Andrew says to the other men, 'Say whatever you say about what she said. I myself do not believe that the Saviour said such things, for surely these are heterodox teachings (ⲉⲛⲕⲉⲙⲉⲉⲩⲉ // ἑτερογνωμονεῖν)' (BG 17,10–17 // PRyl 463 21,9–10). Peter then voices his opinion, saying similar things to Andrew but directing his attack not just at the idea of an ascending soul but also at Mary's person and her relationship with Jesus:

> He asked them about the Saviour, 'Did he speak with a woman secretly (and) not openly to us? Are we to turn and all listen to her? Did he choose her over us?' (BG 17,17–22)

In *GMary*, Peter and Andrew voice the opinions of the 'orthodox' community, who oppose the concept of the ascent of the soul, private instruction and female authority. Through Mary's revelation and character, the gospel expands and challenges the early Christian narrative, presenting a female disciple, led in private instruction, as the esteemed protagonist. *GMary* challenges the basic tenets and boundaries of prevailing beliefs, and inverts the standard rhetoric of orthodoxy and heterodoxy by labelling itself, its protagonist and its teachings as 'heterodox'.

GMary is partially preserved in three manuscripts: the fifth-century Coptic Berlin Codex (BG), in which approximately a third of the text is extant, and two small third-century Greek fragments, POxy 3525 (POxy) and PRyl 463 (PRyl). The text was probably written, in some form, around the turn of the second to third century. Although neither Greek manuscript preserves Mary's teaching, at the beginning of PRyl 463 we catch the end of her revelation regarding the soul finding rest in silence, followed by Mary falling silent 'as the Saviour had spoken to this point' (PRyl 21,3–4). It is then that we find Andrew calling her revelation 'heterodox'. The term ἑτερογνωμονεῖν is pretty uncommon and Andrew's phrase εδοκει γ[αρ ετε]ρογνωμονειν τη εκ[ε]ιν[ου εν]νοια appears to mean something like 'different from his idea', but the ἑτερο- prefix signifies *hetero*-doxy.[2] The fact that this word is used in the early Rylands fragment is striking in that it tells us that already by the third century the author of *GMary* understood its own teachings to be heterodox.

The argument of this paper is that the author of *GMary* self-consciously presents a view of Jesus's message that is counter to the norm, a view that counters the emerging orthodox and dominant position as represented by Peter and Andrew. *GMary*, then, does not present its teachings as one valid voice among many, or as the orthodox voice challenging the heterodox, but reverses the evaluative system of standard heresiological discourse by claiming the heterodox label for itself and

---

2. The prefix is used in words that denote teaching false doctrines, for example, ἑτεροδιδασκαλία and ἑτεροδοξέω. See Lampe, *Patristic Greek Lexicon*, 552b. E.g. 1 Tim 1.3 'so that you may instruct certain people not to teach any different doctrine (ἑτεροδιδασκαλεῖν)'.

rejecting the 'mainstream' apostolic voice. One of the author's basic assumptions appears to be the existence of a dominant 'master narrative', a set of teachings that labels itself as orthodox, and presumably encompasses authority of the twelve male apostles and bodily resurrection and may even include a version of the rule of faith.

Many scholars place *GMary* in the context of the orthodox/heretical debate, arguing that Mary and Peter signify a conflict between orthodox and 'gnostic' Christianity.[3] Karen King warns against this: 'In framing the problem as a conflict between orthodox and heretical Christians, we miss the historical significance of the work's own rhetoric of conflict and the complex dynamics of early Christian social and theological formation.'[4] *GMary* does engage with questions of what was orthodox and what was heterodox, and does present a conflict between 'orthodox' and 'heterodox' Christians, yet, as King states, it is more complex than the usual binary division. *GMary* turns the traditional understanding of 'orthodoxy' and 'heterodoxy' on its head by recognizing that some would consider Mary's teaching as heterodox, but that this heterodox teaching is in fact correct. The label 'heterodox' then becomes something different to how most ancient and modern scholars think of it – it is a descriptor that can be used, transformed, claimed and even reversed.

For a teaching to be proclaimed as heterodox, and for a gospel to qualify as a counter-narrative, the question is what is considered to be orthodox? What is *GMary* countering? The narrative that Andrew and Peter represent is not explicitly made known in the extant gospel. In order to begin to think about these questions, this paper will put *GMary* in dialogue with an 'orthodox' text. This approach is taken to shed light on how the gospel works as a counter-narrative. Here, we will use Tertullian's *Prescription against the Heretics* as the example of the orthodox text, with the help of his slightly later work titled *On the Resurrection* to clarify Tertullian's thoughts on the parousia, judgement and the soul which are mentioned but underexplored in the *Prescription*. The *Prescription* is likely to have been written between 198 and 203, and *Resurrection* around 206/7[5] and this might help to hypothetically date *GMary* towards the end of the second century at the

---

3. Elaine Pagels, *The Gnostic Gospels* (New York: Random House, 1979), 12–14; Pheme Perkins, *The Gnostic Dialogue: The Early Church and the Crisis of Gnosticism* (New York: Paulist Press, 1980), 133–34; Judith Hartenstein, *Die zweite Lehre: Erscheinungen des Auferstandenen als Rahmenerzählungen frühchristlicher Dialoge*, TU 146 (Berlin: de Gruyter, 2000), 135; Christopher M. Tuckett, *The Gospel of Mary* (Oxford: Oxford University Press, 2007), 201. Schaberg argues that 'Magdalene Christianity offers an alternative and a challenge to Petrine Christianity, which has never been able to silence it'; Jane Schaberg, *The Resurrection of Mary Magdalene: Legends, Apocrypha, and the Christian Testament* (London: Bloomsbury, 2004), 19.

4. Karen L. King, *The Gospel of Mary of Magdala: Jesus and the First Woman Apostle* (Santa Rosa, CA: Polebridge Press, 2003), 174.

5. Timothy David Barnes, *Tertullian: A Historical and Literary Study*, rev. edn (Oxford: Clarendon Press, 1985), 55. Other dating ranges between 198 and 206; see

earliest. Tertullian's *Prescription* is one voice from within the mainstream church and *GMary* is one voice that offers a counter-narrative: the *Prescription* does not speak for the entire orthodox community and neither is *GMary* representative of all counter-narratives. However, this pair of texts are interesting dialogue partners. King has made a start on this comparison, concluding that the only commonality between *GMary* and Tertullian is that they both valued prophetic experience and believed that the pure could see God in visions: 'They disagreed on almost every other important issue.'[6] It must be noted that it is not Tertullian's entire corpus of work that is to be discussed here. Tertullian is a complex thinker whose ideas changed over time, and he exemplifies the difficulties of defining orthodoxy or seeing it as a monolithic set of theological doctrines and/or practices.[7] For the purposes of this chapter, the orthodox stance might be summed up through Tertullian's 'rule of faith' as found in the *Prescription*.[8] The rule comprised the belief

> that there is only one God, and that no other besides is the creator of the world; who produced all things out of nothing through his Word, put forth before all things; that this Word is called his Son, and, under the name of God, was variously seen by the patriarchs, constantly heard in the prophets, and was at last brought down by the Spirit and Power of the Father into the Virgin Mary and was made flesh in her womb, and being born of her lived as Jesus Christ. Afterwards he preached the new law and the new promise of the kingdom of heaven, worked miracles, and after being crucified rose again on the third day, ascended into the heavens and sat at the right hand of the Father, sending in his place the power of the Holy Spirit to guide those who believe; who will come with glory to take the saints to the enjoyment of eternal life and the heavenly promises and to condemn the wicked to eternal fire, after the resurrection of both these classes through the restoration of their flesh. (*Prescr.* 13)

Geoffrey D. Dunn, 'Tertullian's Scriptural Exegesis in de praescriptione haereticorum', *JECS* 14 (2006), 141–55, 142.

6. King, *Gospel of Mary*, 64.

7. In such a large body of work, there are inevitable contradictions and developments; Tertullian's ideas changed over time and his later works are influenced by Montanism, which was subsequently regarded as heresy. McGowan writes of 'two Tertullians' as 'scholarship both ancient and modern has almost created dual theological *personae* out of the one historical *substantia* in order to deal with a thinker who came ultimately to be seen as both a pillar of orthodoxy and a promoter of heresy'. Andrew McGowan, 'Tertullian and the 'Heretical' Origins of the 'Orthodox' Trinity', *JECS* 14 (2006), 437–57, 438.

8. As Osborn writes, 'The rule of truth or faith is central to the emergence of orthodoxy'; Eric F. Osborn, 'Reason and the Rule of Faith in the Second Century AD', in *The Making of Orthodoxy: Essays in Honour of Henry Chadwick*, ed. Rowan Williams (Cambridge: Cambridge University Press, 1989), 40–61, 40. See also Devin White's chapter in this volume, who points out that the rule of truth might be understood as an identity-forming metanarrative.

For Tertullian, the rule was taught by Jesus, transmitted by the apostles and recorded in the scriptures. Christians should not deviate from or question the rule of faith. He writes, 'To know nothing in opposition to the rule is to know all things' (*Prescr.* 14). The rule here represents the mainstream voice, the voice to which *GMary* acts as a counter-narrative.[9]

This paper will examine three different aspects of the *Prescription* and *GMary*: (1) the notion of apostolic authority and ignorant apostles, (2) scriptural authority and how to use scripture and (3) philosophy, the body and the soul.

Apostolic authority and ignorant apostles

Throughout the *Prescription*, Tertullian insists that true doctrine was transmitted through the twelve male apostles and should not be disputed: 'In the Lord's apostles we possess our authority, for even they did not of themselves choose to introduce anything on their own initiative but faithfully delivered to the nations the doctrine they had received from Christ' (*Prescr.* 6). Anything that does not originate from the apostles is 'other doctrines' (*Prescr.* 21.6) and so false by definition.[10] The notion that the apostles received their teachings from Jesus provides Christians with a fixed point in history on which to base their arguments. Heretical doctrines, conversely, have no historical basis.

GMary counters the authority of the twelve male apostles. Mary has received secret and higher teachings from Jesus, and she communicates these to the ignorant male apostles. Levi supports her while Peter and Andrew challenge her authority and are represented as unenlightened and ill-mannered. Contrary to Tertullian's opinion that heretics cannot claim that their teachings came from Jesus, *GMary*'s narrative is based at a fixed historical point, and one taken from the *Gospel of John*: the point at which Mary Magdalene meets the risen Lord outside of his tomb. In both texts, Jesus appears first to Mary alone, and afterwards Mary tells the other disciples what she has seen. Mary's words in *GJohn* 'I have seen the Lord' (20.18) are analogous to her words in *GMary*, 'I have seen the Lord' (10,10–11); however, in *GMary* she sees him 'in a vision' (10,11). In *GJohn* Jesus tells Mary that he is ascending (20.17), and in *GMary* Mary's vision is of an ascending soul. In *GJohn* Jesus tells Mary to go to her 'brothers' and to tell them that he is ascending (20.17), and in *GMary* she tells the 'brothers' (9,14) about the soul's ascension. The premise of Mary's revelation and its surrounding narrative in *GMary* appears to be based on *GJohn*.

---

9. It must be stressed here that I am not arguing that the author of *GMary* knew any of Tertullian's writings or even the rule of faith, or that Tertullian had encountered *GMary*, but that these two texts are representative of the mainstream narrative and the counter-narrative.

10. *Superest ergo uti demonstremus, an haec nostra doctrina cuius regulam supra edidimus de apostolorum traditione censeatur et hoc ipso an ceterae de mendacio ueniant.*

In *GMary*, Mary is presented as an exceptional disciple. Not only does she receive a vision of Jesus's ascending soul (or Jesus teaching about this ascension), Mary appears to be an example of the soul. In her vision, which she recounts, the soul overcomes the cosmic powers (or passions) named Darkness, Desire, Ignorance and Wrath and the vision ends with the soul finding heavenly 'rest' in 'silence'. At the end of the vision, Mary herself becomes silent as the soul does, aligning her character with the soul in heaven.[11] Perhaps more explicitly, Jesus calls her 'blessed' (BG 10,14) and the other disciples acknowledge that Jesus loved her.

> [Peter said to] Mary, 'Sister, we know that you were greatly l[oved by the Savi]our like no other woman.' (POxy 14–16) // Peter said to Mary, 'Sister, we know that the Saviour loved you more than the other women.' (BG 10,1–3)

At a later point in the text, Levi confirms that Jesus loved Mary, but in the Coptic manuscript Levi says that not only did Jesus love Mary more than the other women but also more than the male disciples:

> 'For surely he, knowing her i[n]fallib[ly], loved (her)' (PRyl 22,6–8) // 'Surely the Saviour knew her infallibly, and therefore he loved her more than us' (BG 18,13–15)

Mary's beloved status is further emphasized by its juxtaposition with Peter, who is associated with wrath and ignorance.

> Lev[i] says to Peter, 'Peter, wrath is always with yo[u], and so now you are disputing with the woman like an adversary to her.' (PRyl 22,1–4) // Levi answered, he said to Peter, 'Peter, you are always wrathful! I see you now disputing with the woman like the adversaries. If the Saviour made her worthy, who are you to reject her?' (BG 18,5–12)

The term 'wrathful' in the Coptic text puts Peter in line with an evil cosmic power that the soul must overcome called 'the Wisdom [of the] Wrathful One' (BG 16,11–12). Peter is presented as the antithesis of Mary, who is blessed and loved by Jesus and becomes silent and restful.

Peter is also an inferior disciple as he has only been privy to a fraction of Jesus's teachings. Peter knows that Jesus has taught Mary privately, and after Jesus's departure he asks that she shares Jesus's words with the group:

---

11. For further explanation of this, see Sarah Parkhouse, 'Matter and the Soul: The Bipartite Eschatology of the Gospel of Mary', in *Connecting Gospels: Beyond the Canonical/Non-Canonical Divide*, ed. Francis Watson and Sarah Parkhouse (Oxford: Oxford University Press, 2018), 216–32.

[Peter said to] Mary, 'Sister, we know that you were greatly l[oved by the Savi]our like no other woman. Tell us [those words that you know] of the Saviour [which] we have not heard.' [Mary answered, saying, 'What is] unknown to you and I remember, I will pr[oclaim to you.'] (POxy 14–18) // Peter said to Mary, 'Sister we know that the Saviour loved you more than the other women. Tell us the words of the Saviour that you remember, those that you know and we do not, nor have we heard them.' Mary answered and said, 'What is hidden from you, I will proclaim to you.' (BG 10,1–9)

Mary's reply in the Coptic text states that these teachings have been 'hidden' from Peter, further lowering his status. In the Greek text, Peter has not heard them.

A situation in which Peter did not know all of Jesus's teachings is exactly what Tertullian claims that heretics profess. Tertullian is adamant that Jesus did not teach anything in secret (*Prescr.* 27.1; cf. 23–27) and argues against his opponents' allegation that the apostles did not know all things (*Prescr.* 22). Tertullian is particularly irked that heretics would ascribe ignorance to Peter (*Prescr.* 23). He responds, 'Was anything withheld from the knowledge of Peter, who is called the rock on which the church should be built, who also obtained the keys of the kingdom of heaven, with the power of loosing and binding in heaven and on earth?' (*Prescr.* 22.4). For Tertullian, Peter is a special apostle as he is part of Jesus's inner circle who witnessed the transfiguration (*Prescr.* 22.6). The situation described in *GMary* is an example of how Tertullian's opponents represent Peter as an ignorant apostle, who did not receive higher teachings directly from Jesus, and will not accept them upon receiving them from Mary.

Apostolic unity and authority are key criteria for Tertullian's definition of orthodoxy in the *Prescription*. He calls heretics 'strangers and enemies to the apostles' (*Prescr.* 37.7). Tertullian insists that true doctrine originates from the twelve male apostles, who all taught the same thing, and that 'no others ought to be received as preachers than those whom Christ appointed' (*Prescr.* 21.1) as Jesus did not reveal himself to any except the twelve. Thus, anything that comes from outside of the twelve must be regarded as false.

GMary not only introduces different teachings and apostles not traditionally included in the twelve, but it also depicts schism between these apostles. The disciples do not simply follow the teachings of the Saviour: once the Saviour leaves, the male disciples weep and grieve and Mary comforts them and then they begin to 'debate the words of the Saviour' (συν[ζη]τ[ει]ν POxy 13–14//ⲅⲩⲙ[ⲛ]ⲁⲍⲉ 9,23). Peter requests to hear what Jesus told Mary privately and after she reveals her vision, the argument escalates and we see Levi accuse Peter of disputing with Mary like the adversaries. Here again, the words συνζητεις and ⲅⲩⲙⲛⲁⲍⲉ are used (PRyl 22,4 // BG 18,9).

Furthermore, Mary and her champion Levi are characters who do not belong to the twelve. Mary is almost certainly Mary Magdalene due to the narratival connections to *GJohn* 20.14–18.[12] The Levi character is more difficult to identify.

---

12. Most agree that Mary of *GMary* is Mary Magdalene: e.g. Hartenstein, *Die zweite Lehre*, 130; Karen L. King, 'Why All the Controversy? Mary in the Gospel of Mary', in *Which*

In the canonical gospels, the tax collector Levi of *GMark* 2.13–17 (// *GLuke* 5.27–32) has his name changed to Matthew in *GMatthew* (9.9–13), which read together identifies the Markan tax collector with the Matthew of the twelve (*GMt* 10.3). Whether the Levi of *GMary* is supposed to be one of the twelve is possible, but perhaps unlikely – as Judith Hartenstein points out, in the first three centuries most writers assume that Levi and Matthew are different characters.[13] In view of the polemics against Peter and Andrew in *GMary*, it is unlikely that Levi is to be understood as belonging in their group. Mary and Levi stand in contrast with Peter and Andrew who represent the authority and unity of the twelve.[14] Peter and Andrew are the 'orthodox'; they are the poster boys of the 'mainstream' church. Mary is the teacher of 'heterodox' teachings and Levi is the supporter of these heterodox teachings.

Mary's contrast with the twelve is underscored by her gender. The author of the gospel is well aware that Mary being a woman is an issue: it is mentioned three times, twice by Peter. Before she tells them about her vision, Peter acknowledges that Jesus loved Mary 'like no other woman' (POxy 16 // BG 10,3) and after her revelation he asks whether Jesus spoke with 'a woman' in private instead of to everyone or to the male apostles (PRyl 21,13 // BG 17,18–22). Following Peter's outburst, Levi refers to Peter contesting 'the woman' (PRyl 22,3–4 // BG 18,9). The repeated references to Mary as a woman signify that the gospel is making claims about gender equality in discipleship.[15] In the *Prescription*, Tertullian explicitly attacks women for assuming the same authority as men. He associates female authority with heresy and argues that women should not be performing the same tasks as men: 'The very women of these heretics, how wanton they are! For they are bold enough to teach, to dispute, to enact exorcisms, to undertake cures – it may be even to baptize'

Mary? The Marys of Early Christian Tradition, ed. F. Stanley Jones, SBL Symposium Series 19 (Atlanta, GA: Society of Biblical Literature, 2002), 53–74. Marjanen identifies Mary as Mary Magdalene due to the spelling of her name, Antti Marjanen, 'The Mother of Jesus or the Magdalene? The Identity of Mary in the So-Called Gnostic Christian Texts', in *Which Mary?*, 31–42. However, the Magdalene assumption has been challenged by Stephen J. Shoemaker, 'Rethinking the "Gnostic Mary": Mary of Nazareth and Mary of Magdala in Early Christian Tradition', *JECS* 9 (2001), 555–95.

13. Hartenstein, *Die zweite Lehre*, 131. *Contra*, Lührmann supports the identification of Levi of *GMary* with Matthew; Dieter Lührmann, *Die apokryph gewordenen Evangelien: Studien zu Neuen Texten und zu Neuen Fragen*, NovTSup 112 (Leiden: Brill, 2004), 123–24. *Contra*, Tuckett, *Gospel of Mary*, 21–22.

14. Hartenstein, *Die zweite Lehre*, 131–32; *contra*, Tuckett, *Gospel of Mary*, 24.

15. It is a more complicated question whether *GMary* recognizes that women did preach; see Sarah Parkhouse, *Eschatology and the Saviour: The Gospel of Mary among Early Christian Dialogue Gospels*, SNTSMS 176 (Cambridge: Cambridge University Press, 2019), 170–73.

(*Prescr.* 41.5).¹⁶ Certainly, in *GMary* we see Mary being bold enough to teach men and her teaching causes a dispute.

In the *Prescription,* Tertullian has set ideas about apostolic authority, and the whole premise of *GMary* counters these ideas. For Tertullian, authority comes from the twelve male apostles who are united and are not to be contested or questioned. *GMary* uses one of these apostles, and arguably the most important apostle, and presents him as ignorant and wrathful, and narrates Jesus hiding teachings from him and giving them instead to a beloved woman apostle. Both the *Prescription* and *GMary* understand the importance of the true teachings going back to the authority of Jesus, but they make this point in very different ways. For Tertullian, authority comes from apostolic transmission; for *GMary*, Mary has received a vision of Jesus, creatively using *GJohn*.

How to read scripture

For Tertullian, the true apostles had handed down the rule of faith and it was vital that scripture be read through the rule.¹⁷ The rule should not be questioned or deviated from. Tertullian attacks heretics for diverging from the transmitted apostolic preaching and for understanding the scriptures figuratively or symbolically.¹⁸ He writes that heretics use their scriptures selectively, they add and delete material from them and they exploit the more ambiguous passages to offer interpretations that are counter to the rule of faith (*Prescr.* 17).¹⁹ The crux of Tertullian's argument regarding the scriptures is that heretics, who are not Christians, have no right to

---

16. Tertullian is often thought of as one of the serial misogynists of the early church, notoriously calling women 'the devil's gateway' as they represent Eve (*de Cultu Feminarum* 1.1.2). However, Tertullian's thoughts on gender parity are actually more complicated and arguably changed over time, especially due to his conversion to Montanism, through which he submitted to the authority of the female prophets Prisca and Maximilla.

17. I agree with Dunn here that for Tertullian 'the Scriptures are an expression of the *regula*', rather than identical or completely autonomous; see Dunn, 'Tertullian's Scriptural Exegesis', 147–48 and n.37.

18. Tertullian's own method of exegesis, however, was not particularly consistent, even on whether the use of allegory was acceptable. As Dunn writes, 'As someone well-trained in the art of rhetoric, Tertullian knew how to argue in favor of one method of interpreting the Scriptures in one instance and how to argue for exactly the opposite in another. It all depended upon the context and the arguments put forward by his opponents that he was trying to refute' (Dunn, 'Tertullian's Scriptural Exegesis', 142).

19. Tertullian's opponents clearly had a good grasp of the scriptures and their use of scripture was not so dissimilar to the 'orthodox' that non-Christians could tell them apart. In fact, Tertullian warns Christians against entering into conversation with heretics regarding scriptures as it would be easy to fall into confusion regarding which interpretations were orthodox and which were heretical (*Prescr.* 18).

engage with scripture (*Prescr.* 15). The scriptures belong only to those who read within the rule of faith.

The way that scriptural texts are employed in *GMary* is incompatible with Tertullian's instruction. *GMary* uses certain scriptural texts (such as *GJohn*), but whether the author saw these texts as divinely inspired is impossible to say. *GMary* appears to know parts of the canonical gospels but never points to earlier texts explicitly. There are just a handful of echoes or allusions to canonical gospels and Pauline epistles,[20] and there is little to indicate that the Hebrew Bible was used at all. The act of writing a gospel that narrates Jesus revealing new information suggests that the author did not consider previous gospel literature as comprehensive or complete – and the author of *GMary* appears to feel at liberty to use earlier gospel texts selectively and creatively. This practice matches Tertullian's accusation: the author of *GMary* adds to, deletes and opposes material found in other gospels as she wishes.

In Jesus's hortatory speech before his imminent departure, only preserved in the Coptic manuscript, we find a cluster of allusions to the canonical gospels.[21] Here we will look at two examples – (1) the parousia and Son of Man and (2) seek and find – and examine how *GMary* interprets and employs earlier gospel passages contrary to Tertullian's orthodox reading. In his farewell speech, Jesus says,

> Beware, do not allow anyone to lead you astray saying, 'Look in this direction, or look in this place.' For the Son of Man exists within you. Follow him. Those who seek him will find him. (BG 8,14–21)

Here Jesus warns the disciples that they must watch out for misleading information regarding the location of the Son of Man. We find similar material in the synoptic gospels, in which Jesus instructs the disciples to be on guard for false Christ figures and that the true Son of Man will come as the lightning flashes in a future spectacle.

> Watch out that no one deceives you. For many will come in my name, claiming, 'I am the Christ,' and will deceive many. (*GMt* 24.4–5)
>
> At that time if anyone says to you, 'Look, here is the Christ!' or, 'There he is!' do not believe it. For false christs and false prophets will appear and perform great signs and wonders to deceive, if possible, even the elect. (*GMt* 24.23–24 // *GMk* 13.21–22)
>
> So if anyone tells you, 'There he is, out in the wilderness,' do not go out; or, 'Here he is, in the inner rooms,' do not believe it. For as lightning that comes from the east is visible even in the west, so will be the coming of the Son of Man. (*GMt* 24.26–27)

---

20. For an overview of these, see Tuckett, *Gospel of Mary*, 55–74.
21. See Tuckett, *Gospel of Mary*, 57–58.

People will tell you, 'There he is!' or 'Here he is!' Do not go running off after them. For the Son of Man in his day will be like the lightning, which flashes and lights up the sky from one end to the other. (*GLk* 17.23–24)

Each of these synoptic sayings is in an eschatological context: 'the birth pains' (*GMt* 24.8 // *GMk* 13.8) signifying the beginning of the end times, or the appearance of the Son of Man at his return.

GMary uses comparable language to offer a radically different message. In *GMatthew*, the warning directly refutes those who say the Christ/Son of Man is anywhere in the present time. In *GMary*, the look-here-look-there warning is used to counter this exact idea: the Son of Man is already present and exists within the disciples who seek, find and follow him. These passages in themselves may simply reflect two conflicting trajectories of early Christian eschatological thought, yet the juxtaposition of the warning and the reference to the Son of Man in *GMatthew/GMark* is undeniably close to *GMary*, suggesting that the Jesus of this gospel intends to oppose the traditional parousia teaching of its predecessors.[22] The way that *GMary* employs this language from the canonical gospels rebels against a more literal reading of synoptic eschatology, actively contradicting the teaching of the synoptic eschatological discourses.

A literal reading of the synoptic eschatological discourses is reflected in Tertullian's rule of faith. Tertullian does not explain the parousia or judgement beyond the rule in the *Prescription*, apart from a brief reference to the future judgement in which 'we must all stand before the judgement-seat' (44.1; cf. 2 Cor 5.10). However, in *On the Resurrection*, Tertullian writes that the judgement, the kingdom and the resurrection are presented in the gospels with a 'plain and absolute sense so that nothing about them can be forced into allegory' (*Res.* 33.8). Tertullian understands there to be a coming last day, which will be announced beforehand by signs and wonders, the dissolution of the elements and conflicts of nations. The heavens will be shaken and the Son of Man will come in the clouds, as in the synoptic Olivet discourse (*Res.* 22). The coming will be spectacular: Tertullian quotes *1 Thess* 4.13–17, according to which the Lord shall descend from heaven, with noise and commotion, followed by the dead rising and those who are alive being caught up together with them in the clouds to meet the Lord in the air (*Res.* 24).

The future eschatological judgement is also important to Tertullian. As Jaroslav Pelikan points out, Tertullian makes near constant references to the judgement throughout his writings, and it appears to be a point of reference for many of his decisions.[23] In *GMary*, we find a covert critique of the orthodox expectation of a

---

22. *Contra*, Tuckett argues that 'it is uncertain how precise one should make any comparison here', and, in any case, the phrase in *GMary* is closer to *GLuke* 17.23 'in being unspecific about the nature or identity of any false figures'; Tuckett, *Gospel of Mary*, 58–59.

23. Jaroslav Pelikan, 'The Eschatology of Tertullian', *Church History*, 21.2 (1952), 108–22, 112.

judgement. As the soul ascends, it renounces judgement. The soul says to one of the powers, 'Why do you judge me? I did not judge' (15,17–19).[24] In view of the links with *GJohn* 20.14–18, where Jesus tells Mary about his ascension, we might assume that the soul in *GMary* belongs to Jesus, paving the way for souls of the disciples to follow.[25] Thus, the non-judging soul of *GMary* is linked to the Jesus of *GJohn* who states that he judges no one (*GJn* 8.14). Here too we see *GMary* selectively using *GJohn* to critique literal readings of scripture as championed by 'orthodox' thinkers such as Tertullian.

GMary continues Jesus's farewell speech with the line 'Those who seek him will find him.' Variations of the 'seek and you will find' saying (*GMt* 7.7 // *GLk* 11.9) are common in early Christian literature, and Tertullian spends many words attacking heretics for their use of this saying. Heretics, he says, use this saying to account for their symbolic analysis of scriptures and continually seek new explanations of the Christian message: 'Seek and you shall find is everywhere in their minds' (*Prescr.* 43.2). In line with their misinterpretation of most scripture, Tertullian argues that his opponents understand the saying incorrectly: They seek things in the scriptures, but as their seeking is never ending, their interpretation reaches the truth but then goes beyond the truth and further and further beyond what is correct. Tertullian counters this by mandating that 'seek and you will find' should be read in its historical context, which was 'said in respect of the Jews' (*Prescr.* 8.4). The seeking-and-finding saying was not directed at Jesus's own followers. If the seeking and finding is read in its context, then the thing sought and found is belief in Jesus, and thus has an end point. When one has found faith but continues to seek and find, she might find herself into heresies (*Prescr.* 8–11). As Osborn explains,

> The command makes sense if it means that Christ taught *one definite thing* (possessed by the church) which must be believed and which must be sought for the sole purpose of this clearly directed faith. This interpretation of the command is required by the *rule of reason*, for the command has *three parts*: matter, time and limit. These point to the three questions: what, when and how long we have to seek. What is to be sought? Christ's teaching. When is it to be sought? Until it is found. When does seeking stop? When what is found is believed.[26]

GMary uses a variation of the seeking-and-finding saying, putting it in the context of seeking and finding the Son of Man within. For Tertullian, the seeking and finding should culminate in belief; in *GMary*, it refers to finding the internal

---

24. What exactly the soul means by judgement is difficult to understand. King and Tuckett regard this passage as reflecting the Saviour's teachings on sin: without sin, there is no judgement or condemnation; King, *Gospel of Mary*, 71; Tuckett, *Gospel of Mary*, 183.

25. For more on this, see Parkhouse, *Eschatology and the Saviour*, 203–10.

26. Osborn, 'Reason and the Rule of Faith in the Second Century AD', 54–55. See also Dunn, 'Tertullian's Scriptural Exegesis', 149–50.

Son of Man – essentially the Pauline idea of finding Christ within oneself. In both cases, it is about becoming a true Christian. In spite of these similarities, *GMary* is an example of everything that Tertullian despises about this saying: it is outside of the rule of faith and it points towards a heterodox reading of scripture.[27]

Just as Tertullian predicates his faith on his reading of scripture and uses scripture to refute the heretics, *GMary* bases its narrative and message on canonical texts but in a much more subtle way. *GMary* is extremely close to certain parts of the literature that was to be included in the New Testament, but the way that *GMary* uses these earlier texts is creative and free, and would be much to Tertullian's disapproval.

Body, soul and philosophy

Tertullian outlines three main examples of beliefs that heretics profess: that God is not the creator, that Christ is not the son of Mary and that there is a hope other than the resurrection. It is the last one that is important for *GMary*. Whether *GMary* thinks that God is the creator and whether Jesus was born of Mary is not discussed in the extant gospel. However, we do find a hope other than the fleshly resurrection as Mary teaches the disciples about a journey of a disembodied soul to find eternal rest.

Tertullian believes that heretics deny the resurrection of the flesh largely due to philosophical influence, and he is scathing towards philosophers in general. He refers to the famous heretics Valentinus and Marcion as being disciples of Plato and the Stoics, and writes that Paul 'expressly names philosophy as that which he would have us be on our guard against' (*Prescr.* 7.7, citing *Col* 2.8). Consequently, he writes, 'Away with all attempts to produce a mottled Christianity of Stoic, Platonic, and dialectic composition! We want no curious disputation after possessing Christ Jesus, no inquisition after enjoying the gospel!' (*Prescr.* 7.11–12). *GMary* is an example of exactly what Tertullian wants to do away with: it offers a philosophical interpretation of Christianity, followed by the disciples arguing about whether Jesus could have ever taught the ascent of the soul.

Mary's vision in *GMary* narrates a soul journeying through hostile cosmic powers to find eternal rest. It is unclear in the text whether this rest can be realized while still in the flesh, or whether it is attainable exclusively after death. Elsewhere, I have argued that Mary embodies the blessed disciple at rest, no longer under the influence of the passions, but ultimate salvation can only be found after this post-mortem journey.[28] Salvation in this gospel can be understood as spiritual progress;

---

27. King contends that readers who were familiar with both *GMary* and alternative seeking and finding commands 'would not have understood them in terms of borrowing or influence, but as differing, even conflicting meanings of Jesus' command'; King, *Gospel of Mary*, 106.

28. Parkhouse, 'Matter and the Soul'.

and this is what Tertullian warns against in *On the Resurrection*. Here, Tertullian writes that the heretics read scripture in such a way that they understand death and resurrection to refer to spiritual ignorance and enlightenment (*Res.* 19.3).

Mary's teaching may be influenced by the Platonic view that souls descend into bodies, in which they become burdened with passions and movement, and find rest only when they leave the body.[29] Whether the soul pre-existed before its embodiment is not explicitly stated in *GMary*, but this idea is implied during the exchange between the soul and the power named Desire. The soul tells Desire that she saw Desire during her descent from heaven to earth, but that Desire did not recognize her as she was concealed in a garment (BG 15,2–8). This is likely to mean that the soul pre-existed before she came into the fleshly body but the witless power did not see the soul in her true form as all she saw was the fleshly clothing. After leaving the body, the soul ascends to find 'rest' and 'silence' (PRyl 21,2 // BG 17,5–7), which likely suggests a return to an original restful state. Comparable ideas regarding the pre-existence and rest of souls are found in Plato's *Timaeus*, in which we read:

> When, from necessity, they are implanted in bodies, and there is the to and fro movement of their bodies, then the first necessity which would befall them is the innate sense perception common to all, which comes from violent passions; second, desire mixed with pleasure and grief; and added to these, fear and anger and whatever (passions) naturally go with these, along with whatever (passions) are their opposites. (*Timaeus* 42a-b)[30]

In the *Timaeus*, pre-existent souls are stable and restful until they enter into bodies. Once souls are in the flesh, they are moved with passions. The rest in which Plato's pre-existent soul dwells may be a comparable rest to that which the soul of *GMary* attains. Despite the language of violent passions in the passage quoted above, the body in the *Timaeus* is not considered to be entirely negative. Rather, the body is a fabric that holds the soul as a means to protect it but which eventually unravels so that the soul is then released in a natural way (*Timaeus* 73b, 74a, 81d).

GMary's account of a soul conversing with powers may also have a Platonic background. In the *Phaedo*, Plato writes that the soul is not in harmony with the body, but works against it, sometimes 'conversing with the desires and passions and

---

29. The soul presented in *GMary* is not entirely Platonic; for example, there is no indication that the soul is composed of three parts, one rational and two non-rational, as we find in Platonic texts such as the *Phaedrus*, *Republic* and *Timaeus*. *GMary* also shows the influence of Stoicism, as argued by Esther de Boer, 'A Stoic Reading of the Gospel of Mary: The Meaning of "Matter" and "Nature" in the Gospel of Mary 7.1–8.11', in *Stoicism in Early Christianity*, ed. Tuomas Rasimus, Ismo Dunderberg and Troels Engberg-Pedersen (Grand Rapids, MI: Baker Academic, 2010), 199–219.

30. Text from R. G. Bury, trans., *Plato: Timaeus, Critias, Cleitophon, Menexenus, Epistles*, LCL 234 (Cambridge, MA: Harvard University Press, 1929).

fears as though it were quite separate and distinct from them' (94d).[31] The soul and body in *GMary* are likewise divided: during or prior to the ascent, the soul sheds the flesh, as shown through the soul referring to her bodily garment (BG 15,8) and being designated a 'human-slayer' (BG 16,15). Once the soul is disembodied, she converses with the four powers that she meets during her ascent, whose names – Darkness, Desire, Ignorance and Wrath – resemble desires, passions and fears. In *GMary,* the 'rest' that the soul reaches appears to be eternal. After having overcome the final power, the soul says, 'From this time on, I will receive rest from the time of the season of the age, in silence' (BG 17,4–7).[32]

The portrayal of salvation as the infinite heavenly rest of the disembodied soul stands entirely in contradiction to the orthodox position of resurrection of the flesh, as found in the rule of faith in the *Prescription*. In this text, Tertullian does not discuss the unity of the body and soul, but in *On the Resurrection* he asserts that human beings are the union of two natures – soul and flesh. Soul and flesh are joined in the womb (*Res.* 15), and they will be judged and raised together (*Res.* 14). Tertullian's defence of the fleshly resurrection is scriptural, but he also acknowledges that the heretics' derision of it is also based on scripture – but that these heretics use scripture fallaciously. He writes to them: 'You hold to the scriptures in which the flesh is disparaged; receive also those in which it is ennobled. You read whatever passage abases it; direct your eyes also to that which elevates it' (*Res.* 10.1). He also criticizes heretics for reading that which pertains to the flesh figuratively but that which speaks about the soul literally. He writes, 'Since, however, things which belong to the soul have nothing allegorical in them, neither therefore have those which belong to the body. For man is as much body as he is soul; so that it is impossible for one of these natures to admit a figurative sense, and the other to exclude it' (*Res.* 32.6).[33] *GMary* uses Platonic ideas to describe the eternal separation of body and soul, and as *GMary*'s narrative of the soul is based on Jesus's ascension in *GJohn* 20.14–18, the author is prioritising a soul-based reading of Jesus's resurrection at the expense of the scriptural passages in which flesh is given preference or equal importance. There is nothing in *GMary* to suggest that the flesh is unequivocally disparaged and, inspired by Plato, *GMary* might take a more neutral view of the fleshly body than Tertullian suggests of his

---

31. Text from H. N. Fowler, trans., *Plato: Euthyphro, Apology, Crito, Phaedo, Phaedrus*, LCL 36. (Cambridge, MA: Harvard University Press, 1914).

32. The beginning of the Greek is missing, but we have 'the remainder of (the) course of season, of time, of age, (in) rest i[n] silence' (PRyl 21,1–2), also pointing to rest and silence as being eternal.

33. Lehtipuu points out that Tertullian will also read texts figuratively when it suits him, such as *Col* 2.12 in *Res.* 23: 'Passages that mention the body or body parts openly proclaim resurrection in a bodily form. On the other hand, those passages that seem to deny the resurrection of the flesh must mean something else, since Paul and the other apostles cannot contradict themselves'; Outi Lehtipuu, *Debates over the Resurrection of the Dead*, Oxford Early Christian Studies (Oxford: Oxford University Press, 2015), 98, see also 164.

opponents. However, counter to the orthodox position, *GMary* clearly opposes the concept of fleshly resurrection in favour of the salvation of the disembodied soul.

As we saw in the last section, *GMary* may use the canonical gospels to counter ideas found in them, and this points to selective use and figurative reading of earlier texts in order to present 'heterodox' ideas. Tertullian, conversely, endorses a literal understanding of scripture to make the argument against philosophy and for the resurrection of the flesh and soul together. Tertullian claims that the confession of fleshly resurrection was handed down by the apostles, suggesting that his opponents, who reject fleshly resurrection and read scriptures figuratively alongside philosophical ideas, might also deny the authority of the twelve – as we see in *GMary*.

Conclusion

Dominant and resistant narratives in the early Christian world were forever shifting, depending on the time, place, community and so forth. *GMary* self-identifies as a counter-narrative by employing the language of 'heterodoxy', which puts it in a milieu that accepts an emerging dominant, 'orthodox' narrative. Whereas the vast majority of early Christian writers who engage with orthodoxy/heterodoxy rhetoric claim that their rivals are heterodox, and inscribe *hairesis* and *hairetikos* in pejorative ways, *GMary* claimed the ἑτερο- prefix for itself.[34] According to *GMary*, it was those who claimed the title 'orthodox' who were ignorant. They were wrong not only about apostolic authority and how to read scripture but also about fundamentals of Jesus's teachings such as the Son of Man and the nature of the resurrection.

The use of the term *hetero-* in the Greek *GMary* may help to situate this text towards the end of the second century, if not a few decades later. The half century from roughly 180 to 230 CE saw increasingly intense efforts of self-definition and to separate orthodoxy from its opponents. In order to recognize certain teachings as different from mainstream or orthodox ideas, there had to be a sense of orthodoxy within the Christian movement. And so although it is largely correct to say that Christianity in this period was fluid and still defining itself, *GMary* does present an emerging dominant Christian orthodoxy, and one that shared many of the same values as Tertullian's *Prescription*.

On the other hand, the orthodox position that *GMary* alludes to was likely a localized form of orthodoxy. It does not signify a single and continuous Christian history in the way that orthodoxy might be conceived today. It simply indicates

---

34. On labelling others as non-orthodox and thus calling opponents 'deviant', see Lehtipuu. On Tertullian's *On the Resurrection*, the *Treatise on the Resurrection* (NHC 1,4) and the *Testimony of Truth* (NHC 9,3), she writes that 'all three [texts] show similar strategies for labeling their fellow Christians as deviant'; Lehtipuu, *Debates over the Resurrection of the Dead*, 75.

that some Christians were professing to be orthodox as a strategy to identify themselves over against what they were not, and that those employing this label were becoming the dominant and mainstream voice. So, although we talk here of orthodoxy as mainstream, we have to ask to what extent this 'master narrative' really dominated the early Christian world. As this volume shows, there were numerous counter-narratives circulating, and recent studies have shown that the master narrative was hardly homogeneous. The texts and thinkers that we consider as 'orthodox' show great variety, as do those that were labelled 'heterodox'. For example, fleshly resurrection was just one view among texts traditionally labelled as 'orthodox' of how the person continued after their mortal life.[35]

GMary takes an unusual step by self-consciously identifying itself as an outsider and as a counter-narrative. By doing so, the text has the power to oppose the dominant or normative society that surrounds it. The power of counter-narratives is summed up in a special issue of *Critical Psychology*: 'In the stories they tell, the speakers reveal the power of counter stories to expose the construction of the dominant story by suggesting how else it could be told.'[36] *GMary* constructs its own definition of what it meant to be a true follower of Jesus, engaging with ongoing debates concerning authority, reading practices and doctrine as a means of identity formation. There are clearly social issues at stake. Much ink has been spilled on *GMary* as a feminist discourse that challenges patriarchal society especially through its opposition to the male apostles, and this is certainly one of the power dynamics at play. Another dynamic may be local resistance to Roman rule and attitudes, as King argues.[37] Today counter-narratives are used by activists to challenge cultural stereotypes and provide new ways of seeing the world. This purpose can be seen in *GMary*: to challenge gender constructions and social norms in the wider Graeco-Roman world, and to challenge structures of authority, theological teachings and their resultant practices within the Christian community.

---

35. On this topic, see Gonzalez, who helpfully uses the *Passion of Perpetua* to question whether bodily resurrection was even the most widely held view of material continuity within the 'orthodox' community; Eliezer Gonzalez, 'Anthropologies of Continuity: The Body and Soul in Tertullian, Perpetua, and Early Christianity', *JECS* 21.4 (2013), 479–502, esp. 501–2.

36. M. Fine and A. Harris (ed.), 'Under the Covers: Theorising the Politics of Counter Stories', *International Journal of Critical Psychology* 4 (2001), 13.

37. King, *Gospel of Mary*, 158.

6

ATTEMPTING THE IMPOSSIBLE? PTOLEMY'S *LETTER TO FLORA* AS COUNTER-NARRATIVE

Joseph Verheyden

This chapter offers an attempt at reading an ancient Christian text from a particular perspective. Some might think that the perspective taken here may seem too modern, or 'post-modern', to be useful for analysing texts that come from a 'pre-critical' era. The assumption is wrong, as I will try to demonstrate, while admitting that the notion of 'counter-narrative' perhaps needs some nuancing or precision to be helpful at all. The chapter will consist of three parts: a short introductory one in which I define the concept and also provide some caveats, an equally short introduction to the *Letter to Flora* itself and the analysis proper that should illustrate how such an approach can be developed in a fruitful way in studying an ancient text.

Defining 'counter-narrative'

The concept seems to be all over the place these days, but the phenomena it claims to cover have always been around, even if they are not easy to detect or in some cases utterly inaccessible when it comes to applying it to Antiquity. I will not try to survey the history of the concept, nor lose myself in definitions. The following is meant briefly to recall some basic aspects that are naturally linked to it, to show that it is a complicated phenomenon that has often all too easily been 'simplified' and to argue that it can be used for studying ancient texts.

A most straightforward definition can be found in Wiktionary: a counter-narrative is 'a narrative that goes against another narrative'. It is as easy as that. A slightly more complicated definition, also anonymous and randomly picked from the internet, runs as follows: 'A counter-narrative is an argument that disputes a commonly held belief or truth. These beliefs often relate to cultures, people or even institutions.'[1] Today, the concept is used, among others, in sociology, in

---

1. As such, counter-narrative is often associated, indeed almost identified, with counter-culture. While the two are obviously closely related, they are not identical and the former

cultural studies, in literature studies and in several other fields. It got a boost in the realm of postmodern studies emphasizing 'perspectivism', challenging truth claims and promoting diversity and multiplicity over against unity and harmony.[2] At least six aspects or connotations linked to the concept that are also of interest for our purpose should be mentioned.

First, 'counter-narrative' is by definition a secondary concept, for it assumes the existence of something that precedes it. That counterpart is variously called the master narrative, or the dominant, the official or the metanarrative. It is the way the ruling class, or perhaps even the majority in a society, tells the story of its own identity, its principles and values, its way to see 'the facts'. The counter-narrative is its opposite. It is the way a (sidelined) minority, but in other regimes also the masses that are being ruled, define themselves over against the dominant group.[3]

Second, as is clear from the previous point, it is not just about numbers and not only about underdogs. Counter-narratives may originate in sub- or countercultures, but they may also have grown from among the masses, and reflect the latter's aspirations and their way to grasp the world. They may stem from the margins of society or from broader circles – orchestrated by (charismatic) leaders, intellectuals or others, in an attempt to rewrite history and create a new metanarrative.

---

is not the exclusive property of the latter. On counter-culture in an American context, see the classic work by T. Roszak, *The Making of a Counter Culture* (Berkeley, CA: UCA Press, 1968); cf. also J. Milton Yinger, *Countercultures: The Promise and the Peril of a World Turned Upside Down* (New York: Free Press, 1982). In an early Christian context, Gnosticism could perhaps be labelled as 'counter-cultural' – so, e.g., A. D. DeConick, *The Gnostic New Age: How a Countercultural Spirituality Revolutionized Religion from Antiquity to Today* (New York: Columbia University Press, 2016), though it should be noted that its luminaries were most probably not (social) outcasts and that there were also other counter-current trends around (the earliest monastic tradition, to name one).

2. Again with regard to Gnosticism, scholars have not tired of pointing out the differences there are between the several schools and the energy its various prominent members put into creating difference as part of identity creation. See the brief survey of the question by D. Brakke, 'Self-Differentiation among Christian Groups: The Gnostics', in *Cambridge History of Christianity, I. Origins to Constantine*, ed. M. Mitchell and F. M. Young (Cambridge: Cambridge University Press, 2006), 245–60; cf. also his *The Gnostics: Myth, Ritual, and Diversity in early Christianity* (Cambridge, MA: Harvard University Press, 2010).

3. This topic has been dealt with in quite some detail in New Testament studies by Richard Horsley and others, building on the work of the anthropologist James C. Scott and the concept of 'hidden transcript', particularly with regard to the historical Jesus, Paul and Q, for the latter when trying to contextualize the community/ies behind the Sayings Source. Cf., e.g., R. A. Horsley (ed.), *Hidden Transcripts and the Arts of Resistance: Applying the Work of James C. Scott to Jesus and Paul* (Semeia Studies, 48; Atlanta, GA: SBL, 2004); R. A. Horsley (ed.), *Oral Performance, Popular Tradition, and Hidden Transcript in Q* (Semeia Studies, 60; Atlanta, GA: SBL, 2006).

Third, as illustrated in the second definition cited above and also in the first point, counter-narratives have to do with existential questions and with questions of identity building. They are not indifferent, nor trivial. That makes them valuable, socially and historically, and occasionally also dangerous at the same time.

Fourth, and following from the previous, it is important to distinguish between voicing an opinion and devising a counter-narrative. The Canadian novelist Jeyn Roberts in her 2012 novel *Rage Within*, the second part of a trilogy entitled *Dark Inside*, about teenagers trying to survive in a world gone mad and nearing its end, writes somewhere, 'There are three sides to every story. Yours. Mine. What really happened: the truth.'[4] That would be a wrong way to define counter-narrative. It is not about adding another perspective in a dialogue between equals but about challenging (the) one leading opinion (or one that is perceived as such) that mattered so far and about reconstructing the truth anew. It is above all about liberation and emancipation. But that also means it is the clear intention to move from original dissent to creating a new consensus on the terms laid out in the counter-narrative. Ultimately, then, it is a matter of trying to replace 'claimed truth' by 'real truth'.

Fifth, in applying the concept of counter-narrative and studying (ancient) texts along these lines, one should step away from the purely theoretical level of the previous points and realize that all texts and all narratives, meta- or counter-, are historically situated, subject to their own conditions and those of their authors, hence in part contingent in the way they originated and were transmitted and received.

Sixth and finally, in order to avoid ending up in total subjectivity in assessing a particular text in terms of counter-narrative, it is imperative to discover firm indications that this text was indeed meant to function as a counter-narrative. That is often easier said than done. In preparing for this chapter, I came across an interesting work that presents itself as a handbook and toolkit for creating a counter-narrative that has influenced me in several ways. *The Counter-Narrative Handbook* authored by Henry Tuck and Tanya Silverman and published in 2016 by the Institute for Strategic Dialogue (ISD) describes the methods and tools for devising a counter-narrative, in this case a narrative that should 'counter' cases of extremely violent discourse as this can be found on the internet.[5] The authors wish to prepare the reader for mounting a campaign to challenge a dominant and appealing discourse (i.e. in certain milieus, of course). I fully realize that a good part of what can be found in this handbook cannot naturally be transferred to the study of ancient texts and also that not all of the elements listed are equally important to characterize a particular text as a counter-narrative and that other elements can perhaps be added, but for the general outline and also for some aspects I was nevertheless loosely influenced by information gathered from this handbook, especially in the third part of this chapter.

---

4. First published Simon & Schuster (New York, 2012).

5. www.counternarratives.org. ISD describes itself as a London-based 'think and do tank'.

Ptolemy's Letter to Flora *in its current context*

Next to nothing is known about the circumstances in which the *Letter to Flora* was composed, except that its author suggests towards the end that it was solicited by the addressee herself. The work has been preserved only by Epiphanius of Cyprus in his famous *Panarion*.[6] It is found in the chapter against the Ptolemaeans where it takes up a significant part of what Epiphanius has to say about them (33.3–7, i.e., 5 sections out of 12).[7] This 'sect' is the last to be mentioned in the second section of the *Panarion* (21–33). It is preceded in Epiphanius's list by the Valentinians (31) and the Secundians (32) and followed by the Marcosians (34) and the Colarbasians (35).[8]

> 6. Long mistrusted and put away as an ignoramus by modern scholarship, Epiphanius seems to be making a sort of comeback in recent years. See the quite positive views on the man as a well-connected church person, an experienced and respected ascetic, a media figure and even something of an intellectual, in the monographs by R. Young Kim, *Epiphanius of Cyprus: Imagining the Orthodox World* (Ann Arbor: University of Michigan Press, 2015) and A. S. Jacobs, *Epiphanius of Cyprus: A Cultural Biography of Late Antiquity* (Oakland: University of California Press, 2016).
>
> 7. The old edition of the *Panarion* by K. Holl, *Epiphanius, Erster Band: Ancoratus und Panarion Haer. 1–33* (GCS 25; Berlin: Akademie, 1915), has recently been re-edited in a revised form and accompanied by a second volume with (mainly) text-critical notes: M. Bergermann and Ch.-F. Collatz, *Epiphanius I: Ancoratus und Panarion Haer. 1–33* (GCS NF 10/1–2; Berlin: de Gruyter, 2013). The text of the *Letter* remains debated at several points. That is why it is still rewarding to check also the edition provided by G. Quispel, *Ptolémée, Lettre à Flora: Analyse, texte critique, traduction, commentaire et index* (SC 24; Paris: Cerf, 1949; SC 24 bis; Paris: Cerf, 1966). The latter should in turn be checked against the comments of W. A. Löhr, 'La doctrine de Dieu dans la Lettre à Flora de Ptolémée', *RHPhR* 75 (1995), 177–91. English citations here are, as a rule, from the revised version of the translation by F. Williams, *The* Panarion *of Epiphanius of Salamis, Book I (Sects 1–46)* (NHS 35; Leiden: Brill, 1987; NHMS 63; Leiden: Brill, 2009²). For other English translations of the *Letter*, see W. Foerster, *Gnosis: A Selection of Gnostic Texts*, I. *Patristic Evidence*, English translation edited by R. McL. Wilson (Oxford: Clarendon Press, 1972), 154–61; the original appeared as *Die Gnosis, I: Zeugnisse der Kirchenväter* (Zürich: Artemis, 1969; repr. 1997), 204–13. See also B. Layton, *The Gnostic Scriptures* (Garden City, NY: Doubleday, 1987), 306–15.
>
> 8. It has been noted that this represents the order of Irenaeus, to which he adds at the end Heracleon who is mentioned by Hippolytus (who follows the order Valentinus, Ptolemy, Secundus, Heracleon, Marcus, Colarbasius); so A. Pourkier, *L'hérésiologie chez Épiphane de Salamine* (Christianisme antique 4; Paris: Beauchesne, 1992), 104. But maybe it is more correct to say that Epiphanius mixed up the two. They are not the only Gnostic groups Epiphanius mentions in his work. He has a keen interest, though not always matched with knowledge, of the phenomenon and also lists the Sethians (*Pan.* 39) and a group he calls the Archontics (*Pan.* 40), as well as a more shadowy one to which he refers as the Borborites or simply as the Gnostics (*Pan.* 26) along with several other, apparently minor, groups that are packed together at the beginning of *Pan.* 25. For his comments on these various Gnostic

The chapter's structure is reasonably well organized, certainly when compared to others in the *Panarion*. Basically, it can be divided into six parts of quite uneven length. It opens with a short note on Ptolemy's network (33.1.1), then continues with rather extensive presentations of two topics from his teachings, the second of which is the *Letter* (33.1.2–2.5 and 33.3–7), followed by refutations of each of these topics (33.8 and 9–11), to conclude with a thanksgiving-cum-insult, in which the bishop thanks God for his assistance in refuting the heretic and damns the latter by comparing him to some sort of vermin, as he ends almost all the chapters of his *Panarion* (33.12).[9]

According to Epiphanius, the sect is named after its frontman as a sign of respect from his followers. In his typically messy style, he presents Ptolemy as a follower of Secundus and a certain Epiphanes and more generally as one who belongs to the Valentinians, but then also adds that Ptolemy held certain opinions that single him out from his fellow Gnostics (33.1.1). It looks as if Ptolemy at one point had gone his own way and founded his own group, but no further details are given and it is not clear if this group considered itself 'a school', though that may well have been the case.[10] It all remains rather fuzzy and Epiphanius does not really care to explain things any further. The nature of Ptolemy's relation with Valentinus remains a bit of an open question also in modern scholarship.[11] I will not dwell on this or on

---

movements, see Foerster, *Gnosis*, 234–38 (Valentinus), 293–98 (Sethians and Archontics), and Layton, *Gnostic Scriptures*, 184–90 (Sethians), 191–98 (Archontics) and 199–214 (Gnostics).

9. See my analysis of this motif in 'Epiphanius of Salamis on Beasts and Heretics: Some Introductory Comments', in *Heretics and Heresies in the Ancient Church and in Eastern Christianity*, ed. J. Verheyden and H. Teule (Eastern Christian Studies 10; Leuven: Peeters, 2011), 143–73.

10. In the *Summary* (*Anacephalaeosis*) of the *Panarion*, which is most probably by a later hand, the Ptolemaeans are said to be 'disciples' of Valentinus and to hold the same ideas as the latter and the Secundians with regard to the syzygies of the aeons, but otherwise also differ from these, though it is not said in what respect.

11. See W. A. Löhr, 'Ptolemäus, Gnostiker', *Theologische Realenzyklopädie* 27 (1997), 699–702, 699: 'das genaue Verhältnis von Ptolemäus zu Valentin ist unklar. ... Ebenfalls unklar bleibt die Stellung des Ptolemäus zur Grosskirche.' It sometimes translates into referring to him merely as 'the Valentinian Ptolemy' or in speaking of 'Ptolemy's version of Valentinianism' without making much of an effort to point out similarities or distinctions; see, e.g., A. H. B. Logan, *Gnostic Truth and Christian Heresy: A Study in the History of Gnosticism* (Edinburgh, T&T Clark, 1996), 19, 30 (and *passim*); M. A. Williams, *Rethinking 'Gnosticism': An Argument for Dismantling a Dubious Category* (Princeton NJ: Princeton University Press, 1996), 14–18, 26–27; J. Lahe, *Gnosis und Judentum: Alttestamentliche und jüdische Motive in der gnostischen Literatur und das Ursprungsproblem der Gnosis* (NHMS, 75; Leiden: Brill, 2012), 327–28; R. van den Broek, *Gnostic Religion in Antiquity* (Cambridge: Cambridge University Press, 2013), 94–96. Building on Tertullian, some scholars have called him a leader of the Valentinian school, and indeed perhaps the one who was at the origins of its split into a Western and an Eastern branch, though this may

other aspects of Ptolemy's teaching that have been preserved by other ancient authors.[12] Suffice it to say that Ptolemy has received relatively little coverage in modern scholarship when compared to some other luminaries associated with Gnosticism.[13] However, it is not immediately relevant for our purpose as Ptolemy does not say that he depends on anyone for the views he presents in the *Letter*, which some have taken to be an early work.[14] One has the strong impression that in this case he rather wished to stand up for his own views (see below).

Epiphanius takes issue with two aspects of Ptolemy's teachings that in his view are interconnected, as the one offers proof for the other. The first has to do with Ptolemy's argument for the existence of a 'lesser' God. In this regard, he seems to have further fine-tuned some of the opinions of his predecessors on the pairs of aeons. What Epiphanius has to say about it basically consists of a combination of an unidentified excerpt and a paraphrase of Irenaeus's views on the matter, including the latter's criticism of the misrepresentation of God and God's attributes and capacities, which he 'enriches' with some further observations on the unfavourable comparison between what Ptolemy says about God and Homer about Zeus: 'Ptolemy mimicked Homer speaking of Zeus' (33.1.2–2.5, and compare *Adv. Haer.* 1.12.1–3). So much for aeons, syzygies and Ptolemy's image of

---

also have been the work of his disciples; so E. Thomassen, *The Spiritual Seed: The Church of the 'Valentinians'* (NHMS 60; Leiden: Brill, 2006), 128–29. Cf. also C. Markschies, *Valentinus Gnosticus? Untersuchungen zur valentinianischen Gnosis mit einem Kommentar zu den Fragmenten Valentins* (WUNT 65; Tübingen, Mohr Siebeck, 1992), 371–72.

12. See the evidence from Irenaeus (and Clement) in W. Foerster, 'Die Grundzüge der Ptolemaeischen Gnosis', *NTS* 6 (1959–60), 16–31 (assuming that the *Letter* does not differ significantly from the rest of Ptolemy's teaching and interpreting the former in light of the latter); Foerster, *Gnosis*, 121–54 (citing the relevant texts); Layton, *Gnostic Scriptures*, 276–302; D. Wanke, 'Irenäus und die Häretiker in Rom: Thesen zur geschichtlichen Situation von *Adversus haereses*', *ZAC* 3 (1999), 202–40, here 207–16.

13. On the figure and teaching of Ptolemy in general, see Löhr, 'Ptolemäus', 699–702; C. Markschies, 'New Research on Ptolemaeus Gnosticus', *ZAC* 4 (2000), 225–54, here 246–53. Not infrequently, his views are discussed within the broader Valentinian context; see, e.g., the discussion of Gnostic cosmogony in G. May, *Schöpfung aus dem Nichts: Die Entstehung der Lehre von der creatio ex nihilo* (Arbeiten zur Kirchengeschichte, 48; Berlin: de Gruyter, 1978), 92–119; cf. also Markschies, *Valentinus Gnosticus?*, 392–402. Sometimes he gets a short chapter of his own at the fringes of studies on Valentinus and his school, but then it is above all to demonstrate how difficult it is to get a good grasp of the man and his teachings. See, among others, Thomassen, *Spiritual* Seed, 119–29; B. A. Pearson, *Ancient Gnosticism: Traditions and Literature* (Minneapolis, MN: Fortress, 2007), 155–61, with a few words also on the *Letter*. The latter, though, gets a separate treatment in F.-M.-M. Sagnard, *La Gnose valentinienne et le témoignage de saint Irénée* (Études de philosophie historique 36; Paris: Vrin, 1947), 451–79; I. Dunderberg, *Beyond Gnosticism: Myth, Lifestyle, and Society in the School of Valentinus* (New York: Columbia University Press, 2008), 77–94.

14. Thomassen, *Spiritual Seed*, 129.

God, one could say. As Epiphanius sees it, the presentation of his opinion is at the same time also its refutation.

Next to the representation of God, it is the way divine Law is tackled by Ptolemy that raises Epiphanius's ire. Here too he relies on a source, but this time it is a work of the opponent himself on this topic – a letter he wrote to one of his companions. He claims to cite the text out of intellectual honesty so that readers can check that what he says about it is true (33.2.6). He does not say that he quotes it in full – there is no formal address or greeting at the beginning and the end, but the overall impression is that apart from these the excerpt may pretty much cover the complete text of the letter. It is not the first nor the only time Epiphanius quotes at length from the work of a 'heretic'.[15] In cases where this can be checked against other sources, it appears that he as a rule quotes rather accurately. There is no reason to doubt that this would have been the case here. He has nothing to tell about the circumstances of writing, nor does he inform the reader about how he came in possession of a copy of the work. Since he makes it the second of two items on which to pin down Ptolemy, he obviously considers it to be a topic of great importance within this group. The letter gives the name of the addressee, a woman, and contains some hints about her status and knowledge of Christian doctrine. Ptolemy calls her 'my good sister' (33.3.1), which may indicate that she was a member of the group, or maybe only an aspiring member, for she is expected to benefit from these teachings 'in what follows as well' (33.7.10).[16] Flora must have had some basic knowledge, and probably more, of Christian and perhaps even Jewish doctrine on the Law.[17] In the final lines Ptolemy notes that he was quick to respond to her demand for some further instruction (33.7.10).[18] Epiphanius notes in the introduction that the work has a certain appeal, which makes it a dangerous item (33.2.6).

Even though Epiphanius does not give any such indications, the *Letter* can rather easily be divided into five sections that reflect the common structure of an ancient letter: *exordium* (33.3.1), *narratio* (33.3.2-7), *divisio* (33.3.8), *argumentatio* (33.4.1-7.7, subdivided into three parts [33.4.1-14, 33.5.1-6.6, 33.7.1-7], each with its own threefold division) and *conclusio* (33.7.8-10).[19] In the Introduction,

---

15. Most famous perhaps are the lengthy citations from Marcion in *Pan.* 42.

16. Quispel (*Lettre*, 75) leaves it open whether Flora had already joined 'the spiritual family'.

17. 'Tout indique d'ailleurs que Flora est chrétienne' (Sagnard, *Gnose valentinienne*, 452).

18. It is tempting to try and identify the addressee a bit further but all such attempts must of necessity remain hypothetical, including the one that suggests Flora was a kind of patron of the movement or school. So Dunderberg, *Beyond Gnosticism*, 90-92. P. Lampe assumes that the woman Justin speaks about in his second *Apology* (2.2) on the topic of a second marriage after divorce may well be Ptolemy's Flora: *Die stadtrömische Christen in den ersten Jahrhunderten* (WUNT II 18; Tübingen: Mohr Siebeck, ²1989), 200-3; criticized by Markschies, 'New Research', 248-49.

19. So Dunderberg, *Beyond Gnosticism*, 80. A somewhat different proposal in Löhr, 'Doctrine de Dieu', 180: 33.3/4/5-6/7.1-7/7.8-10. In summarizing the contents of the

Ptolemy reviews opposite opinions on the origin of the Law (33.3). He then proposes his own solution, which consists of introducing a threefold division in what is commonly understood by the Law, distinguishing between divine commandments and those devised by Moses and by 'the elders' (33.4). Next (33.5–6), Ptolemy introduces a further subdivision, again in three parts, of the first category he had mentioned previously, speaking of 'pure legislation' (τὴν καθαρὰν νομοθεσίαν), legislation that is 'mixed with inferior matter and injustice' (τὸν συμπεπλεγμένον τῷ χείρονι καὶ τῇ ἀδικίᾳ) and 'typical and allegorical legislation' (τὸ τυπικὸν καὶ συμβολικὸν ... νομοθετηθέν). The fourth section deals with the implications of this position for identifying the author of this part of the Law (33.7.1–9). The work ends with a brief conclusion with some summary advice for the addressee (33.7.10). I will come back to the details of the argument below.

Epiphanius has the *Letter* followed by a rebuttal of his own making, but somewhat unexpectedly, yet well in line with his often rather chaotic approach elsewhere in the *Panarion*, he first comes back once more to the first topic, even though one might have thought that all was said about it by paraphrasing Irenaeus, in order to ridicule Ptolemy and compare him to ancient mythologists who also did not know how to distinguish between lie and truth. Those who like this sort of irony will probably well appreciate the way Epiphanius refers to the latter indulging in divine genealogies as 'midwives as though of some heavenly mothers' (33.8.4). Ptolemy and his followers are not different. They pretend to know things humans cannot know, and in this way not only fool others but also themselves. Their speculations have no basis in Scripture. Stopping for nothing, Epiphanius even recalls (without mentioning it by name) the old Euhemeristic explanation for the existence of the gods of Greek mythology when asserting that these are mere human beings 'turned into names of gods' (33.8.9).

Epiphanius's criticism of Ptolemy's views on the Law first of all focuses, most naturally, on the proposed threefold division of the Law that is dismissed as nonsensical, because all true commandments obviously come from God and God only (33.9.7, 13) and because one should distinguish between such commands and rabbinic traditions that are not found in Torah (33.9.3). Moreover, Ptolemy is accused of misrepresenting some of the divine commandments, which shows him to be a trickster (33.9.12). Epiphanius then turns to the second triad, which is perhaps even worse in his eyes because it threatens to introduce a division in God and reveals Ptolemy as a charlatan (33.10.1). There evidently cannot be such a thing as a second-rank divine Law (33.10.6). Against Ptolemy, he argues that the *lex talionis* is not an inferior commandment compared to Jesus's teaching about turning the other cheek (*GMt* 5.39). The latter is a way to avoid any need for the

---

letter, Quispel (*Lettre*, 11–44) divides it into thirteen sections, but these do not really reflect the structure of the work. Markschies ('New Research', 232) proposes a threefold division (33.4/5–6/7) according to the characteristic genre of the letter as a διαίρεσις (see below n. 22), but that may be a bit artificial as he then considers the first two parts to be 'two branches' of the same διαίρεσις on 'the law of god'.

former, but it does not nullify it (33.10.7-8, and again in 33.11.6-7). Rather, it is a more advanced understanding of the consequences of some of the commandments in the Law on the principle that humankind has grown more mature and has been thought worthy to be initiated into 'the full mysteries' (33.11.1-5). As clear proof, finally, that the old commandment is still in force Epiphanius cites *GMatthew* 24.50-51 – the Lord having his vengeance and executing judgement in a most horrible way (33.11.8). One thing he grants the opponent: it is his view that some parts of the Law are to be understood allegorically (on circumcision or the Sabbath), but this does not excuse him from his other mistakes regarding the Law and the person of God (33.11-13). This latter part is interspersed with direct attacks on the credibility of the opponent (33.11.9-10). Epiphanius ends in the usual way, thanking God for having given him the power to conquer the enemy and raging against the evil heretic who is compared to 'bad fish' and damned for trying to delude others (33.12).

I deliberately started with a short presentation of Epiphanius's refutation because it already gives a taste of what the *Letter* is about. Epiphanius was clearly far less favourably impressed than modern scholars have been who have praised its language, its structure and its author's pedagogical skills.[20] But let us leave the old bishop in his wisdom and instead turn to the text itself.

Reading Ptolemy's Letter to Flora *as a counter-narrative: Pros and cons*

Planning the Project. This is a most important stage as it has direct consequences for the way the project is to be conceived and received. It involves defining the intended audience, setting goals and objectives, choosing the appropriate medium, reflecting on the form one thinks is most appealing to the audience and informing oneself about the views of the opponents.

The *Letter* offers very little information in this regard and Epiphanius is hardly of any help. As stated above, it was written on demand and delivered quite promptly. Actually, Ptolemy sent Flora a text that had already been prepared. 'I have not been slow to send you these few words, my sister Flora, and had written the brief statement already, making the matter sufficiently clear' (33.7.10).[21] If this information can be taken at face value, it would mean that Ptolemy had somehow anticipated the request. Or maybe it was part of a larger project that came in handy when Flora asked for it? We do not know what the addressee concretely required

---

20. See, famously, E. Norden, *Die antike Kunstprosa vom VI. Jh. v. Chr. bis in die Zeit der Renaissance*, 2 vols (Leipzig: Teubner, 1909; Stuttgart: Teubner, 1983⁹), II, 920-22. Cf. Sagnard, *Gnose valentinienne*, 451; Lampe, *Die stadtrömischen Christen*, 255, but with some nuancing (in line with Quispel).

21. Exceptionally I cite here from Williams's first edition, which still reads ἠτόνησα (with Holl and Bergermann/Collatz), but which he replaced with Petavius's conjecture ἐφθόνησα in the second edition.

from Ptolemy. Was she particularly interested in the status of the Law, or had she asked, rather more generally, what he thought was a major point of contention between their group and the mainstream church? In any case, Ptolemy makes it clear right from the start that his addressee was aware that there circulated 'discrepant opinions' about the role and function of the Law for Christians (33.3.1, τὰς διαφωνούσας γνώμας). She may have been confused by it, or perhaps she was just looking for confirmation of the view she had heard about as a member of the group.

All of this means that the project was perhaps not so much planned by the author as provoked by the addressee. Ptolemy conceives of it as a private answer to an unknown individual (to us at least, though not to Ptolemy) who is naturally thought to be sympathetic to his views and to benefit from his instruction. The letter genre, formally a διαίρεσις, fits this purpose well. However, it is not said that the text cannot be circulated. Hence, it cannot be excluded that Ptolemy hoped, or perhaps even assumed, that it would also come to be known by other sympathizers. Also by outsiders?[22] The work looks like a kind of small treatise that relies upon no other authority than that of Scripture, the Saviour as Lawgiver and Ptolemy himself in the role of the exegete who is capable of explaining Scripture without any help from colleagues.[23] He clearly thought this should work.

In terms of creating a counter-narrative, it means the project was from the outset intended for one individual or perhaps a small audience of sympathizers

---

22. On the genre, see W. A. Löhr, 'Die Auslegung des Gesetzes bei Markion, den Gnostikern und den Manichäern', in *Stimuli: Exegese und ihre Hermeneutik in Antike und Christentum. FS E. Dassmann*, ed. G. Schöllgen and C. Scholten; JbAC Ergänzungsband 23 (Münster: Aschendorff, 1996), 77–95, here 80, and above all the detailed and convincing analysis of Markschies, 'New Research', 228–233 (with the nuance mentioned in n. 19 above).

23. See 33.3.8: 'But as I have been vouchsafed <knowledge> of both [i.e., the God of justice and the Father of all], it is left to me to declare to you and accurately describe both the nature of the Law itself and the person by whom it was given, the lawgiver. I shall provide the proofs of <the> things I shall say from the words of our Saviour, by which alone we are surely guided to the perception of the truth.' Quispel (*Lettre*, 81–82) notes the difference (contradiction?) between the way Ptolemy accounts for his knowledge in this instance and at the end of the *Letter*. Here it is presented as a spiritual gift: 'Ptolémée a reçu la grâce de recevoir la gnose'; in 3.7.9, he says his knowledge comes from apostolic (i.e. secret, so Quispel) tradition. The two are not necessarily to be taken as contradictory and could also be read as if the latter, compared to the former, further explains the origin of that knowledge. In any case, Ptolemy does not seem to make much of the potential tension. On the other hand, as Quispel notes, both ways to access knowledge are known from ancient literature (Hippolytus, *Refutatio* 6.42.2, for the first, Ps-Clementine Homilies, *Epistula Petri*, for the second). The word 'knowledge' (γνῶσις) is not in the text but was added by Holl for clarity and kept by later editors. Quispel (*Lettre*, 82) notes the use of 'ignorance' (ἀγνοεῖν) in the immediately preceding context.

who apparently did not so much need to be convinced as to be instructed. The immediate goal is therefore rather limited, but as said, the addressee is not forbidden to spread and talk about the contents of the letter; as a matter of fact, the work was circulated more broadly and even survived into the fourth century and was known to at least one outsider, the author of the *Panarion*. It remains the case that a (apparently) private letter to a sympathizer is obviously not the best way to reach out to a larger audience, let alone to one's opponents, but I guess that not all counter-narratives are by definition intended to become common knowledge.

Creating content (1): the trouble with the Law. When the audience, the goal and the form of the medium are set, it remains to start creating content – the most important element of all, but one that is intrinsically linked to the others. As said above, the topic Ptolemy will deal with seems to have been suggested by his addressee. It has to do with the status assigned to the Law as it is found in Scripture (and in Jesus's disputes with his opponents). Ptolemy has a clear idea of the core of the problem and of the solutions that have been proposed, though he does not tell the reader what his sources are. Actually, he does not mention anyone by name, but rather presents two diametrically opposing opinions that by this very fact are considered to be the two ruling narratives on the matter. On the one hand, there are those who think that the Law stems from 'our God and Father'; on the other, those who argue, by contrast, that it is a creation of the devil, 'the father and maker of this universe' (33.3.2).[24] The latter view may refer to the Marcionites,[25] though it cannot be excluded that Ptolemy may also have had in view rival Gnostic groups. The situation is more complex still with regard to the former view.[26] The formula

---

24. The label assigned to the devil is Platonic in origin (*Timaeus* 28e) but had become 'un lieu commun' (Quispel, *Lettre*, 76). Quispel is right in pointing out the parallel in Irenaeus, *Adv. Haer.* 1.5.1 (but here applied to Yahweh as seen by Gnostics). In 33.7.4–5, Ptolemy, by contrast, clearly opposes the Father and the Demiurge/Creator. Löhr ('Doctrine de Dieu', 186) explains this with reference to Numenius of Apamea (*Fragments* 12 and 13) who makes a similar distinction and notes a possible echo of the latter at the end of the *Letter* in the motif of the seed (33.7.10). A more general comment on the spread of the motif in Markschies, 'New Research', 235.

25. So Quispel, *Lettre*, 76, with the important qualification, twice repeated, that Ptolemy is not fully correct in rendering their position. See also Markschies, 'New Research', 234; G. Lüdemann, ‚Zur Geschichte des ältesten Christentums in Rom, I. Valentin und Marcion; II. Ptolemäus und Justin', *ZNW* 70 (1979), 86–114, here 97–114. Lüdemann situates Ptolemy's *Letter* in the broader Roman context and points out similarities with Justin Martyr's views on Jewish Law and on how to tackle Marcion; S. Pétrement, *A Separate God: The Christian Origins of Gnosticism* (London: Darton, Longman and Todd, 1996), 47. Löhr, on the other hand, thinks that Ptolemy represents a sort of 'marcionitisme modéré' ('Doctrine de Dieu', 191). Cf. also his 'Auslegung', 80–84.

26. The reference may be to Jews (Harnack) or to Christians (Quispel, *Lettre*, 76, who actually speaks of 'Catholics'). Cf. Markschies, 'New Research', 233.

'our God and Father' might give the impression that he is thinking of 'orthodox' Christians, but shortly afterwards he criticizes this position for not recognizing that the Law needs to be fulfilled (33.3.4), which is a core Christian notion that would naturally identify this first group as being Jews (or perhaps Jewish Christians strictly holding on to Torah). While this is not impossible in itself, such a conclusion raises the further question of why Ptolemy would be interested in opposing these two 'extreme' views[27] while relegating the good Christian concept of the need for fulfilment of the Law, attested in the gospel and quite possibly the mainstream Christian position, to the mere level of an argument against the first group. He uses the concept in a positive way, but he clearly does not regard it as the full and correct answer, for he will move in quite a different direction. But why then not present it as a third option along with the two others and discuss (and reject it) in its own right? As I see it, there are two options for a way out. Either one has to assume that Ptolemy deliberately downplayed this third position to the point that it is virtually obscured and offered only an incomplete picture of the whole situation in a strongly dichotomizing format. This format has the advantage that things are clearly stated, but it runs the risk of being criticized because it is not the full scene. Or one has to assume that he preferred to give precedence to how the different groups looked at the figure of God as the giver of the Law and made this the distinctive criterion for dividing up the positions. On such a hypothesis, Ptolemy might well have felt he was right in assimilating the mainstream Christian position to the Jewish(-Christian) one, for they both hold to the view that it is the same 'just' (and 'good') God who gave the Law over against those who claim it comes from the devil. It is not easy to make a decision, but in view of what will follow in the fourth section of the work, which deals with the consequences of his position on the Law for the image of God that goes with it, the second option seems to be the more plausible one.[28] Ptolemy cannot be accused of being incomplete. His presentation is guided by the question what kind of God it is who produced the Law. Within this constellation he proceeds in a perfectly logical way when speaking of two main positions. For one like Ptolemy who shows a strong interest in logic and systematization, as will be seen below, that may well have been a major factor in his decision. It also allows him to make a limited use of the notion of fulfilment when it suits him without having to counter it as such, even if this cannot be the full answer to his question. Ptolemy is not just interested in the contents of the Law but also in the person of God as lawgiver.[29]

---

27. Cf. Sagnard, *Gnose valentinienne*, 453.

28. The old debate about whether these are 'Jews' or Christians is thus in a sense a moot discussion.

29. On the (delicate/difficult) relationship between Gnosis and Judaism and the hypothesis of the Jewish origins of Gnosticism in general, see, e.g., Lahe, *Gnosis und Judentum*, 189–386; cf. also K. L. King, *What Is Gnosticism?* (Cambridge, MA: Harvard University Press, 2003), 40–47 (45–46 on Ptolemy).

Ptolemy thus aims not at one but at two major narratives, which in his eyes are both wrong and will both be refuted.[30] The two positions are introduced as if they stand on the same level. This presentation is not wholly incorrect in so far as the second group really was intent on challenging the other position and was not just content with putting forward a possible alternative but also wished to promote the one and only view they thought was the correct one. Ptolemy's presentation is more than just a sketch of the status quo. It involves certain decisions and offers him some advantages for his own purpose. He could have presented things differently and have spoken of one major narrative ('the Catholics') that is being challenged by a minority opinion ('the Marcionites'). The possible danger of going down that path would be that his own position could then more easily be dismissed as yet another minority view, which it actually was. By presenting a picture of two competing narratives, apparently on an equal basis, his own position is enhanced and comes out as the true alternative. So there may well have been some strategy and tactics behind his presentation.

As Ptolemy sees it, the problem with both alternatives is a basic lack of logic. That is a strong argument and one that claims to rely on objective factors rather than impressions or theological axioms. He says this in so many words in presenting the flaw in their reasoning. 'It is evident, since logical' (ἑπόμενον γάρ ἐστιν), so Ptolemy,[31] that the Law is imperfect and cannot (as a whole) be ascribed to a perfect God, as the Christian God evidently is. It needs fulfilment and (some of) its commandments cannot be brought into harmony with the nature of this God (33.3.4). For now, Ptolemy confines himself to the general principle and feels no need to illustrate this, but examples will follow later in the letter. It is worth noting that he formulates his criticism in an absolute way, as if the whole of the Law were defective. However, that is not the spirit of the text (hence the brackets around 'some of', above), for in his critique of the second position, which is also expressed in absolute terms (and which I likewise nuanced), he readily admits that

---

30. Markschies is right when noting, 'Ptolemy certainly simplifies both positions', though maybe not just 'for didactic reasons' ('New Research', 234). It is important to note, both for our purpose and for what I think is a correct understanding of Ptolemy's purpose with the *Letter*, that he begins by clearly delineating his position over against two others that, by the mere fact that they are singled out as his main targets, are considered to be majority positions. This does not mean that Ptolemy's *Letter* cannot be seen as a counter-narrative. A counter-narrative does engage with majority views to a certain point, but with the explicit purpose of refuting or at least of surpassing these. Ptolemy is more of an innovator than a parasite, to use M. A. Williams's terms, in that he finds some common ground with 'the larger intellectual and religious culture of the day' in addressing certain topics (*Rethinking 'Gnosticism'*, 85–89, esp. 89).

31. Quispel (*Lettre*, 77) persists in reading ἑπόμενος ('secondaire') while recognizing that 'all editors' read ἑπόμενον ('conséquent'), and actually follows this reading in his translation when rendering the word as 'évident'. Williams paraphrases it a bit but is true to its meaning.

(part of) the Law does indeed tackle iniquity, which makes it logically impossible that it would stem from the devil. He illustrates this with a quote from *GMatthew* 12.25 about the fate of a house divided against itself, hence with an argument from Jesus himself (33.3.5). The Law is not perfect, but neither is it an absolute evil.

Ptolemy feels certain he has made a strong case, but for some reason he also adds a more general comment, or rather a kind of axiom, about the Creator of all things and creation as the product of a righteous God. To help clarify things, it may be useful to cite the text in full:

> And further, depriving the liars beforehand of their unfounded wisdom, the apostle says that the creation of the world is his own [i.e., the Saviour's], that all things were made by him and without him nothing is made, and that creation is the work of a righteous God who hates iniquity, not of a god of corruption. <This latter> is the view of thoughtless persons who take no account of the Creator's providence and are blinded, not only in the eye of the soul, but in the eye of the body as well. (33.3.6)[32]

The syntax is anything but clear, the reasoning seems twisted and the passage indeed is something of a crux. The reference to the authority of 'the apostle' and the paraphrase of *GJohn* 1.1, 3 is not really helpful, since it applies only to creation by the Saviour but says nothing about a righteous God. It seems there are two options to make sense of the phrase as a whole. One is to consider it a (not really excellent) representation of the creation of the world that involved three entities: Wisdom who has produced unformed matter, Christ who created the visible world and the just God, who rules this world. This interpretation relies heavily on Valentinian creation mythology and on Heracleon's exegesis of verse 3 from John's Prologue.[33] The other, quite the opposite, concludes from the fact that Christ the Saviour is made identical to the demiurge/creator that Ptolemy went his own way and cannot be correctly understood from Valentinian doctrine.[34] The problem with this interpretation is that Ptolemy elsewhere in the *Letter* clearly distinguishes between Saviour and demiurge, the latter being an 'intermediate' being, the former sharing in the nature of the perfect God.[35] It seems to me that in both options the context

---

32. ἔτι τε τὴν τοῦ κόσμου δημιουργίαν αὐτοῦ ἰδίαν λέγει εἶναι τά τε πάντα δι᾽ αὐτοῦ γεγονέναι καὶ χωρὶς αὐτοῦ γεγονέναι οὐδὲν ὁ ἀπόστολος, προαποστερήσας τὴν τῶν ψευδοηγορούντων ἀνυπόστατον σοφίαν, καὶ οὐ φθοροποιοῦ θεοῦ, ἀλλὰ δικαίου καὶ μισοπονήρου· ἀπρονοήτων δέ ἐστιν ἀνθρώπων τοῦτο, τῆς προνοίας τοῦ δημιουργοῦ μὴ αἰτίαν λαμβανομένων καὶ μὴ μόνον τὸ τῆς ψυχῆς ὄμμα, ἀλλὰ καὶ τὸ τοῦ σώματος πεπηρωμένων.

33. So Quispel, *Lettre*, 77–79.

34. See the extensive argument, which I cannot repeat here in all details, of Markschies, 'New Research', 239–46.

35. In a lengthy response to Markschies, see H. Schmid, 'Ist der Soter in Ptolemäus' Epistula ad Floram der Demiurg? Zu einer These von Christoph Markschies', *ZAC* 15 (2011), 249–71.

in which this passage occurs has been ignored or abstracted. The text does not stand on its own but is part of a polemic in which Ptolemy is positioning himself against two opposite views that are both said to be wrong and 'to have completely missed the truth' (33.3.7 οὗτοι μὲν οὖν ὡς διημαρτήκασι τῆς ἀληθείας δῆλόν σοί ἐστιν). One side ignores 'the God of justice' and thinks it is all the work of an evil agent; the other sticks to this God and fails to accept that the true God as he was made known by Christ is more than justice alone.[36] The way Ptolemy formulates this in 33.3.6 may not be his best moment, but the reasoning and purpose are quite clear. As Ptolemy sees it, it is all about a lack of truth and logic on either side of the opponents. Again, the implications of such a presentation for his own purpose are obvious. His position will be logical and therefore true. Unlike that of the others, his narrative is grounded in firm soil. This is good counter-narrative stuff. The claims are made, the arguments for it have yet to follow.

From the preceding it may already have become clear that Ptolemy is intent on bringing forward a radically new narrative, not just a few emendations left and right. This is not about nuancing or fine-tuning existing positions but about changing the parameters by which to look at a problem. That is again a major characteristic of any counter-narrative.[37] In a first step, Ptolemy bluntly dismisses the idea that one source ('one legislator', as he writes in 33.4.1) stands behind the whole of the Law. Actually, there are three such sources – God, Moses and the elders of the people. Part of Torah is man-made.[38] Startling as this may sound, certainly in view of the two major narratives Ptolemy had evoked, perhaps even more disturbing is the twice-repeated assertion that this is not the author's invention but was stated and defended by Jesus himself (33.4.1 and 4.3–14). Consequently, any criticism of what follows is by definition a critique not of an ingenious exegete but of Christ himself.

Ptolemy illustrates his claim with two examples from the gospels – one relating to Moses, the other to the tradition of the elders. The first is taken from Jesus's teaching on divorce (*GMt* 19.3–9 par. *GMk*), where a contrast is drawn between what God had ordained and what Moses had changed for the sake of the people

---

36. Quispel (*Lettre*, 80) is right when noting that Ptolemy is not totally fair to the Marcionites, for they do know the God of justice, only they think He is not to be found in Jewish Scripture; it is more doubtful if his second critique is fuelled by Gnostic doctrine about the 'unknowable God'.

37. This does not necessarily mean that he is really entering completely unknown territory, but he at least presents it as such and does not mention any predecessors. Marcion and Justin Martyr were exploring much the same topic (see above) and long before that Philo had pondered on the possibility that not all in the Law had the same origin. For the latter, see F. T. Fallon, 'The Law in Philo and Ptolemy: A Note on the Letter to Flora', *VC* 30 (1976), 45–51.

38. Quispel (*Lettre*, 84) tends to go beyond what is said by Ptolemy when translating this observation in Gnostic terms and speaking of hylic and psychic in this regard.

(19.8: 'your hardness of heart').³⁹ Ptolemy stresses the distinction to the point that he can claim these are two different laws (33.4.5 ἕτερον μὲν τὸν τοῦ θεοῦ δείκνυσι νόμον ..., ἕτερον δὲ τὸν τοῦ Μωσέως). Such a conclusion may well be called typical for the author's mindset and for his taste for clear-cut distinctions. Actually, he pushes things even further, arguing that these are not just different but as a matter of fact contradictory statements (33.4.6 ἐναντία τῷ θεῷ νομοθετεῖ ὁ Μῶσης).⁴⁰ And this too may be said to be characteristic of the author. Ptolemy cannot or does not wish to think of the question in terms of nuancing a divine commandment – that would be utterly impossible in his opinion – but of changing the parameters. What was once forbidden has now been allowed – that is the issue. Ptolemy takes care to point out that Moses is not to be blamed for this; he was forced because of the unwillingness of his own people to abide with God's Law. 'He did it of necessity' (33.4.6 κατὰ ἀνάγκην). Moses acted on his own initiative when creating 'a second law', 'a lesser evil' (33.4.8 δεύτερόν τινα ... ἧττον κακόν), out of concern for his people, lest they might be damned for not upholding the divine commandment (33.4.7). Ptolemy concludes by assuring his addressee that other such examples could be cited, though he refrains from doing so (33.4.10). One can hardly overestimate the novelty of this presentation. Moses is said to have created new laws, apparently without explicitly consulting with God, and indeed laws that substantially alter ('contradict') the divine commandments.⁴¹ As far as Ptolemy is concerned, Moses is truly a second source of jurisdiction. The major narratives mentioned at the start completely missed this point when solely focusing on God as the exclusive lawgiver of the Jewish people. And it does not stop there.

Jesus also addressed the question of rules initiated by Jewish religious authorities ('the elders') and that he argued changed the essence of an existing divine commandment. Ptolemy keeps this section much shorter (33.4.11–13). The example that is cited is that of the *korban* mentioned in *GMatthew* 15.4–9 (par. *GMk*). In this instance, Ptolemy can rely on the very wording of Jesus about rendering void the word of God (15.6 ἠκυρώσατε). The (slightly adapted) quotation speaks for itself – no need for any further comment.⁴²

---

39. I am not sure that in Ptolemy's view, 'Moïse en sort totalement excusé' (Sagnard, *Gnose valentinienne*, 458).

40. Quispel (*Lettre*, 86) refers to Justin Martyr, *Dialogus cum Tryphone*, 65, and Irenaeus, *Adv. Haer.* 2.28.3.

41. The motif that Scripture (Jewish and Christian) had been corrupted was well known in Gnostic circles and was also used against them by mainstream Christian authors accusing their opponents of being at the origin of it, as Quispel amply illustrates (*Lettre*, 83), but Ptolemy plays this out in a radical way and applies it also to Moses. The possibility that he was inspired by the same Palestinian-Christian milieu that gave us the so-called *Kerygmata Petrou*, a supposed source of the Ps.-Clementine Homilies, has a history that goes back to Hilgenfeld and is accepted by Quispel (*Lettre*, 85) and Markschies ('New Research', 236), but without really offering any proof for it.

42. One more reason for Quispel to praise Ptolemy's literary qualities (*Lettre*, 88).

The reasoning and the examples may well have impressed the addressee, though we do not know if Flora ever reflected on any of the following two items. First, Ptolemy does not point out that the qualification 'second law', which he used with regard to Moses, is not found in the gospels but is his way to assess what Moses has been doing. Similarly, he passes over in silence the inherent difference in status there is in *GMatthew* 15.6 between 'the word of God' and human 'tradition', and the plain fact that this particular tradition never was a formal part of the written Torah. It is not per se an indication that Ptolemy was unfamiliar with what was and was not in Torah. Nor is it an indication that the first of the two positions he presented at the start exclusively referred to the Jewish understanding of (written and oral) Torah. There is to my knowledge no evidence that Jewish Christians, let alone other Christians, ever were tempted to invoke the *korban* principle, though the Matthean and Markan story could be read as a warning not to try and do this; but that is not the point. What concerns Ptolemy are rulings that are clearly denounced by Jesus as devised by the elders, hence of purely human origin, but that apparently indeed received such a status that they could be invoked against a true divine commandment, hence that are 'almost' like a commandment from the Law, regardless of whether they are part of written Torah. Actually, if such rulings can exist along with the latter, some may also have crept into it. So even if Ptolemy is generalizing for the sake of the argument, he must have thought that his take on the problem was not completely wrong and that it did concern Christians as well as Jews.

Second, and perhaps more important still, Ptolemy cites only one example from the gospels for each of the two categories he dismisses as not having their origin in God. He gives the impression that other examples could be cited (at least for the first category), but he does not do so and leaves the reader pondering what these might be. He does not seem to care much about it but is only interested in the principle as it had been formulated by Jesus. From there, so it seems, one is entitled to go on and work along the same lines. If true, this would give him (and other exegetes) the right to sift out from Torah what could be assigned to the second or third category, even without the explicit backing and consent of Jesus. Something of this kind is apparently hinted at in 33.7.1 when Ptolemy says he has given concise but sufficient proof for his position. It is a mighty principle and a great tool the Lord has given us to find our way through the many commandments.

In the conclusion, while continuing to uphold the general image of the one Law, Ptolemy draws the consequences of his threefold division; they are immense. The Law has been interpolated by material that should never have had its place in a document containing God's divine commandments, and it has been infected by material of clearly secondary origin with the sole purpose of contaminating the original or even putting it out of force. It is a complicated task for the exegete to find out what is truly God's Law (33.4.14).

Focusing then on 'the Law of God himself' (33.5.1), Ptolemy, like a scholastic author of later times, urges his addressee to open her mind for yet another threefold division. That part of the Law that can truly be assigned to God (by whom and on which criteria, apart from those formulated by Jesus, is not said) is itself to be divided into three. First, as already indicated above, there is 'the pure legislation, unmixed with evil'; then, material that is 'mixed with inferior matter and injustice'; and finally, laws that are to be interpreted 'typically and allegorically' (33.5.1–2).[43] One will note the imagery used – '(un)mixed', 'inferior matter', 'injustice', which is itself a mixture of philosophical and ethical vocabulary. Again, this is in a way a revolutionary idea, but for various reasons these categories are not without problems.

The problems start already with the first category, which as Ptolemy presents it is basically limited to the Decalogue. Even this summa of Jewish jurisdiction, 'unmixed with inferior matter', needed to be 'fulfilled' by Christ and 'lacked perfection' (33.5.3 μὴ ἔχοντες δὲ τὸ τέλειον).[44] It is a disconcerting thought. The Jewish people has always lived with an illusion, even when reciting the Decalogue. But the situation can be and has been remedied so that there is no need to side with those who would radically reject all of Torah. Ptolemy has nothing further to say about what fulfilment would mean.

The second category receives some more attention, but again things get a bit blurred. Here the example is the *lex talionis*.[45] It is contradictory by definition, for it allows one party to do (in revenge) what a first party is accused of having done. Such laws fundamentally undermine God's authority and make him 'an unwitting victim of necessity', as Ptolemy phrases it (33.5.6 ἑαυτὸν ὑπ᾽ ἀνάγκης κλαπείς).[46] What he means is that God would have been 'forced' to introduce such laws, in open contradiction to his own commandments about not killing another person and against his own nature, for the sake of humankind that seeks retaliation when being victimized. Yet Ptolemy is not willing to dismiss this kind of law completely,

---

43. 'Nous allons jouer maintenant sur ces trois cordes' (Sagnard, *Gnose valentinienne*, 460). Quispel (*Lettre*, 88–89) thinks it is possible that Ptolemy got the motif of the threefold divine Law from Justin's *Dialogus cum Tryphone* 44, and compares it with the Valentinian motif of a threefold prophecy, arguing that the tripartite division reflects the latter's distinction between what comes from the spiritual seed (σπέρμα), from Sophia and from the demiurge, but the parallel is not that clear-cut and in any case Ptolemy will use it in a quite different way; so correctly A. Le Boulluec, *La notion d'hérésie dans la littérature grecque (IIe-III{e} siècles)*, 2 vols (Paris: Études augustiniennes, 1985), I, 206: 'La tripartition de la Loi n'aboutit pas à une reconnaissance partielle de la doctrine "orthodoxe", mais devient un moyen d'affiner la critique de l'Ancien Testament tout en affaiblissant l'efficacité d'instruments polémiques analogues à la représentation de Justin.'

44. 'Le Sauveur, désigné sous le nom de *Fils* … opère cette rectification' (Sagnard, *Gnose valentinienne*, 461), a position that was opposed by mainstream Christians such as Clement of Alexandria, *Stromateis* 3.46.2 (so Quispel, *Lettre*, 92). I have cited Williams's first edition; in the second he renders the phrase, rather more weakly, as 'were incomplete'.

45. 'Dans ce passage Ptolémée prend position dans le débat entre Marcion et l'Église' (Quispel, *Lettre*, 92).

46. 'Ainsi Ptolémée n'hésite pas à envisager la possibilité que la loi du talion corresponde à la nature du Père – mais, aussitôt, il se corrige' (Löhr, 'Doctrine de Dieu', 182).

for he calls it 'perhaps appropriate' (33.5.6) and even 'just', though it is evidently a 'violation of the pure law' (33.5.5 ἐν παρεκβάσει τοῦ καθαροῦ νόμου). Fortunately, this kind of (unwilled) injustice has now been abolished through the teaching of Jesus Christ (33.5.7).[47] One will note the change from the more usual title 'Saviour' to that of 'Son' in referring to Jesus and the pointed contrast that comes from it after God had been called 'the Father'. The Son completes and brings to another level what the Father apparently was not able to withstand.[48] It is a daring thought, but one that in Ptolemy's logic inevitably follows from the premise: laws intermixed with injustice have no place in the Kingdom.

The third category also receives due attention. This time it is not about fulfilment, nor abolition, but about transformation, though Ptolemy is not always consistent in the use of the concept (see 33.5.9 ἀνῃρέθη, 'abrogated'). Divine laws are being transformed by interpreting them spiritually. Ptolemy lists a number of such rituals and commandments, without intending to be exhaustive, that were all taken literally by the Jews but should be given a spiritual meaning, as 'the Saviour' taught us (33.5.8). One should not be mistaken about the nature of this transformation as Ptolemy sees it. This is not a move from good to better. It is a move from an imperfect and indeed evil law, a symptom of God's weakness for the sake of humankind, to a perfected form, for the sake of our salvation. The keyline, it seems, is the opening words of 33.5.9: 'Since all these were images and allegories, they were transformed when the truth appeared.'[49] Only now have we come to understand the true meaning of these many laws and ritual commandments. The literal has given way to the spiritual. Ptolemy duly mentions the new meaning. Sacrifices take the form of praise of God and charity towards one's neighbours

---

47. Quispel seems to have become a victim of his own hypothesis about Valentinian Christology when emphasizing that this cannot be anyone else but the 'psychic Christ', 'qui doit être distingué du Rédempteur' (*Lettre*, 94). Löhr's (correct) reaction: 'Donc, encore une fois, G. Quispel veut expliquer un passage difficile par référence aux subtilités du système valentinien. Mais, encore une fois, l'explication de Quispel n'emporte pas la conviction' ('Doctrine de Dieu', 183). The Son and Saviour is Jesus Christ, as proven by 33.6.2.

48. The citation from *GMatthew* 15.4 that concludes 33.5.7 is clearly meant to be spoken by Jesus and not by the demiurge as some have argued. So correctly Quispel, *Lettre*, 94 (but with the nuance that this is the psychic Christ); Löhr, 'Doctrine de Dieu', 183–4. The lex talionis was invented by necessity; it does not reflect God's nature: 'On pourrait même remarquer que la loi du talion signale les limites de la puissance du Dieu de l'Ancien Testament' (Löhr, 'Doctrine de Dieu', 183–4). The reading καταριθμεῖται is to be preferred over Quispel's ingenious καταρυθμεῖται.

49. πάντα γὰρ ταῦτα, εἰκόνες καὶ σύμβολα ὄντα, τῆς ἀληθείας φανερωθείσης μετετέθη. The notion of the Law being only a preliminary entity that needs fulfilment was of course not a completely new one. Long ago, B. Lohse pointed out similarities in this regard with Melito of Sardes, without specifying the nature of their relationship: 'Meliton von Sardes und der Brief des Ptolemäus an Flora', in *Der Ruf Jesu und die Antwort der Gemeinde: FS Joachim Jeremias*, ed. E. Lohse et al. (Göttingen: Vandenhoeck & Ruprecht, 1970), 179–88.

(33.5.10).⁵⁰ Circumcision is of the heart, not of the body (33.5.11).⁵¹ Keeping the Sabbath means desisting from evil works (33.5.12), and fasting likewise translates as 'abstinence from all evil' (33.5.13), though Ptolemy hastens to add that in this last case the literal meaning is not totally to be given up, since bodily fasting is useful also for the soul, as an image of the true fast; but it should at least be disconnected from all sorts of calendrical purposes and concerns (33.5.14). The literal has given way to the spiritual, but not to the full hundred percent. The reader might ask why this modification applies to fasting and not to any of the other rituals and commandments, but Ptolemy clearly does not wish or expect Flora to ponder this. The same ambiguity plays in what he has to say about Jewish festivals. Pesach has lost its meaning since Christ has become our Passover lamb,⁵² and the Feast of the Unleavened Bread serves no purpose anymore, for we have become 'a new lump' (citing *1 Cor* 5.7). One feast is given up on, the other is duly changed in form and meaning. It seems it is only a thin line between transformation and abrogation. Again, Ptolemy clearly does not expect to hear any comments or questions for clarification. The new narrative is self-evident and transcends any critical comments from the readers or hearers.

Yet Ptolemy apparently also thinks there is a need for some recapitulation. The better part of chapter 6 does just that. One part of the Law has been fulfilled; one has been annulled; and one has been transformed, as Ptolemy puts in, thereby repeating some of the examples he had given before for the first and second category. The turning point came with Jesus Christ. He brought the truth; images or outright 'evil' laws have faded (33.6.1–5).⁵³ The purpose for this rather lengthy recapitulation is not really clear. Two possible explanations come to mind. First, it is an opportunity for Ptolemy to emphasize once more that it is all a matter of truth versus falsity. The Law, even the better parts of it, was sorely in need of being perfected. It is a harsh judgement on the Law as a whole. Second, the paragraph serves as a transition from Jesus, the prime authority for Ptolemy's position, to Paul, who serves as a sort of second authority, confirming and supporting the

---

50. 'C'est ici l'atmosphère de l'Épître aux Hébreux' (Sagnard, *Gnose valentinienne*, 462). Quispel speculates about the origin of this spiritual reading of the divine commandments and thinks Ptolemy might be heir to apocryphal traditions, but he then also notes, rather more to the point, that the notion of spiritual sacrifice is known from Scripture (*Ps* 49.14) and was on its way to become 'un lieu commun' in Christian polemics with Judaism or Judaizing tendencies (*Lettre*, 95–96). Readers may also appreciate his care for clarifying the meaning of Christian charity: 'Il n'est pas ici question de "communisme"' (96).

51. This too, just as the interpretation of the Sabbath commandment, had its distant origins in Jewish Scripture and came to be accepted in Christian controversy literature.

52. A motif that was known to Heracleon and Tertullian alike; cf. Quispel, *Lettre*, 98.

53. Quispel (*Lettre*, 99) again takes away of the force of Ptolemy's reasoning by mixing in his thoughts on the input of Sophia in this instance. The motif that the image does not surpass truth itself, as expressed in 33.6.5, is a most forceful one also without his speculations.

former (33.6.6). It is not the author's most fortunate move. If Paul had rightly been cited for the third category (see *1 Cor* 5.7 above),⁵⁴ thereby in a sense completing what Jesus had said about other commandments, and if he could also be cited with good reason for the second category (here Ptolemy gives a loose citation of *Eph* 2.15: 'The Law of commandments contained in ordinances is abolished'), it is less clear how the citation of *Rom* 7.12 should function to illustrate the first category – commandments in need of fulfilment. The verse upholds and glorifies the Law, but it does not speak of its need for perfection. It is true, of course, that taken for itself the prohibition of killing is 'holy and just and good', but Jesus's expansion of it to include all forms of anger is not mentioned in this instance.⁵⁵ Have we come across a flaw in Ptolemy's logic and presentation? In itself, this is not impossible, but in view of the author's overall interest in logic and structure, it looks rather improbable to me. A possible way out is to assume that Ptolemy expected the addressee to read the quote in its context. It supposes that Flora was rather well versed in Paul's letters and in such a method of interpreting the text. On such an hypothesis it is immediately clear that Paul's first interest is not in glorifying the Law, but in pointing out how the Law cannot be upheld because sin reigns in all of us. It gives rise to some of Paul's stronger statements about the limits of the Law to bring humankind to salvation. It is Torah that made us aware of our sinfulness. 'Apart from the law sin lies dead. I was once alive apart from the law, but when the commandment came, sin revived and I died' (*Rom* 7.8–9). It means that the statement in v. 12, while in itself not completely false, is then a rather more theoretical one. In reality, Torah cannot conquer sin. Salvation comes from another corner. When read from such a perspective, the quotation makes sense. The problem is, first, that we have no clue whether Ptolemy really wished his addressee to read the passage in this way and, second, that Paul speaks of Torah in general and does not indicate in any way that he is only dealing with what Ptolemy regards as the best part of it. Alternatively, one might argue that his first purpose was to show that the threefold division of the Law he proposed not only found its origins in Jesus's teaching but was also readily accepted in the church from early on, even if no one so far had spoken of three categories in the strict way as Ptolemy suggests. His point is to demonstrate this with a quotation from Paul for each of these three categories, without bothering too much about the nuance he had brought in for the part that belonged to 'the pure legislation'.⁵⁶

---

54. The reading δείξας δι' ἡμᾶς makes good sense; there is no need to follow Quispel's conjecture and read διὰ τοῦ πάσχα δι' ἡμᾶς (*Lettre*, 99).

55. Cf. Le Boulluec (*Notion d'hérésie*, I, 208), who thinks Ptolemy relies on apocryphal tradition, all while recognizing that the citations from Paul here and the reference to John 'the apostle' in 33.3.6 show he has a more outspoken sense for 'canon' than Justin and other mainstream Christians. I am afraid one can question both aspects of this position.

56. Quispel (*Lettre*, 100) thinks ἐν δόγμασι specifically refers to the commandments addressed in the Sermon on the Mount, but how is this to be linked to Paul?

This concludes the first major part of the *Letter* in which Ptolemy addressed the question of gradations and outright invalid material in the divine Law. He offered more illustrations for his first category than for the second (Moses) and third one (the tradition of the elders), but there is no need to think he wished to be exhaustive in this regard, and so again, as with the other categories, a whole exercise lies ahead for exegetes to sift through the Law according to the principles formulated by Jesus and repeated by Paul and Ptolemy. He does not take that direction, but instead proposes to move to his second topic, which is integrally linked to the former – the figure of God as Lawgiver that stands behind such a model (33.7.2). Now Ptolemy's counter-narrative reaches its climax.

Creating content (2): the author of the Law. A perfect God cannot have produced an imperfect Law – that is utterly illogical; but neither can it be ascribed to the work of the devil – that would just be plain wrong: 'If, as we have explained, the Law was not given by the perfect God himself, and certainly not by the devil – it is not proper even to say this – then this lawgiver is someone other than these' (33.7.3).[57] As one might perhaps have expected, the solution lies in the middle,[58] in a figure that stands in between perfection and total chaos and evil – the demiurge or 'the Intermediate' as Ptolemy proposes to call him (33.7.4).[59] The solution is rooted in the broader cosmological views of fellow Gnostics, and it is as simple as it must have been un-Christian for a representative of the mainstream church. By the same token God is saved from all imperfection, and the devil gets no credit whatsoever. His position 'in the middle' defines this demiurge in all other respects – his status, his nature and his interests.[60] For one, the notion that stands in between 'perfect good' and 'perfect evil' is that of the just one, and that is what this middle figure is and represents. He is interested in justice; Christ and the Father are interested in doing the good.[61] Justice alone is not enough. The categories are

---

57. εἰ γὰρ μήτε ὑπ' αὐτοῦ τοῦ τελείου θεοῦ τέθειται οὗτος, ὡς ἐδιδάξαμεν, μήτε μὴν ὑπὸ τοῦ διαβόλου, ὃ μηδὲ θεμιτόν ἐστιν εἰπεῖν, ἕτερός τίς ἐστι παρὰ τούτους οὗτος ὁ θέμενος τὸν νόμον. 'Ce tiers personage' (Sagnard, *Gnose valentinienne*, 468–69).

58. Cf. Markschies, 'New Research', 234, who draws attention to the 'skilful' use of the same Platonic phrase Ptolemy had used already in 33.3.2.

59. οὗτος δὲ δημιουργὸς καὶ ποιητής ... ἕτερος ὢν παρὰ τὰς τούτων οὐσίας μέσος τε τούτων καθεστώς, ἐνδίκως καὶ τὸ τῆς μεσότητος ὄνομα ἀποφέροιτο ἄν.

60. Quispel (*Lettre*, 100) not only connects it with the place where Sophia resides but also cites evidence from Heracleon, Hippolytus and Clement of Alexandria who all use the notion, though with different connotations.

61. Löhr ('Doctrine de Dieu', 186) formulates it slightly differently: 'Le démiurge est une image (εἰκών) du premier Dieu [cf. 33.7.7], c'est-à-dire garde une relation ontologique avec son origine; il n'est ni bon ni mauvais, mais juste, bien qu'inférieur à la justice du premier Dieu.' I would rather replace 'just' with 'good' when speaking of the Father or the true God, as Ptolemy does in 33.7.5: ἕνα γὰρ μόνον εἶναι ἀγαθὸν θεὸν τὸν ἑαυτοῦ πατέρα ὁ σωτὴρ ἡμῶν ἀπεφήνατο. The reference obviously is to *GMatthew* 19.17 (see also *Adv. Haer.* 1.8.3; Sagnard, *Gnose valentinienne*, 470), but several other similar passages can be cited from early Christian literature; cf. Quispel, *Lettre*, 101.

divided in this way without any further justification. This distinction is taken for granted as if part of the grand scheme in which Ptolemy, and others like him, were working. Naturally, this demiurge is inferior to the one God, hence begotten and answerable to this God, as Ptolemy adds in what looks like an afterthought that he will not further develop (33.7.6 'subject to his justice'). But as naturally, he must be of a different nature and stature also than the devil. God and the devil are both defined by four qualities that are each other's opposite (33.7.7 corruption and incorruptibility; light and darkness; simple and material; and uniform and composite). The demiurge stands above the one and under the other, sharing in the essence of both without being fully absorbed in it, though more leaning towards the better than towards the evil one. How exactly one has to represent this 'dual capacity' (33.7.7 ἡ δὲ τούτου οὐσία διττὴν μέν τινα δύναμιν προήγαγεν, αὐτὸς δὲ τοῦ κρείττονός ἐστιν εἰκών) is left to the imagination of the addressee who for now is comforted with the words 'do not let this trouble you' (33.7.8), the promise that she will soon learn more about this (33.7.9), and a foretaste of what is to come that in its conciseness sounds rather confusing.[62] For indeed how should poor Flora be able to make sense of a doctrine that assures her that the devil and the demiurge, in all their difference, both stem from the same first and simple principle that is itself 'unbegotten, imperishable and good' and can only 'produce its like and its own kind' (33.7.8 τὰ ὅμοια ἑαυτῷ καὶ ὁμοούσια γεννᾶν τε καὶ προφέρειν)?[63] Maybe she should just stick to the short formula Ptolemy intersperses into his description that says 'we confess and believe it to be' (33.7.8 ὁμολογουμένης ἡμῖν καὶ πεπιστευμένης), and that may well be the best indication we have of how he thinks the addressee should receive this particular part of her instruction, and perhaps also everything else she has heard so far.

So the lesson is not over yet and more is to come, but that part of the correspondence has not survived, if it was ever written. The *Letter* ends with words of encouragement at the address of the interlocutor, who is judged 'worthy of the apostolic tradition', which sounds like a sort of initiation,[64] and will bear fruit from the seeds she has received (33.7.9, 10),[65] and an explicit statement on how the author sees his role and status. He is the instructor, but what he teaches his pupil is solidly grounded in the apostolic tradition he himself had received and has the

---

62. Quispel once more interprets the phrase within the system, the demiurge producing the hylic and the psychic (*Lettre*, 102). Löhr brings us on the right track again when explaining it in a more ontological sense ('Doctrine de Dieu', 187–88).

63. Quispel (*Lettre*, 103–4) in correcting Harnack that this is not about the nature of Christ.

64. Something Irenaeus holds against the Valentinians because they use the argument for their own cause (Sagnard, *Gnose valentinienne*, 473). Quispel (*Lettre*, 104) traces this tradition back to Paul himself, but that is Clement of Alexandria speaking, not Ptolemy who sees no interest in explaining the concept any further.

65. 'C'est la signature du Valentinien' (Sagnard, *Gnose valentinienne*, 473).

blessing of the Saviour (33.7.9). What more can a reader wish to read to be assured of the truth of what s/he is reading?

Making sure the message goes down. With this last comment Ptolemy has devised a way to make sure the reader is and continues to be convinced that truth is to be found here. It is a proven tactic. The correspondent is said to have been initiated into a narrative that started long ago and is part of a long-standing tradition, going back all the way to Christ. The tone and the formulation differ greatly from the way Epiphanius speaks about Flora who is referred to, most dismissively, as 'your girl' and 'a silly woman laden with sins' (33.9.1; cf. *2 Tim* 3.6), while addressing Ptolemy as 'you there' (33.9.2 ὁ οὗτος). By contrast, Ptolemy stresses that the one who brings the message is sanctioned by his loyalty to Christ and to the tradition he initiated. As a consequence, anything that differs and anyone who teaches differently is by definition not part of that venerable tradition. The argument is solid as a rock for the one who wishes to believe in it.

A second, rather more risky tactic is to test and be aware of the limits of the proof one can produce for what one is claiming or arguing. In some instances, it is perhaps better not to try to prove too much and to leave some things unsaid. A fine example of this approach is met in 33.7.8 where Ptolemy confidently asserts that the highest God is the principle from which the demiurge and even the devil originated – that principle is defined by the same features as the Father – and that this principle can only produce what is of its own nature. But how is it that this God is the origin of all things and yet allows the imperfect Law to exist and the devil to rage in the world? The question is not posed, an answer is not expected. One does not address what is impossible to answer. Instead, Ptolemy urges Flora 'to confess and believe'.

A third proven way in Christian texts to create comfort and confidence is to refer to the ultimate authority of Jesus, who is never referred to by his own name, but only by highbrow Christological titles such as the Saviour and the Son. His teaching is evoked, but more often explicitly quoted, and in a couple of instances also merely referred to in the expectation that the addressee will either know the relevant passage or believe that what is identified as a word of the Lord is actually also found in the gospels. The latter is the case with the way Jesus is said to have made known the Father in 33.7.5: 'And if, in his own nature, the perfect God is good – he is indeed, for our Saviour has declared that his Father, whom he made manifest, is the one and only good God.' There is no explicit quotation, but the wording recalls *GJohn* 14.6–7 (9?) and *GMatthew* 19.17, and for the believer that may suffice.

A further way to enhance the importance of what one has written is to make the addressees fully aware of the great things that are at stake. In this case, these topics are the Law and the person of God. The first retains significance also in Christian tradition, but it has to be made manageable, it has to be adapted to the criteria laid out by Christ and to be interpreted accordingly. The Law is purified of its imperfections and safeguarded against its own contradictions. The same happens to God. He too is safeguarded against being substituted by the devil and against being made the source of imperfect lawgiving. But it comes at a cost – a complication that Ptolemy presents as a logical, natural and harmless solution, but that ultimately does not explain how the introduction of a middle figure who takes upon him the blame for the imperfect Law fully excuses the Father-God who is the source of all that exists. Here Ptolemy shifts the level of discourse and moves from argument to faith claim. One may call it a wise decision, but it does not hide the problem that was created.

Maybe also the fact that the *Letter* does not refer to other writings of the author or of others with similar views can be interpreted as part of the tactic. The *Letter* stands on its own and appears to voice Ptolemy's principal position on the issues at stake. He does not make much of an effort to point out any similarities to or differences from other works used by Irenaeus in *Adv. Haer.* 1.1–9 to tackle him.[66] It does not have to mean that Ptolemy had developed or changed his position, and certainly not that one or the other would be inauthentic. The first of these options is certainly not impossible, but it is hard to prove.[67] Rather, the way he formulates his views, the form in which they are communicated and the contents themselves – two crucial topics – all contribute to strengthen the overall impression that this is what Ptolemy stands for on these matters.

Finally, there is the status of the author. He is at the same time an expert exegete and a guru. He explains Scripture in line with the teaching of Christ, and he poses as the one who brings the truth and the solution – his own solution[68] – to an eternal problem. He is loyal to Christ and at the same time the one who is protecting the true God from being discredited. Such credentials should count for much.[69]

Evaluating the results. A last important aspect in the whole procedure is to check on the effect and the results to see if the message caught on. This can of course not yet be done in the medium by which the message is conveyed, and we do not know if Ptolemy made any efforts to find out if Flora was convinced by what he wrote her. But some preliminary steps can be made and that part of the procedure can in any case already be announced. The implicit promise to continue the correspondence, or at least to show an interest in the further development of the addressee, is at the same time a way to tell her that some sort of check will

---

66. I have refrained from going into this issue, in part because it has perhaps been exploited a bit too much in the past to prove Irenaeus right over the whole line (so Sagnard, *Gnose valentinienne*, 479 and *passim*), but in part also because it does not do full justice to Ptolemy's endeavour in the *Letter*, which the same Sagnard correctly characterized as something different than constructing a system. The system is found in Irenaeus, but in the *Letter* 'la gnose s'habille de chair et devient vivante' (Sagnard, *Gnose valentinienne*, 479).

67. See the comments of Löhr ('Doctrine de Dieu', 190–91) in this regard, reckoning with the possibility that Ptolemy may have changed his views over time ('On pourrait conjecturer').

68. So emphatically and correctly, Markschies, 'New Research', 237.

69. I would not say that Ptolemy 'does not commit himself completely' (*pace* van den Broek, *Gnostic Religion*, 96).

follow – by Ptolemy himself or by others. It is not said that this version of the story should be taken as a sort of identity marker of the group (the author hardly ever speaks of 'we', but he does so in the crucial passage in 33.7.8 about confessing), but the addressee is clearly expected to interiorize the message and the contrast that was created at the beginning between the two alternatives and Ptolemy's version at least gives the impression that three approaches by three separate groups are being discussed. This is not a purely theoretical discussion. It is something one has to adhere to and of which the results should be reflected in one's convictions and can be checked. It is about the most that could be done at this stage.[70]

Conclusion

It seems that it was worthwhile to adopt this perhaps slightly unorthodox approach and to try and read the *Letter* as a counter-narrative. The hypothesis has several pros and very few cons. Maybe the letter form is not the best way to spread a doctrine on a larger scale, but it was a known and not totally uncommon way to go about. The decision not to mention the adversaries by name is part of the strategy, rather than a mistake; their identity is supposed to be well known to all who care about it, and the confusion there possibly may be is part of the approach that is favoured. It is not so much about persons or groups as about distinct positions and opinions.

On a more positive note, one can single out the following features that all fit well in any attempt at devising a counter-narrative. The author has picked out a crucial question, actually two interrelated ones, that concerns religious life as a whole and maybe can be said to be an identity marker for the group to which he belongs. He pleads for a radical approach in which there is no place for compromise. His take on the issue is not one account among others, but the *true* one. He disclaims all other positions as 'fake news' and offers instead 'alternative facts' that are presented and argued for in a strictly logical way and with repeated reference to the sole authority he is ready to accept – the teaching of our Lord Jesus Christ and those who followed in his footsteps (Paul, the evangelists). He shows an interest in asserting that the message comes over and in creating confidence in the addressee and in the author himself. Finally, he is well aware that he may perhaps not have said everything he needed to say, but he is clever enough to stay away from issues that would complicate things and turns to the appeal to believe. All of this may be enough to claim that the *Letter* not only can be read as a counter-narrative but most probably was also meant to function in such a way.

---

70. Perhaps something can be derived from how Ptolemy was received in the wider Roman community, but much here remains shaky because of the lack of evidence. Cf. Lüdemann's attempt at comparing him with Justin (above n. 23).

7

COUNTER-NARRATIVES OR COMPETING VOICES? EARLY CHRISTIANS AND THE RESURRECTION OF THE FLESH

Outi Lehtipuu

What constitutes a counter-narrative? In its most simple definition, a counter-narrative is a narrative that goes against another narrative. Narration – be it a personal anecdote of an everyday incident or a historiographical analysis of the past – always involves position-taking, and, thus, each narrative can be countered by a different version. In social, political and cultural studies, the concept of counter-narrative has recently developed into a methodological tool to analyse the complexities of sociopolitical and cultural discourses. In this essay, I explore how helpful this perspective is when studying ancient Christian texts. In my opinion, engagement with the category of counter-narrative needs to take into account the great diversity of early Christ followers' beliefs. To illustrate this, I examine the ways in which resurrection is discussed in two Nag Hammadi texts, the *Gospel of Philip* and the *Treatise on the Resurrection*.

Counter-narratives and master narratives

In recent years, the concept of counter-narrative has been widely used in, among others, literary studies, historiography, sociology, education, psychology, law and gender studies. As an analytical category, counter-narratives have been defined as 'stories ... which offer resistance to ... dominant cultural narratives'.[1] In other words, counter-narratives offer alternate visions to an authoritative, 'official' version – also called the 'grand narrative' or 'master narrative'. The counter-narrative is, by definition, a positional category; it is only meaningful in relation to that which it is countering. To posit a 'counter-narrative' thus presupposes a 'master narrative'.

---

1. Molly Andrews 'Counter-Narratives and the Power to Oppose', in *Considering Counter-Narratives: Narrating, Resisting, Making Sense*, ed. Molly Andrews and Michael G. W. Bamberg (Amsterdam: John Benjamins, 2004), 1–6, 1.

Resistance to dominant narratives can be either implicit or explicit. In the latter case, counter-narratives aim to deconstruct existing patterns of power and hegemony and at constructing alternative means through which to gain power.[2] One important feature in this conceptualization is that those who construct counter-narratives position themselves at the margins. Indeed, contemporary studies often emphasize the ability of counter-narratives to inspire, empower and liberate groups or individuals who perceive themselves as marginalized by the dominant narratives. Counter-narratives resist hegemonic discourse by giving voice to those who feel silenced. By offering an alternative, a counter-narrative has the potential to emancipate, enabling the oppressed to assert their own stories rather than being defined by stories told about them by those in power.[3]

While master narratives present what purports to be the normative experience and counter-narratives resist such culturally privileged forms of discourse, the two are not necessarily or even primarily opposed to one another.[4] Counter-narratives vary widely in the degree to which they resist the master narrative, and, as a whole, counter-narratives often utilize and appropriate existing master narratives and their culturally accepted plot lines.[5] Counter-narratives can thus transform the dominant narrative and, if they prove persuasive, even become new master narratives.

In the context of ancient Christianity, then, what was the dominant narrative, and where did it stand in relation to the belief in the resurrection of the flesh? In the formative centuries of Christianity, the small communities of Christ believers were at the margins of society and thus represented minority views. From this perspective, Christian beliefs and practices could be characterized as counter-narrative.[6] Indeed, scholars have traditionally viewed the belief in bodily resurrection as running counter to the widespread Greek notion of the immortality of the soul, and maintained that most ancient people would have found the idea of receiving the dead body back in the afterlife both repulsive and ridiculous. However, as Dag Øistein Endsjø, among others, have noted, this is

---

2. L. Stephanie Cobb, *Divine Deliverance: Pain and Painlessness in Early Christian Martyr Texts* (Oakland: University of California Press, 2016), 122–23.

3. Kagendo Mutua, 'Counternarrative' in *The SAGE Encyclopedia of Qualitative Research Methods*, ed. Lisa M. Given (Thousand Oaks, CA: Sage). https://dx.doi.org/10.4135/9781412963909, 132.

4. Andrews, 'Counter-narratives', 2; Matti Hyvärinen, 'Analyzing Narratives and Story-Telling', in *The SAGE Handbook of Social Research Methods*, ed. Pertti Alasuutari, Leonard Bickman and Julia Brannen (Thousand Oaks, CA: Sage, 2008), 447–60, 455.

5. Michael Bamberg, 'Considering Counter Narratives', in *Considering Counter-Narratives*, ed. Molly Andrews and Michael G. W. Bamberg (Amsterdam: John Benjamins, 2004), 351–71, 360.

6. For example, Stephanie Cobb analyses Christian martyr texts as narratives that counter the values and experiences of pain in the dominant Roman culture; see her *Divine Deliverance*.

an oversimplification of ancient belief systems.[7] There were in fact several ways in which immortality and the eternality of life were conceptualized in the Greek and Roman worlds, just as there was a variety of ideas related to resurrection and immortality among early Christians (and Jews). According to Endsjø, the Platonic teaching of the soul's immortality represented only one minority opinion, whereas most Greek myths portrayed immortality as encompassing both body and soul.[8]

The boundaries between different notions of resurrection and immortality thus did not run between Christians and non-Christians but among Christians themselves. A telling example is Origen's discussion in *Contra Celsum*. While refuting Celsus's criticism of the Christian belief in the resurrection of the body, Origen actually accepts many of his arguments. In Origen's view, Celsus is right to deem the return of the deceased body repulsive and unworthy of God; however, Origen argues, this notion is a misunderstanding of the Christian teaching. Celsus was recounting the ideas of 'simpler' believers (οἱ ἁπλούστεροι) who do not have the capacity to understand Paul's teaching on resurrection correctly, thinking rather that it is the flesh and blood that will be risen.[9]

From ancient sources, it is impossible to ascertain which variants represented the dominant narratives and which were the counter-narratives among Christians. There were, of course, claims to dominance. According to Irenaeus, for example, the church to which he belonged represented the truth, since it traced itself back to the apostles and ultimately to Jesus himself. Even though it had spread everywhere, it remained unanimous in all essential beliefs.[10] Such language not only creates the impression that Irenaeus and others like him represented the master narrative of the majority, but it also marginalizes other Christians, excluding them from membership in the 'true' church.[11] Even though we cannot determine from Irenaeus's description alone whether the form of Christianity he represented had indeed become normative, his rhetoric has proven successful, for, over the course of subsequent centuries, his definitions of the norm of Christianity and what deviated from it became axiomatic.

Only in recent decades have scholars sufficiently noted that this is only one side of the story. There were competing voices who also appealed to apostolic authority

---

7. Dag Øistein Endsjø, *Greek Resurrection Beliefs and the Success of Christianity* (New York: Palgrave Macmillan, 2009). Cf. George W. Nickelsburg, *Resurrection, Immortality, and Eternal Life in Intertestamental Judaism and Early Christianity*, Expanded Edition (Cambridge, MA: Harvard University Press, 2006), 219–23.

8. Endsjø even claims that the teaching on the resurrection of the body was one of the keys to the success of Christianity. For a critical assessment of this view, see Outi Lehtipuu, *Debates over the Resurrection of the Dead: Constructing Early Christian Identity* (Oxford: Oxford University Press, 2015), 62–65.

9. Origen, *c. Cels* 5.18–19.

10. *Adv. Haer.* 1.10.1–2; 4.41.4.

11. Denise K. Buell, *Why This New Race: Ethnic Reasoning in Early Christianity* (New York: Columbia University Press, 2005), 150–51.

and who maintained that they were the ones who followed the true and original teachings of the Saviour. According to Clement of Alexandria, for example, the Valentinians claimed that their teacher, Valentinus, was a disciple of Theudas, who in turn was a disciple of Paul.[12] Similarly, the Valentinian teacher Ptolemy refers to the 'apostolic tradition which we too have received by succession', one that ultimately goes back to Jesus: 'we too are able to prove all our points by the teaching of the Saviour.'[13] Beliefs in resurrection were controversial and became a central topic of debates, because there were no means of power to silence opposing voices. In its formative centuries, when Christianity was still in its infancy, there were no universally accepted structures – no canon or creed, no church organization that could have established boundaries for different interpretations, no normative master narrative. All these would develop gradually over the subsequent centuries – as the result of fierce disputes.

In what follows, I present two examples of resurrection narratives that challenge other types of Christian beliefs. The first one is the *Treatise on the Resurrection* (NHC I,4), for which resurrection is taken to coincide with the moment of death and the believer is considered to be already resurrected in this life. The second is the *Gospel of Philip* (NHC II,3), for which resurrection is taken likewise as something to be attained in this life, prior to one's physical death. Despite the emphasis on the present state of resurrection, both texts also speak of the resurrection of the flesh, which, however, does not mean the salvation of the earthly body. These two texts provide an incisive case study in the sense that scholars have traditionally treated the Nag Hammadi texts as representing the 'other' in early Christianity and their teachings as constituting a counter-narrative to normative Christian beliefs. Yet, neither of the texts studied here seems to presuppose that the way they conceptualize resurrection constitutes a counter-narrative from the margins. On the contrary, both defend what they consider the true faith against others who resist this faith.

The Treatise on the Resurrection

As the name indicates, ⲡⲗⲟⲅⲟⲥ ⲉⲧⲃⲉ ⲧⲁⲛⲁⲥⲧⲁⲥⲓⲥ ('The Treatise on the Resurrection') offers an exposition on the resurrection and is thus a natural place to look for a resurrection narrative. The text itself illustrates the complexity of early Christian resurrection beliefs, discussing resurrection in often ambiguous 'symbols and images' (ⲛ̄ⲥⲩⲙⲃⲟⲗⲟⲛ ⲙⲛ̄ ⲛ̄ⲧⲁⲛⲧⲛ̄ ⲛ̄ⲧⲁⲛⲁⲥⲧⲁⲥⲓⲥ).[14] For example, the text speaks of the 'spiritual' resurrection as 'swallowing' up the 'psychic' and the 'fleshly' (ⲧⲉⲧⲁⲛⲁⲥⲧⲁⲥⲓⲥ ⲛ̄ⲡⲛⲉⲩⲙⲁⲧⲓⲕⲏ ⲉⲥⲱⲙⲛ̄ⲕ ⲛ̄ⲧⲯⲩⲭⲓⲕⲏ ϩⲟⲙⲟⲓⲱⲥ ⲙⲛ̄ ⲧⲕⲉⲥⲁⲣⲕⲓⲕⲏ).[15] It is

---

12. Clement of Alexandria, *Stromateis* 7.17.
13. Ptolemy's *Letter to Flora* in Epiphanius, *Pan.* 33.7.9.
14. *TrRes* 49,6–7.
15. *TrRes* 45,39–46,2.

not entirely clear whether this is a description of a three-stage transformation, where the spiritual resurrection denotes the highest level, or whether it refers to three different kinds of destinies of three different groups of people, or whether it simply means that other types of resurrection are destroyed and do not exist, as they have been swallowed up by the spiritual one.

As a whole, the text is written in the form of a letter addressed to 'my son Rheginos', but the author refers to the recipients of the letter in plural.[16] They are constantly reminded not to doubt the resurrection; it is not an illusion but the truth, and something one can already attain in this life.[17] Yet the text also conceptualizes resurrection, alongside the potential for its present manifestation, as an immediate ascent to heaven at the physical death of the believer:

> The Saviour swallowed up death – (of this) you are not reckoned as being ignorant – for he put aside the world which is perishing. He transformed [himself] into an imperishable Aeon and raised himself up, having swallowed the visible by the invisible, and he gave us the way of our immortality. Then, indeed, as the Apostle said, 'We suffered with him, and we arose with him, and we went to heaven with him.' Now if we are manifest in this world wearing him, we are that one's beams, and we are embraced by him until our setting, that is to say, our death in this life. We are drawn to heaven by him, like beams by the sun, not being restrained by anything. This is the spiritual resurrection which swallows up the psychic in the same way as the fleshly. (*TrRes* 45,14–46,2)[18]

The argumentation leans heavily on the authority of the apostle Paul. In this respect, it does not differ from most early Christian resurrection discourses. Indeed, Paul, 'the apostle of resurrection (ἀναστάσεως ἀπόστολος)',[19] served as the single most important authority for questions concerning resurrection.[20] Beyond quoting 'the Apostle',[21] the passage is also rich with terminology familiar

---

16. See *TrRes* 50,2, 4, 7–8, 15–16.

17. *TrRes* 47,2–3 (cf. 47,36–37); 48,10–13; 49,15–16 (cf. 49,22–24).

18. Translation here and elsewhere from Malcolm L. Peel, 'The Treatise on the Resurrection (I,4)', in *The Nag Hammadi Library in English*, ed. James M. Robinson (Leiden: Brill, 1996⁴), 52–57.

19. *Excerpts of Theodotus* 23.2. Cf. Christine Jacobi, '"Dies ist die geistige Auferstehung": Paulusrezeption im Rheginusbrief und im Philippusevangelium', in *Receptions of Paul in Early Christianity: The Person of Paul and His Writings through the Eyes of His Early Interpreters*, ed. Jens Schröter, Simon Butticaz and Andreas Dettwiler (BZNW 234; Berlin: de Gruyter, 2018), 355–75, 356.

20. Lehtipuu, *Debates*, 87–90.

21. Despite the formula 'as the Apostle said', this is not a direct citation from any of the Pauline letters. The sentence resembles several Pauline passages but comes closest to *Rom* 8.17b and *Eph* 2.6.

from Paul's Corinthian correspondence.[22] Even though the idea that the believers would be drawn to heaven at death differs from many other interpretations of Paul's teaching, this resurrection narrative is not written in resistance to Paul but is clearly meant to be taken as a continuation of his teaching.[23]

The immediacy of salvation at death is also emphasized in another passage, where the text makes clear that salvation does not pertain to the earthly body:

> But there are some (who) wish to understand, in the enquiry about those things they are looking into, whether he who is saved, if he leaves his body behind, will be saved immediately. Let no one doubt concerning this.... indeed, the visible members that are dead shall not be saved, for (only) the living members that exist within them would arise. What, then, is the resurrection? It is always the disclosure of those who have risen. (*TrRes* 47,31–48,6)

Contrasting 'the visible members that are dead' with 'the living members that exist within them', the text claims that only the latter will arise. The visible members comprise the outer body, which will be left behind at death, when the inner self is saved at the very same moment. Such an understanding of an inner and outer human being, where the inner constitutes the true being that alone will be saved, is hardly unique within early Christian literature.[24]

What is somewhat surprising is that the text speaks of the flesh in what seems to be a positive manner:

> Never doubt concerning resurrection, my son Rheginos! For if you were not existing in flesh, you received flesh when you entered this world. Why will you not receive the flesh when you ascend into the Aeon? That which is better than the flesh is that which is for it (the) cause of life. (*TrRes* 47,1–10)

This is the single most controversial passage in the whole text, and scholarly opinions about its meaning vary greatly. Is the passage promoting or rejecting the resurrection of the flesh? The key is whether the question 'why will you not receive the flesh when you ascend into the Aeon?' is a rhetorical question or whether it represents the opinion of an imaginary interlocutor to whom the writer objects. The latter makes sense if receiving the flesh while ascending is at odds with the rest of the teaching in the treatise. This is not, however, necessarily the case, as the flesh that ascends may represent an 'inner' or 'spiritual' flesh and correspond to 'the living members' inside the human being.[25] Again, the text combines several

---

22. These include 'swallowing', 'imperishable', 'Aeon', 'transformation', 'wearing him [Christ]', and so forth.

23. See Lehtipuu, *Debates*, 98–102.

24. See, e.g., Origen, *Dialogue with Heraclides*, 10–11, 16–24. For a more detailed discussion and further examples, see Lehtipuu, *Debates*, 152–56.

25. For a more detailed analysis, see Hugo Lundhaug, "'These Are the Symbols and Likenesses of the Resurrection": Conceptualizations of Death and Transformation in the

Pauline ideas, such as the Pauline taxonomy of flesh, the dichotomy of the inner and the outer human being and the idea of a spiritual resurrection body.[26] Like most ancient texts, *TrRes* presumes that the spirit or the soul always exists in embodied form;[27] however, the body that is saved will not be of earthly flesh and blood.

In sum, resurrection in the Nag Hammadi *Treatise on the Resurrection* is taken to be a present reality and, at the same time, an ascent of the soul to heaven at the moment of one's physical death. The ascending soul is not itself without flesh, though this flesh is not earthly flesh but some sort of 'spiritual flesh'.

Does this understanding of resurrection then constitute a counter-narrative? In the more general sense of the word, the answer is in the affirmative. *TrRes* is a highly polemical text that self-assertively counters other ways of understanding the resurrection. At the outset of the letter, the writer reminds Rheginos that there are 'some' (ϩⲁⲉⲓⲛⲉ) who wish to understand resurrection but have deviated from the truth, and there are 'many' (ϩⲁϩ) who do not believe in resurrection at all.[28] Who these people are and what exactly they teach about resurrection are never explicated. Later in the text, the writer belittles 'philosophers of this world' (ⲛ̄ⲫⲓⲗⲟⲥⲟⲫⲟⲥ ⲉⲧⲛ̄ⲛⲓⲙⲁ) and their capacity to be persuaded, warning his audience 'not to fall into the foolishness of those who are without knowledge'.[29] The writer thus offers his Christian narrative of resurrection in opposition to dominant philosophical accounts of reality and to other Christian versions of the belief.

Resurrection, understood as an immediate ascension of the soul to heaven at death, may also sound like a counter-narrative to other known early Christian texts. For example, Justin Martyr considers those who reject the resurrection of the flesh and teach that the soul alone ascends to heaven to be false Christians. In his *Dialogue with Trypho*, Justin writes,

> For if you have fallen in with some who are called Christians ... who say there is no resurrection of the dead, and that their souls, when they die, are taken to heaven, do not imagine that they are Christians. (*Dial.* 80.4)

From the point of view of the writer of *TrRes*, however, it is Justin's version of the resurrection that is the counter-narrative, whereas his version represents the 'word of truth', – an expression that must have been of some importance to the author given that he repeats it.[30] It is the same truth the apostles proclaimed and the many

---

Treatise on the Resurrection (NHC I,4)', in *Metamorphoses: Resurrection, Taxonomies and Transformative Practices in Early Christianity*, ed. Turid Karlsen Seim and Jorunn Økland (Ekstasis 1; Berlin: de Gruyter, 2009), 187–205.

26. Cf. *1 Cor* 15.39–40, 44; *2 Cor* 4.16; *Rom* 7.23.

27. In ancient anthropological discourses, spirit and soul were mostly conceptualized as being made out of matter, only much finer matter than the body, such as fire, aether, etc. See Lehtipuu, *Debates*, 56–59.

28. Cf. *TrRes* 43,25–37; 44,4–10.

29. Cf. *TrRes* 46,3–14, 25–34.

30. *TrRes* 43,33–34; 45,3–4.

allusions to the Pauline letters show that the writer considered his text to stand firmly within this tradition.[31] Only over the course of time would Justin's point of view become the dominant one and other narratives, such as the one in *TrRes*, the deviant and marginal ones. This judgement has even influenced twentieth-century scholarship on the text. That is, even though *TrRes* explicitly draws inspiration from Pauline tradition,[32] scholars have often taken it to represent a dubious interpretation, accusing its writer of twisting scriptures to support his thinking. But does not every early Christian writer read biblical texts to find support for their beliefs? In this respect, there is very little difference between Justin and the writer of *TrRes*.

The Gospel of Philip

The *Gospel of Philip*, the third text in Nag Hammadi Codex II, is a collection of loosely connected sayings, making it difficult to discern its overall teaching on the resurrection. Some scholars argue that the text is best understood as an anthology of excerpts without coherence or any organizing principle.[33] Its overall tone is polemical, and the beliefs in resurrection reported in it form a part of its polemics, as the following sayings make clear:

> Those who say that the Lord died first and then rose up are in error, for he rose up first and then died. If one does not first attain the resurrection he will not die. (*GPhil* 56,15-19)[34]

> Those who say they will die first and then rise are in error. If they do not first receive the resurrection while they live, when they die they will receive nothing. (*GPhil* 73,1-4)

In both passages, resurrection is taken to denote something that must take place in this life, prior to death. The text also inverts the concepts of life and death: only the one who has attained resurrection can die.[35] Such a deliberate inversion of the

---

31. The expression 'the word of truth' (ὁ λόγος τῆς ἀληθείας) is another reference to Pauline tradition; cf. *2 Cor* 6.7; *Eph* 1.13; *Col* 1.5; *2 Tim* 2.15. This became a stock phrase that several early Christian teachers used to characterize their own teaching; cf. Ps-Justin, *On the Resurrection* 1.1; Theophilus of Antioch, *To Autolycus* 2.14.

32. Mark J. Edwards 'The Epistle to Rheginus: Valentinianism in the Fourth Century', *Novum Testamentum* 37 (1995), 76-91.

33. Bentley Layton, *The Gnostic Scriptures: A New Translation* (New York: Doubleday, 1987), 325-26.

34. Translations of *GPhilip* follow Wesley W. Isenberg in *The Nag Hammadi Library in English*, 141-60.

35. Cf. Hugo Lundhaug, *Images of Rebirth: Cognitive Poetics and Transformational Soteriology in the Gospel of Philip and the Exegesis on the Soul* (NHMS 73; Leiden: Brill, 2010), 229.

culturally accepted meanings of these concepts might itself already be called a counter-narrative, but the text goes on more specifically to denounce the dominant view that resurrection overcomes physical death as false.

This resurrection in the present life is also closely connected with rituals, for 'baptism includes the resurrection and [the] redemption'.[36] On the other hand, baptism alone is insufficient, as the text claims that those who think that they will live because they are baptized are in error.[37] Baptism must be accompanied by chrismation (anointing).[38]

Even though the resurrection must take place in this life, *GPhilip* also implies that something will happen after one's physical death:

> While we are in this world it is fitting for us to acquire the resurrection, so that when we strip off the flesh we may be found in rest and not walk in the middle. (*GPhil* 66,16–20)

Stripping off the flesh here seems to denote death. However, elsewhere, the text claims that the resurrection must take place in this flesh, because everything in this world exists in it:

> Some are afraid lest they rise naked. Because of this they wish to rise in the flesh, and [they] do not know that it is those who wear the [flesh] who are naked … 'Flesh [and blood shall] not inherit the kingdom [of God]'. What is this which will not inherit? This which is on us. But what is this, too, which will inherit? It is that which belongs to Jesus and his blood. Because of this he said, 'He who shall not eat my flesh and drink my blood has not life in him.'[39] What is it? His flesh is the word, and his blood is the Holy Spirit. He who has received these has food and he has drink and clothing. I find fault with the others who say that it [i.e., the flesh] will not rise. Then both of them are at fault. You say that the flesh will not rise. But tell me what will rise, that we may honour you. You say the spirit in the flesh, and it is also this light in the flesh. (But) this too is a matter which is in the flesh, for whatever you shall say, you say nothing outside the flesh.[40] It is necessary to rise in this flesh, since everything exists in it. (*GPhil* 56,26–57,19)

---

36. *GPhil* 69,25–26.
37. *GPhil* 73,5–8.
38. *GPhil* 74,12–15, 18–20. The author seems to imply that those who have only been baptized do not deserve the name Christian. The true Christians are those who have received the chrismation. Cf. *GPhil* 64,22–27.
39. *GJohn* 6.53.
40. The meaning of this sentence is unclear and remains disputed. See the detailed discussion in Herbert Schmid, *Die Eucharistie ist Jesus: Anfänge einer Theorie des Sakraments im koptischen Philippusevangelium (NHC II,3)* (VCSup 88; Leiden: Brill, 2007), 187–94.

Again, the text is highly polemical, countering two different positions. It first rejects the idea that the resurrection will include earthly flesh ('this which is on us'). Those who believe that one needs the earthly flesh at the resurrection are disparaged for naively thinking that the human spirit is naked if it is not covered with flesh. The author justifies this point by quoting the apostle Paul: 'flesh and blood shall not inherit the kingdom of God.'[41] On the other hand, however, he rejects the idea that only the 'naked' spirit or soul will rise.[42] To avoid nakedness, a certain kind of flesh and blood must be taken on to inherit the kingdom – namely, the flesh and blood of Jesus. Resurrection must take place in the flesh; the spirit cannot rise alone. The true clothing for the spirit is not the earthly body but the flesh and blood of Jesus. By referring to Jesus's words in the *Gospel of John* ('he who shall not eat my flesh and drink my blood has not life in him'), the author thus links the resurrection to the Eucharist, the ritual that provides the believer with the proper flesh and blood.[43]

In many respects, *GPhilip* and *TrRes* share a similar understanding of resurrection. Both texts maintain that resurrection is a present reality and that, even though resurrection involves flesh, the flesh that rises is a kind of 'spiritual flesh' – an idea that may be inspired by Paul's teaching of the 'spiritual body'.[44] Indeed, both texts invoke apostolic authority by quoting scripture and claim to represent the (only) truth, which runs counter to the beliefs of other Christians, the latter of which are, from the perspective of the authors of these texts, Christians in name only, ones who have fallen short of the true teaching of the Saviour.

However, their objection to other ways of conceptualizing resurrection as well as their polemical tone hardly constitute a counter-narrative, if we take counter-narrative to mean resisting hegemonic discourses. Belief in resurrection and rituals that, in some sense, convey resurrection are important elements in the construction and maintenance of the Christian identity reflected in *GPhilip*.[45] From the writer's point of view, he is not challenging a more dominant or normative narrative; he is distinguishing the true faith from the teachings of those who falsify the Christian tradition. It is easy to be deceived, he argues, as the same terminology can be used to promote wrong ideas:

> Names given to the worldly [things][46] are very deceptive, for they divert our thoughts from what is correct to what is incorrect. Thus one who hears the word 'God' does not perceive what is correct, but perceives what is incorrect.

---

41. *1 Cor* 15.50.
42. Further in the gospel, the writer states that 'no one will be able to go in to the king if he is naked' (58,15–17).
43. *GJohn* 6.53. Cf. Schmid, *Eucharistie*, 171–78; Jacobi, 'Geistige Auferstehung', 371–73.
44. Cf. *1 Cor* 15.44.
45. Minna Heimola, *Christian Identity in the Gospel of Philip* (Publications of the Finnish Exegetical Society 201; Helsinki: Finnish Exegetical Society, 2011), 168–69.
46. Here I have added the word 'things' to Isenberg's translation to clarify that the names are given to worldly things rather than worldly people.

> So also with 'the Father' and 'the Son' and 'the Holy Spirit' and 'life' and 'light' and 'resurrection' and 'the church' and all the rest – people do not perceive what is correct but they perceive what is incorrect, [unless] they have come to know what is correct. (*GPhil* 53,23–35)

To know correctly is rather to adhere to the master narrative of the apostolic tradition, passed on to the believers through anointment. For this reason, chrismation is the ritual that truly makes a Christian Christian:

> It is because of the chrism that 'the Christ' has his name. For the Father anointed the Son, and the Son anointed the apostles, and the apostles anointed us. He who has been anointed possesses everything. He possesses the resurrection, the light, the cross, the Holy Spirit. (*GPhil* 74,15–24)

Resurrection as something that must be achieved in the present life is not an idea unique to *GPhilip*. Similar ideas appear, for instance, in several apocryphal acts, most prominently in the *Acts of John* where 'rising up' is a metaphor for conversion; 'the dead' are those who are spiritually dead and who can be brought to life. Only the one who has become a believer has woken up from sleep and been truly resurrected.[47] This notion has its roots in earlier tradition – e.g. in the *GJohn* and *Colossians*.[48] It represents but one popular way of understanding resurrection in ancient Christian texts, and *GPhilip* defends it against countering beliefs.

Conclusion

History is written by the winners. Beneath official constructions of the past, however, there are always counter-narratives that differently recount the past and understand the present. The master narrative of the early centuries of Christianity, developed by ecclesiastical writers, long remained unchallenged. Only in recent decades have scholars learned to listen to other voices and to appreciate the diversity that characterized ancient Christianity. The story of the formation of Christianity is more complex than a battle between the one true faith and its misrepresentations. There were several competing claims to authenticity and as many complaints against those who distorted the one truth.

The two texts I have studied here, *TrRes* and *GPhilip*, represent but two voices that have often been ignored when studying early Christian resurrection beliefs. One of the major challenges in interpreting them is the fact that we know practically nothing about the historical and social contexts where they were produced. The texts are also difficult to date; and it is unknown why they were written, who read them or what language they were originally written in. Both

---

47. For a more detailed analysis, see Lehtipuu, *Debates*, 173–77.
48. *GJohn* 5.24; 11.25–26; *Col* 2.11–12.

texts are preserved in one manuscript only, and there are no references to them in other ancient literature. For centuries, both texts remained unknown and, hence, exerted no direct influence on later texts. It may well be that they were not widely known and that their understanding of resurrection was not shared by many. It is subsequently easy to dismiss them as relatively late compositions, as counter-narratives to more established views – as earlier scholars have done.

In this essay, I have used the concept of counter-narrative to denote stories that resist hegemonic narratives from a marginal position. When early Christian narratives are viewed in relation to the dominant culture within which they emerged, it is easy to note several counter-narratives at play. These include, for example, interpreting the execution of a criminal on a cross as a salvific act, resisting the imperial power, venerating those who died because of their disobedience as martyrs and so forth. However, there was never just one Christian narrative – opinions about martyrdom, the worldly powers and the significance of the crucifixion varied widely, just as they did about resurrection. Over the course of time, some variants acquired a hegemonic position – these included the belief in the resurrection of the earthly body. Later definitions and power arrangements, however, do not necessarily reflect which beliefs were hegemonic and which were marginal at the time and place of composition, nor are the texts studied here written from a marginal position. On the contrary, the inner logic of both *TrRes* and *GPhilip* presupposes that they represent mainstream beliefs, true apostolic teaching.

In light of these different ways of understanding the resurrection of the dead in general and the resurrection of the flesh in particular in ancient Christianity, the counter-narrative is a useful category only if we allow that the dominant and the counter-hegemonic are not static but in a constant state of renegotiation. If we lose this perspective, we easily end up supporting the outdated view that ancient Christianity formed only one established master narrative, which different counter-narratives tried to challenge.

8

RESURRECTION IN THE *EXEGESIS ON THE SOUL* (NHC II,6)

Kimberley A. Fowler

The *Exegesis on the Soul* (*ExegSoul*) is found as the sixth tractate in Nag Hammadi Codex II. The text offers by way of an allegorical narrative an account of the feminine, personified soul's fall from and return to her Father's heavenly home. Soul is characterized as a wayward daughter who descends to earth from her Father's side and subsequently becomes trapped in a material body, using this to commit sexually inappropriate acts (ⲡⲟⲣⲛⲉⲓⲁ) with numerous adulterous males, defiling her original purity. Soul eventually realizes the error of her ways, and begs her Father to allow her to return to his side. Upon seeing her heartfelt penitence, the Father provides Soul with the means to her salvation – a male saviour who is both her brother and bridegroom (to be interpreted as Christ), and marital union with whom will enable her to undergo a rebirth and return to purity. The role of Soul's femininity has been much debated, especially given that we are told by the author of *ExegSoul* that she was originally androgynous (ϩⲟⲩⲧⲥϩⲓⲙⲉ),[1] and only became female when she fell to earth. Through marriage with her Saviour-bridegroom, the balance of male-female unity is restored. The tractate claims to be an 'exegesis' (ⲉⲝⲏⲅⲏⲥⲓⲥ), and some interpreters have preferred to understand this Greek loan word in the sense of a 'story' due to the narratological nature of the tractate.[2] Madeleine Scopello views the text as a 'gnostic novel' which takes influence from Greek Hellenistic novels, which also centralized themes of love, separation and reunion, all of which are extremely prominent in *ExegSoul*.[3] However, in addition to this, the author of *ExegSoul* can certainly be credited with

---

1. *ExegSoul* 127,24.

2. On the appropriateness of this term, see Rodolphe Kasser, 'L'Eksêgêsis etbe tpsukhê [NH II, 6]: Histoire de l'âme puis exégèse parénétique de ce mythe gnostique', *Apocrypha* 8 (1997), 71–80.

3. Madeleine Scopello, 'Jewish and Greek Heroines in the Nag Hammadi Library', in *Images of the Feminine in Gnosticism*, ed. Karen L. King (Harrisburg, PA: Trinity Press International, 2000), 71–90, 72, 78.

hermeneutical ability. Indeed, the manner in which scripture is utilized by the author of the text will form the major part of this paper's argument.

Due to the complex process by which the author narrates Soul's salvific restoration, it has been suggested that *ExegSoul* presents an understanding of resurrection that is largely based in earthly redemption, rather than something eschatological and post-mortem. In this sense, the text might be seen to offer a counter-narrative to more mainstream Christian ideas of resurrection, which focus on an event after the believer's death. Despite this, however, a version of the Johannine resurrection promise is cited in *ExegSoul* amidst the narration of Soul's salvation: 'No one can come to me unless *my Father* draws him *and brings him to me*; and I will raise him up on the last day' (*ExegSoul* 135,1–4 / *GJn* 6.44 with italics indicating a substitution for 'the Father who sent me' and an addition). This raises the question of whether a futuristic view of the resurrection of believers at the end of time does actually underpin the author's understanding. It is worth noting from the outset that *ExegSoul* only explicitly refers to 'resurrection from the dead' on one occasion (134,9–15), and I shall argue in what follows that the meaning of this phrase is symbolic. The essential question is whether we have in *ExegSoul* a case of the often cryptic and hermeneutically dense writing that is common across the Nag Hammadi literature obscuring what is essentially a view of resurrection in line with that presented in *GJohn* and other early Christian writings, i.e. a future eschatological resurrection. Or, alternatively, whether the citation from *GJohn* 6.44 is not intended by the author of *ExegSoul* to be read in this sense within the context in which it is reproduced. I will argue that neither view is entirely correct. The author of *ExegSoul*, I suggest, is interpreting the Johannine Jesus's words so as to emphasize the role of earthly atoning actions and the Father's mercy. Building on studies of *ExegSoul* which have understood its mythical narrative as a poetic explanation of Christian penitence and salvation through a ritual of baptism and rebirth, I will argue that despite the use of *GJohn* 6.44 in the tractate's culminating statements regarding 'resurrection', futuristic eschatology is not of concern. However, far from countering *GJohn*'s resurrection perspective as a whole, *ExegSoul* actually shares the Fourth Gospel's predominant emphasis on soteriological gains during one's earthly life – often termed 'realized eschatology'.

In order to better understand how *ExegSoul* and its use of *GJohn* could have been interpreted differently over the course of the text's history, discussion will turn in the final part of the paper to the relevance of the likely monastic provenance of the manuscript of *ExegSoul*. I will suggest that in the anti-Origenist climate of late-fourth-/early-fifth-century Egypt the tractate's argument for the resurrection as something entirely un-fleshly (for Origen, the resurrection was a spiritual event), along with its narrative of the fall of the pre-existent soul (another Origenist idea), became unacceptable for those championing 'orthodoxy'. Despite the Johannine emphasis on 'realized eschatology', comparable with the perspective in *ExegSoul*, the rejection of the other major component of *GJohn*'s resurrection theology, which acknowledged a future eschatological raising, rendered *ExegSoul* a counter-narrative at least from the perspective of its fourth-century readers. In this sense, we can view the text as *becoming* a counter-narrative later on in its reception, at the point at which ascetic Egyptian monks were reading it and likely interpreting it in line with Origenist ideology, which was popular among the monasteries of Upper Egypt during late antiquity.

I will begin by overviewing other relevant accounts of 'resurrection' in the Nag Hammadi corpus and the New Testament in order to highlight a stream of thought in early Christianity to which *ExegSoul* seems to belong.

Alternative resurrections at Nag Hammadi

The redemptive ritual that is described in *ExegSoul* as, among other things, a 'resurrection' does indeed bear some similarities to other Nag Hammadi texts which appear to see the resurrection as something achieved on earth, and downplay the idea that Christians could look forward to some sort of eschatological resurrection at Christ's return. Specifically, the *Treatise on the Resurrection* (NHC I,4), the *Gospel of Philip* (NHC II,3) and the *Testimony of Truth* (NHC IX,3) either reject the views of resurrection held by arguably more 'mainstream' Christian groups or present an additional understanding of its nature and function. For context and comparison, then, and in order to better establish *ExegSoul*'s place within what is arguably a resurrection counter-narrative among certain early Christian teachers and their followers, let us very briefly overview these narratives before turning more specifically to that presented in *ExegSoul*.

In *TrRes*, addressed to a certain Rheginos who has apparently inquired as to the nature of the resurrection, the author explains that the Saviour overcame death and raised himself up imperishable, allowing his followers to likewise gain immortality (46,14–19). Citing Paul but apparently not understanding the resurrection as the raising of a spiritual body at Christ's Parousia, the author states that, having suffered with the Saviour, believers rise with him and enter heaven at the end of their earthly life, which is the 'resurrection (ⲁⲛⲁⲥⲧⲁⲥⲓⲥ) of the spirit' (45,23–40; cf. *Rom* 8.17, *Eph* 2.5–6, *1 Cor* 15.44–46). It is made very clear that the human person of Christ was raised from among the dead, and Rheginos is urged strongly not to doubt the truth of the resurrection – belief in the resurrection is integral to the elect believers who have been predestined not to fall into ignorance (46,14–34). However, the ultimate resurrection into the aeon (Pleroma), which believers are rewarded with, is not one of the flesh but purely of the spirit (47,4–10). The mortal body and all its parts which die on earth will not be saved – there is no 'physical' resurrection of the body. What is raised is the inner enlightened spirit: the resurrection is 'the revelation of those who have risen' (47,37–48,6). That the resurrection, or enlightening of the wise believer, is something which occurs prior to death is emphasized by the assertions near the end of the treatise that fleeing from fleshly temptations means one already has the resurrection. The believer who has overcome ignorance is already risen and need not worry about the physical body dying and decaying. Effectively, for the author of *TrRes*, resurrection equates to true enlightenment regarding Christ's conquering of death, and the knowledge that the spirits of the elect believers will rise to be with the Saviour in the eternal heavenly realm. Resurrection is very much an event which is achieved during a person's earthly life. The final departure of the spirit from the physical body does still occur at the moment of death (45,34–39; 47,19–24, 35–38), but there is no eschatological aspect to resurrection. The 'raising' of the elect believers, i.e. their knowledge of being in Christ, has already happened during their lifetime.[4]

The discussion of resurrection in *GPhilip* engages with Paul's comments on the subject in *1 Corinthians* 15, where the apostle deals with divisions caused by a group of believers questioning the form of the resurrected body. This can be deciphered from Paul's quotation (whether real or rhetorical) in 15.35, 'Someone will ask, "how are the dead raised? With what sort of body do they come?"' Their worry is seemingly shared by the author of *GPhilip*. Within pages 56–57 we are informed that the author's audience are afraid of 'rising naked' (ⲧⲱⲟⲩⲛ̄ ⲉⲩⲕⲁⲕⲁϩⲏⲩ) and as a consequence wish to 'rise in the flesh' (56,26–29). This is a concept that the author himself disapproves of, stating that 'it is those who wear the [flesh] who are naked' (56,29–30). The author's initial denouncing of ἀνάστασις ἐν σάρκι, however, is soon after seemingly contradicted with the statement 'I find fault with the others who say that it will not rise' (57,9–10). This also appears to be the sentiment of 57,18, where the author remarks that 'it is necessary to rise in the flesh'. When it comes to when the resurrection will take place, *GPhilip* suggests that it is (at least in part) a pre-death event.[5] In 66,16–17 it is stated,

> While we are in this world it is necessary for us to attain the resurrection, so that when we strip off the flesh we may be found in rest and not walk in the Middle.[6]

Equally, *GPhilip* 73,1–4:

> Those who say they will die first and then rise are wrong. If they do not first receive the resurrection while they live, when they die they will receive nothing.

---

4. For a more detailed treatment of resurrection in this text, see Hugo Lundhaug, '"These are the Symbols and Likenesses of the Resurrection": Conceptualizations of Death and Transformation in the Treatise on the Resurrection (NHC I, 4)', in *Metamorphoses: Resurrection, Body and Transformative Practices in Early Christianity*, ed. Turid Karlsen Seim and Jorunn Økland (New York: de Gruyter, 2009), 187–205; Outi Lehtipuu, *Debates over the Resurrection of the Dead: Constructing Early Christian Identity* (Oxford: Oxford University Press, 2015), 189–93; Thomas D. McGlothlin, *Resurrection as Salvation: Development and Conflict in Pre-Nicene Paulinism* (Cambridge: Cambridge University Press, 2018), 135–47; and Einar Thomassen, *The Spiritual Seed: The Church of the 'Valentinians'* (Leiden: Brill, 2006), 83–85.

5. On the notion of a 'realized eschatology' in *GPhilip*, see Michael Allen Williams, 'Realized Eschatology in the *Gospel of Philip*', *Restoration Quarterly* 14 (1971), 1–17.

6. This may be referring to a 'Valentinian' myth about Sophia-Achamoth, the 'Middle' being the temporary place in which she waits until leaving to unite with the Saviour (see Irenaeus *Adv. Haer.* 1.7.1). Regardless, it is a place of dread to be avoided.

Crucially, it is not only believers whose resurrection is at issue for *GPhilip*, but that of Christ too:

> Those who say that the Lord died and (then) rose are wrong. For he rose first and (then) died. If one does not first attain the resurrection, he will not die.[7]

The experience of Christ therefore gives precedence for the process that believers must undergo. As Hugo Lundhaug has demonstrated, the terms life and death are understood by the author as referring not simply to their usual temporal states but rather to the situations of individuals in relation to the important rituals of baptism, anointing (chrismation) and Eucharist. By partaking in these rituals fully, the believer is able to participate in Christ's resurrection, which he achieved during his life through his own baptism and anointing – the act of arising from the baptismal waters seems to be an important part of this.[8]

Finally, the author of the *Testimony of Truth*, like *GPhilip* and *TrRes*, speaks against a purely fleshly resurrection, and seems to suggest that this view misinterprets the Scriptures (36,29–37,9). The author quotes certain Christians who claim that they will be raised 'on the last day' but states that these individuals are mistaken about the 'last day' (34,26–35,4). Unfortunately, extensive lacunae make the subsequent text difficult to interpret. However, true knowledge (ⲅⲛⲱⲥⲓⲥ) appears to be the way that one is raised up by Christ (35,25-36,22).

Caution must be exercised when making comparisons between these texts in order not to assume a unified resurrection position among these authors represented at Nag Hammadi (such an approach risks falling victim to the heuristic problems that the category of 'Gnosticism' has engendered).[9] Scholars have traditionally understood the above texts, as well as *ExegSoul*, as representing a 'Valentinian' position on the resurrection, somewhat based on the claims of Tertullian (*On the Prescription of Heretics* 33.7; *On the Resurrection of the Body* 19.2–7) and Irenaeus (*Against Heresies* 2.31.2). However, there are significant hermeneutical problems with basing such categorizations on the polemical testimonies of such authors, and as such I prefer to approach these texts simply as Christian, while recognizing

---

7. *GPhilip* 56,15–19.

8. For a detailed interpretation of resurrection prior to death in *GPhilip*, and the importance of rituals in this process, see Hugo Lundhaug, *Images of Rebirth: Cognitive Poetics and Transformational Soteriology in the Gospel of Philip and the Exegesis on the Soul* (Leiden: Brill, 2010), 229-36. See also Minna Heimola, *Christian Identity in the Gospel of Philip* (Helsinki: Finnish Exegetical Society, 2011), 114–69.

9. See the seminal critiques of Michael Allen Williams, *Rethinking 'Gnosticism': An Argument for Dismantling a Dubious Category* (Princeton, NJ: Princeton University Press, 1996); and Karen King, *What Is Gnosticism?* (Cambridge, MA: Harvard University Press, 2003). Subsequent scholarship, while not all in agreement that the category of 'Gnosticism' should be abandoned, has been urged to be more cautious in its analysis of material traditionally labelled in this way.

that their specific viewpoints depart on various issues from those found in the canonical literature of the New Testament and other early Christian writings, and have enough in common to be considered together for the purposes of tracing a current of thought among particular early Christians.[10] I will now briefly consider the various opinions related to resurrection and/or Christian immortality among the New Testament writings, before moving to *ExegSoul*.

The New Testament

The issue of resurrection apparently caused some worry among early Christian communities, to the degree that various teachers sought to address the issue, and this is not limited to those texts outside what would later become the New Testament canon. In the New Testament, resurrection is linked at various points with the second coming of Christ, and is often characterized by an eschatological hope of immortality. However, as Outi Lehtipuu cautions, we should remember that for Paul at least, this future event was not something distant, but something expected to happen imminently.[11] Paul's first letter to the Thessalonians addresses worry among members of the congregation regarding the fate of those who died prior to Christ's Parousia, and assures them that when Christ returns the dead will be raised first, followed by all the faithful still living, who will be gathered together with them to meet the Lord (*1 Thes* 4.13–18). That there was confusion regarding the precise point at which resurrection would happen is evidenced by *2 Timothy* 2.17–18, in which the author warns against the teachings of Hymenaeus and Philetus, who apparently falsely claim that the resurrection had happened already. In *Romans* 6.4 Paul argues that through baptism believers are buried into death with Christ, which affords them 'new life'. However, he maintains that resurrection is a future event (*Rom* 6.5), and this is of course also the sentiment of *1 Corinthians* 15.1–34, where the truth of the resurrection is strongly emphasized in the face of apparent doubts among certain believers. The author of *Colossians* 2.12, on the other hand, interprets Paul's teaching about being buried with Christ through baptism as meaning that followers could already be raised with him. Similarly, *Ephesians* 2.6 claims that God has already 'raised us up with Christ' (cf. 5.14). As we have suggested in the example of *GPhilip* above, and as we shall see in our discussion of *ExegSoul*, rituals were important in connection with resurrection to many early Christians, and we see this to a degree in the New Testament also. *GJohn* connects immortality with the Eucharist in 6.51–58, and 8.51 and 11.26

---

10. There has been significant research in relatively recent years into the so-called Valentinian School, but there is not space to enter into discussion of the merits of this category here. See the detailed treatment by Thomassen, *The Spiritual Seed*; Ismo Dunderberg, *Beyond Gnosticism: Myth, Lifestyle, and Society in the School of Valentinus* (New York: Columbia University Press, 2008).

11. Lehtipuu, *Debates over the Resurrection*, 160.

suggest that immortality is directly linked with living life ethically in line with Jesus's commands.[12]

In order to better understand to what degree *ExegSoul* is responding to or countering the position on the resurrection in *GJohn* 6.44, it is necessary first to reflect in a little more detail on how resurrection and eternal life are presented in the Fourth Gospel.

The Gospel of John

Discussion of the resurrection in *GJohn* has been exhaustive, and I do not intend to replicate the entirety of the debate here.[13] Rather, I wish to highlight the most important themes running through the Fourth Gospel in order to provide a fuller background against which to consider how *ExegSoul* could be interpreting and using *GJohn* 6.44. Of the four canonical Gospels, *GJohn* gives the most space to the resurrection accounts and appearances of Jesus (chapters 20–21), and the concept of resurrection is intrinsically linked to death from the very first mention of Jesus's death and resurrection in 2.13–22. Moreover, the theme of eternal life through Christ, which is crucial throughout *GJohn*, is directly connected to resurrection. Seventeen of the thirty-six occurrences of 'life' in *GJohn* are qualified by the adjective 'eternal', and Jesus's teaching frequently equates eternal life with resurrection (notably of course in 11.25: 'I am the resurrection and the life'). Scholars have long debated how exactly the message of the resurrection in *GJohn* fits with the author's presentation of Jesus's crucifixion, which is understood as the culmination of his exaltation; Jesus's earthly death is what gives him glory, not his resurrection. His dying words 'It is finished' (19.20) exemplify this, as do the author's frequent references to Jesus's 'hour/time' of glory (e.g. 2.4; 7.6, 8; 12.3, 27; 13.1, 31, 32; 17.1) – the cross is very much seen as a moment of resolution in *GJohn*'s narrative, despite the importance of the subsequent resurrection.[14]

Particularly interesting when considering *GJohn* in relation to *ExegSoul* is their respective views of the divine coming down into human, fleshly form. *GJohn* 1.14

---

12. Dunderberg, *Beyond Gnosticism*, 42.

13. Recent discussions and further bibliography can be found in Craig R. Koester and Reimund Bieringer (ed.), *The Resurrection of Jesus in the Gospel of John* (WUNT 222; Tübingen: Mohr Siebeck, 2008); Sandra M. Schneiders, *Jesus Risen in Our Midst: Essays on the Resurrection of Jesus in the Fourth Gospel* (Collegeville, MN: Liturgical Press, 2013). For slightly older, but still highly useful treatments, see Andrew T. Lincoln, '"I Am the Resurrection and the Life": The Resurrection Message of the Fourth Gospel", in *Life in the Face of Death: The Resurrection Message of the New Testament*, ed. Richard N. Longenecker (Grand Rapids, MI: Eerdmans, 1998), 122–44; John P. Heil, *Blood and Water: The Death and Resurrection of Jesus in John 18–21* (Catholic Biblical Quarterly Monograph Series 27; 1995). See 172–80 of Heil's study for bibliography on the resurrection in *GJohn*.

14. See Lincoln, 'I Am the Resurrection', 123.

famously states that 'the Logos became flesh', and as Lincoln identifies, it is this very act of the divine doing something new by descending into a human body, experiencing fleshly weakness and ultimately death, that provides the conceptual background for the 'newness of life' that Christ's followers can experience. Just as the divine took on a new form by entering into flesh, human beings can take on a new form at their resurrection after death.[15] In *ExegSoul* of course, the situation is quite different – Soul is trapped in the fleshly form and is degraded by it; her imprisonment is not for the soteriological good but rather is something to be escaped and left behind. Soul's return to God the Father requires the complete abandonment of the flesh and its temptations, whereas in *GJohn* one's access to the Father is granted precisely *because* the Logos appeared in a bodily form. We have in the two texts very different representations of the blending of the divine and the human.

In the Temple cleansing narrative of *GJohn* 2.13–22, it is made clear that the Logos will die an earthly death, yet will be raised in a bodily form – the 'temple of [Jesus's] body' will be raised (2.21). Moreover, the Logos himself will be the instigator of his own resurrection: 'I will raise it (i.e. Jesus's body) up' (2.19) and will replicate this for believers with the authority granted to him by God: 'The hour is approaching when all those who are in their graves will hear his voice and will come out: those who have done good to the resurrection of life' (5.28–29). Jesus's powers in this regard are of course exemplified through the raising of Lazarus in *GJohn* 11.[16] Earlier, however, *GJohn* 5.21 asserts that the Son has the authority from the Father to 'raise the dead and give them life', and this is followed by an account of an end reckoning, when the dead who have believed will be raised:

> Truly, truly, I say to you, the hour is coming, and is now here, when the dead will hear the voice of the Son of God, and those who have heard will live. For just as the Father has life in himself, so too he has given the Son also to have life in himself; and he has given him authority to make judgment, because he is the Son of Man. Do not be surprised at this; for the hour is approaching when all those who are in their graves will hear his voice and will come out: those who have done good to the resurrection of life, and those who have done evil to the resurrection of judgement. (5.25–29)

However, the idea that believers *already* have life or eternal life in Christ is recurring (3.15–16; 3.36; 5.24; 6.40; 6.47; 6.54; 10.10; 20.31),[17] and as Lincoln emphasizes, the ability of Jesus to judge on the issue of eternal life and its alternative, condemnation, is presented in 5.19–29 as being a God-given right that the Logos

---

15. Lincoln, 'I Am the Resurrection', 126.

16. For a discussion of the Lazarus narrative and its significance for *GJohn*'s understanding of the interconnectedness of eternal life, and Jesus's death and resurrection, see Lincoln, 'I Am the Resurrection', 140–42.

17. See also Dunderberg, *Beyond Gnosticism*, 42.

exercises both in the present (i.e. during his earthly life) and in the future at the end of time.[18] The connection of eternal life and resurrection, then, is not purely something futuristic for *GJohn*, but something which has meaning in the present also. We can in this sense, then, speak of a type of 'realized eschatology' in *GJohn* wherein future expectation is grounded very much in the earthly person of Jesus. John's insistence on eternal life beginning in the present, and not only being a future reality, is one of the Gospel's most significant features, with God's present acts of salvation and the believer's role in these clearly emphasized. This is nicely illustrated in the fact that as acknowledged above, *GJohn* connects immortality with the Eucharist at 6.51–58. Jesus is the 'bread from heaven', the 'living bread' (ὁ ἄρτος ὁ ζῶν ὁ ἐκ τοῦ οὐρανοῦ καταβάς) (6.51), the consumption of which ensures eternal life, and actions carried out during one's lifetime are on more than one occasion linked to immortality. At 8.51 Jesus claims that 'whoever keeps my word will never see death', and 11.26 further links living (ζάω) and trusting (πιστεύω) in Jesus with eternal life.

It is my contention that *ExegSoul* actually echoes something of the 'realized eschatology' that seems to be suggested in *GJohn*, whereby important aspects of the soteriological process occur during the believer's earthly life. If *ExegSoul* counters a part of *GJohn*'s resurrection viewpoint, it is that which emphasizes the raising of the fleshly body, the sentiment of which the ascetic character of the former text speaks against. In the section that follows, we shall see that 'resurrection' in the *ExegSoul* amounts to an earthly redemptive process, not a futuristic eschatological raising of the flesh. When it comes to the citation of *GJohn* 6.44, I will argue that the author of *ExegSoul* interprets this text as a metaphor for the ascension of the redeemed soul, achieved through repentance and ritual practices.

Resurrection, redemption, restoration and reascent in the Exegesis on the Soul

As Outi Lehtipuu has noted, in the section of *ExegSoul* where *GJohn* 6.44 is cited the process by which Soul undergoes salvation is referred to in several different ways: 'resurrection (ⲁⲛⲁⲥⲧⲁⲥⲓⲥ) from the dead (ⲙⲟⲟⲩⲧ)' (134,12), 'ransom (ⲥⲱⲧⲉ) from captivity (ⲁⲓⲭⲙⲁⲗⲱⲥⲓⲁ)' (134,13), the 'upward journey (ⲁⲛⲁⲃⲁⲥⲓⲥ) to heaven' (134,14) and the 'ascent (ⲃⲱⲕ ⲉϩⲣⲁⲓ̈) to the father' (134,15).[19] Understanding precisely how the author of *ExegSoul* conceives of resurrection is therefore complicated by the fact that a range of terminology, including 'resurrection', is employed to describe what is arguably one soteriological journey. This is something I have discussed in more detail elsewhere.[20] Lehtipuu suggests that

---

18. Lincoln, 'I Am the Resurrection', 128.
19. Lehtipuu, *Debates over the Resurrection*, 193.
20. See Kimberley A. Fowler, 'The Ascent of the Soul and the Pachomians: Interpreting the Exegesis on the Soul (NHC II,6) within a Fourth-Century Monastic Context', *Gnosis* 2 (2017), 63–93.

resurrection for the author of *ExegSoul* is a 'mystical experience' conceived of as rebirth and heavenly ascent, the end result of which is the soul returning to its pre-fallen state. Noting the citation of *GJohn* 6.44, Lehtipuu argues that this reveals a certain tension between the 'already' and the 'not yet'.[21] In other words, she views the resurrection for the author of *ExegSoul* as having both connotations of an earthly process by which one atones for sin, and an eschatological event. However, I do not think that we have tension here, so much as an appropriation of Jesus's words in *GJohn* 6.44 to support an alternative, non-eschatological explanation of resurrection. The process of Soul's ultimate ascent (ⲃⲱⲕ ⲉϩⲣⲁⲓ) to the Father in *ExegSoul* is strongly connected to her gender identity, which over the course of her journey changes from androgyny (her original virginal state prior to her fall to earth), to distinct female, and finally to a state of gender balance, whereby her union with her Saviour/bridegroom enables her to rectify the damage done when her female body prostituted itself upon the earth. Among the strangest features of *ExegSoul* is the description of her womb, which characterizes her fall from the heavens in unmistakably anatomical language that makes her femininity clear.[22] The author states that Soul's immoral behaviour on earth has made her womb external so that it resembles male genitalia (131,23–27), and scholars have debated whether such a characterization in *ExegSoul* should be viewed either as presenting femaleness in a negative light or viewing maleness pejoratively, as predatory and sexually aggressive.[23] I do not think that either perspective quite

---

21. Lehtipuu, *Debates over the Resurrection*, 193.

22. As has been noted by Martin Krause, 'Die Sakramente in der "Exegese über die Seele"', in *Les textes de Nag Hammadi: Colloque du Centre d'Histoire des Religions (Strasbourg, 23–25 octobre 1974)*, ed. Jacques-É. Ménard (Leiden: Brill, 1975), 47–60, 49 n. 23; and Lundhaug, *Images of Rebirth*, 90, Philo of Alexandria also gives the soul a womb, which he explains can be made pregnant with godly virtues, and bring them into being (*De Sacrificiis Abelis et Caini* 1.102).

23. For Lundhaug, *Images of Rebirth*, 91, the author clearly identifies Soul's fallen, polluted state with maleness, as the male-like genitalia is the result of her fornications. However, this does not fit neatly with the suggestion that it was her sins upon the earth that made her female in the first place. Rose Horman Arthur has argued along these lines that *ExegSoul* views nearly all of Soul's feminine aspects in a negative light. See *The Wisdom Goddess: Feminine Motifs in Eight Nag Hammadi Documents* (Lanham: University Press of America, 1984), 42. Frederik Wisse's view ('On Exegeting "The Exegesis on the Soul"', in *Les textes de Nag Hammadi*, 68–81, 73) is that Soul's fornications on earth involved her indecently exposing herself, which resulted in the adulterers committing offenses with her, while Richard Smith reads this aspect of the text in light of ancient medical theories where male and female genitalia were virtually identical apart from the fact that male genitalia are outwards and female genitalia turned inwards. He therefore concludes that the picture the author presents of Soul's womb is an allusion to her former androgynous state. See Richard Smith, 'Sex Education in Gnostic Schools', in *Images of the Feminine in Gnosticism*, 345–60, 354–55.

accounts for the complexity of the text's argument and imagery – especially given that both females and males are represented variously at certain points in the text. For instance, while the male adulterers are responsible for drawing Soul into sinful acts and defiling her, she (at this point specifically identified as female) is a willing accomplice, and not a helpless victim. We learn that the beginning of Soul's restorative journey is when she realizes the trouble that she is in and weeps before the Father, repenting of her wickedness (131,16–18). This is achieved by the Father turning her externalized womb back inside again, a process which is directly associated with baptism (131,27–132,2):

> When the soul's womb, through the father's will turns itself inward, it is baptised and at once cleansed of the outward pollution that pressed on it, just like [garments when] they are dirty are placed into the [water and] turned until their dirt is removed and they become clean. And so the cleansing of the soul is in order to regain the [newness] of her previous nature, and turn herself inward again. That is her baptism.

Later on in the text, Acts 13.24, John the Baptist's 'baptism of repentance' is cited (135,22–24) as proof that salvation truly begins with repentance, and throughout the text the desperate anguish of Soul to overcome her past sins is recalled and is even likened to a woman pained in childbirth (132,2–5). The sacrament of baptism is central to Soul's redemption, then, which as we have noted above is also described as her 'resurrection from the dead' (134,12). For Lundhaug, the baptismal sacrament that is alluded to in *ExegSoul* is metaphorical,[24] and this may indeed be the case in that her baptism seems to be understood at 132,2 as the moment at which the Father sees her penitence and decides to forgive her sins. It may be, however, that the author views the actual water baptism of the individual believer as a moment when their desire to repent from former sins and focus on joining with Christ is formalized. The elaborate narrative of the tractate need not detract from the fact that more fundamental Christian ideals such as this are identifiable.

The next step in Soul's soteriological journey is her marital union with the Saviour-husband, whom she should submit to like a wife and become one with, allowing her to partake in his life-giving seed (133,34–134,6). Soul's male counterpart is sent by the Father, and their union in the 'bridal chamber' (ⲙ ⲁⲛϭⲉⲗⲉⲉⲧ) is entirely opposed to 'fleshly marriage'.[25] Essentially, the process describes the believer's union with Christ, which having begun with renunciation of earthly sins, and the desire to be renewed, culminates in 'marriage' with the

---

24. Lundhaug, *Images of Rebirth*, 94–99.

25. In Song of Songs, the bridegroom is also the bride's brother, which we see replicated in *ExegSoul*, and Ephesians 5 also utilizes the motif of the bridegroom as the Saviour. See Lundhaug, *Images of Rebirth*, 102, on the relevance of this biblical material for the author of *ExegSoul*, and the way that he alludes to it in the narrative without specific reference.

Saviour, whose life-giving spirit (134,1–2) enables the soul to be 'resurrected from the dead' (134,12). We shall discuss in the next section what 'dead' means to the author, and see that it is not a reference here to the death of the physical body, thereby making resurrection in this case nothing to do with eschatological raising of believers. Having contextualized the way in which 'resurrection' is understood in *ExegSoul* as part of an earthly redemptive process, we will now move to consider more closely the role that *GJohn* 6.44 plays in the author's argument, beginning with an introduction to the text's use of scripture more generally.

Creative use of scripture: GJohn 6.44 in the Exegesis on the Soul

ExegSoul makes extensive use of scriptural citations (both Old and New Testament) in addition to inexplicit allusions, drawn upon as support for the author's contentions and sometimes to dramatize the events being described in the narrative of Soul's trials and tribulations. The tractate quotes directly from *Jeremiah, Hosea, Ezekiel, Psalms* and *1 Corinthians*, with *Ephesians, Genesis, Isaiah* and *GJohn* cited without specific identification. Other biblical material is also paraphrased, yet presented as quotation, and introduced with formulas such as 'as it is written'.[26] One notable example is *ExegSoul* 133,4: 'the master of the woman is her husband', which draws upon *Genesis* 3.16, *1 Corinthians* 11.3 and *Ephesians* 5.23, each of which refer to the authority of man over woman. Scholars have approached these with varied attitudes over the years. Wilson's 1975 study was particularly sceptical, arguing that the author had taken biblical passages carelessly out of context and reused them without any consideration of their original meanings.[27] For William Robinson, the biblical citations are entirely supplementary, having been added in by a subsequent redactor of *ExegSoul* who seemingly wished to 'Christianize' the existing narrative. Lifting the biblical citations out of the text, Robinson maintained, would have absolutely no effect upon the coherence of the mythical tale about Soul and her plight.[28] However, not all were as negative about the author's abilities or the text's integrity and coherence. Early on the view of Robinson in particular was challenged by Frederik Wisse, Bentley Layton and Martin Krause, and more recently Hugo Lundhaug has convincingly demonstrated that even taking out the explicit citations of Scripture from *ExegSoul* would not obliterate the biblical material detectable within its narrative, as the author makes complex

---

26. See Lundhaug, *Images of Rebirth*, 70. This sort of paraphrasing utilizes material from *Genesis, GMatthew, GLuke, Acts, 1 Thessalonians, 1 Corinthians, 2 Corinthians* and *Ephesians*.

27. Robert McL. Wilson, 'Old Testament Exegesis in the Gnostic Exegesis on the Soul', in *Essays on the Nag Hammadi Texts in Honour of Pahor Labib*, ed. Martin Krause (Leiden: Brill, 1975), 217–24, 223.

28. William C. Robinson Jr., 'The Exegesis on the Soul', *NovT* 12 (1979), 112–17.

use of implicit scripture through allusions.²⁹ Besides, the experience of Soul is very often based in biblical concepts, the most prominent example being her salvation by the 'bridegroom'. The fact that the author also cites on three occasions Homer's *Odyssey* (136,28–35; 136,35–137,1; 137,1–5) has led some to question whether this text is viewed with equal authority to biblical material.³⁰ However, I do not believe this to be a necessary conclusion, especially given that the biblical references far outnumber the non-biblical. Rather, a Christian author well versed in a variety of Greek literature, and perhaps keen to demonstrate this within his intellectual environment, saw how the passages chosen from the epic poem complemented the theme and subject matter at hand.

It is worth considering more carefully the way each biblical citation is utilized in *ExegSoul*, particularly to highlight any creative exegesis on the author's part, or deliberate use of ambiguity. This would not mean that *ExegSoul*'s author did not view biblical Scripture with spiritual authority, but rather that he was willing to be imaginative or free and loose with hermeneutics. For the purposes of the present discussion, then, we will consider to what degree *GJohn* 6.44 has been used creatively within *ExegSoul* in order to better assess whether there is in fact a tension between more 'mainstream' Christian notions of a future post-mortem resurrection and resurrection conceived of as a process undertaken during one's earthly life, that seems to be present also in texts such as *GPhilip*, *TestTruth* and *TrRes*.

GJohn 6.44 is introduced with the words 'the Saviour cries out' and comes within the following section of *ExegSoul* (134,25–135,4) towards the conclusion of the narration of Soul's salvation:

> Then when she becomes new (ⲃⲣ̄ⲣⲉ) she will ascend, praising the father and her brother who rescued her. Therefore, it is by being reborn (ϫⲡⲟ ⲛ̄ⲕⲉⲥⲟⲡ) that the soul will be saved. This is not due to ascetic words (ϣⲁϫⲉ ⲁⲛ ⲛ̄ⲁⲥⲕⲏⲥⲓⲥ) or technical skills (ⲧⲉⲭⲛⲏ) or from writings (ⲛ̄ⲥϩⲁⲓ̈). Rather, it [is] the grace (ⲭⲁⲣⲓⲥ) of the […, it is] the gift (ⲇⲱⲣⲉⲁ) of the [...]. For such is this heavenly thing. Therefore the Saviour (ⲥⲱⲧⲏⲣ) cries out: 'No one can come to me unless my

---

29. See Lundhaug, *Images of Rebirth*, 67. See also Wisse, 'On Exegeting', 80–81; Bentley Layton, 'The Soul as a Dirty Garment (Nag Hammadi Codex II, Tractate 6, 131:27–34)', *Mus* 91 (1989), 155–69, 163–64; Wilson, 'Old Testament Exegesis', 217–24; Krause, 'Die Sakramente', 49.

30. See Birger Pearson, 'Use, Authority and Exegesis of Mikra in Gnostic Literature', in *Mikra: Text, Translation, Reading and Interpretation of the Hebrew Bible in Ancient Judaism and Early Christianity*, ed. Martin Jan Mulder and Harry Sysling (Peabody, MA: Hendrickson, 2004), 635–52, 642; and Arthur Droge, 'Homeric Exegesis among the Gnostics', in *Historia, Theologica, Gnostica, Biblica et Apocrypha: Papers Presented to the Tenth International Conference on Patristic Studies Held in Oxford 1987*, ed. Elizabeth A. Livingstone (Leuven: Peeters, 1989), 313–21.

Father draws (ⲥⲱⲕ) him and brings him to me, and I myself will raise (ⲧⲟⲩⲛⲟⲥ) him on the last day (ⲫⲁⲉ ⲛ̄ϩⲟⲟⲩ).'

When the reader familiar with the wider context of *GJohn* reads the citation of 6.44 in *ExegSoul* 134,35-135,4 it may be tempting to focus on the mention of raising up on the last day, and therefore assume that the author of *ExegSoul* is including these words of the Saviour in order to support the idea of an end-time resurrection. However, in order to understand the way the text is being employed, I suggest we must shift attention initially to the earlier part of the citation, where we find the language of being drawn to Christ at the behest of the Father. This is entirely fitting within the broader narrative context of *ExegSoul*, whereby the Father himself sends Soul's Saviour, her bridegroom, to be understood as Christ. While Christ's union with Soul is a central part of her redemption, it is the Father who has sent him to her, in an effort to 'draw in' the soul in need of salvation. The process is essentially as follows, and the Father is instrumental at every stage: the Father sees the suffering, penitent Soul in need of help (128,26–129,5); the Father has mercy on Soul and instigates the process of her cleansing through baptism (131,19–132,2); the Father sends Soul's Saviour-bridegroom (132,7–10), who comes to Soul's bridal chamber very much due to the Father's will (this is re-emphasized at 132,21-25); their union is the 'perfect' (ϫⲱⲕ) marriage (ⲅⲁⲙⲟⲥ), and again this is the will of the Father (134,5-6). Soul is then able to be renewed, and return to her original home. It is this, *ExegSoul* states, which is 'the resurrection (ⲁⲛⲁⲥⲧⲁⲥⲓⲥ) from the dead (ⲙⲟⲟⲩⲧ)', the 'ransom (ⲥⲱⲧⲉ) from captivity (ⲁⲓⲭⲙⲁⲗⲱⲥⲓⲁ)' and the 'journey of ascent (ⲃⲱⲕ ⲉϩⲣⲁⲓ̈) to heaven' (134,6–14).

The role of the Father is repeatedly made clear, and therefore *GJohn* 6.44, with its assertion of the Father drawing the believer to Christ is extremely fitting within this context. Indeed, it is made clear immediately prior to the citation (134,29–34) that acts undertaken by the individual to attempt to ensure their salvation, such as 'ascetic words', 'technical skills' or the reading of 'writings' (this term is non-specific, and it is not clear whether the author has in mind Scripture, other literature, or a combination of the two), are useless without the gift of grace. This is presumably from the Father – lacunae obscure the identity of the one from whom the gift of grace comes, but the emphasis on the Father's role in facilitating Soul's redemption due to his mercy make it more than likely that he is referred to here. So, with this in mind, let us now consider the latter part of the Johannine citation concerning 'the last day' (ⲫⲁⲉ ⲛ̄ϩⲟⲟⲩ). In light of *ExegSoul*'s broader argument relating to the process by which Soul is able to be restored to her original state, and ultimately ascend back to the Father, I argue that instead of interpreting the 'last day' here eschatologically, informed by inherited understanding of the citation in its Johannine context, in *ExegSoul* this is understood as the culmination of the believer's redemptive process, when the soul is able to 'resurrect' as purified and renewed, and be 'raised up' to the Father's side. For the individual Christian reader of the tractate, this redemptive process may have started with their desire to undergo baptism and leave their former earthly preoccupations behind. Their renewed lifestyle and constant desire to receive the Father's mercy, probably in combination with sacramental participation (see the above discussion about the meaning of baptism in the text), allow a union with Christ and a renewal of the soul: the resurrection.

The final part of the tractate continues to show repeated concern with individual repentance and desire for atonement. There can be no mistaking that this is how salvation is achieved – by appealing to the Father's mercy and making the soul's wish for salvation plain. Both the biblical and non-biblical reference texts and the language used to emphasize this key point are extremely poignant in this regard. Immediately following the citation of *GJohn* 6.44 we read in *ExegSoul* 135,4–15 that as a result of the Father's mercy and his power to 'draw'[31] individuals to their Saviour, Christ, it is necessary to pray tirelessly night and day from the inward depths of one's soul, begging forgiveness for sin and past ignorance, and imploring the Father to take pity when he sees the self-hatred for the individual's transgressions. Terminology of 'weeping', 'distress', 'grief', 'pity', 'hatred' and 'mourning'[32] accompanies the frequent reminders that repentance is synonymous with salvation. The author paraphrases *GMatthew* 5.4, 6 and *GLuke* 6.21, in addition to *GLuke* 14.26:

> Blessed are those who mourn, for they will be pitied; blessed are those who are hungry, for they will be satisfied.[33]
>
> If one does not hate his soul he cannot follow me.[34]

Just as John's 'baptism of repentance' (ⲡⲃⲁⲡⲧⲓⲥⲙⲁ ⲛ̄ⲧⲙⲉⲧⲁⲛⲟⲓⲁ) prefigured Christ, repentance prefigures salvation. Making use of the Old Testament (*Is* 30.15, 19–20 LXX; *Ps* 6.6–9, or 6.7–10 LXX),[35] as well as words attributed to 'the prophet' but seemingly inspired by *1 Clement* 8.3–4 and Clement of Alexandria's *Paedagogus* 1.91.2,[36] the author then proceeds to demonstrate that the Father's love for souls in distress is great, and he will hear his children in their times of crisis. Odysseus's weeping on Calypso's isle (136,29–35; *Odyssey* 1.48–1.59) and Helen lamenting that Aphrodite has tricked her into leaving her home and her family (136,36–137,5; *Odyssey* 4.260–264) are also drawn upon following the biblical and other citations and paraphrases to further highlight the type of anguish that the soul desirous of forgiveness and redemption suffers through. The first Homeric references in particular (1.48–1.59) might also be more directly connected to the theme of

---

31. Outi Lehtipuu makes the observation that the terminology of being 'drawn' (ⲥⲱⲕ) to the Father in *ExegSoul* is reminiscent of that in *TrRes* 45,36–37, where Christ draws believers into heaven (*Debates over the Resurrection*, 194 n. 193).

32. *ExegSoul* 135,4–26.

33. *ExegSoul* 135,16–19.

34. *ExegSoul* 135,19–21.

35. *ExegSoul* 136,4–8, 136,8–16; 137,15–22.

36. *ExegSoul* 135,31–136,3.

GJohn 6.44, in that it highlights the divine role in Odysseus's return to his village. Some portions of the text have been reconstructed (and we can also compare the Greek text of the Odyssey), but even without these the most crucial elements for constructing meaning are present, namely that help comes from heaven for Odysseus, whose aim is to return home: 'Had he not [received] help (ⲃⲟⲏⲑⲉⲓⲁ) from heaven (ⲡⲉ), [he would] not [have been able to return] to his village.'[37] If we compare this with the notion of God 'drawing' believers back to him in the Johannine citation discussed above, further thematic coherence is illuminated. Like the degraded Soul, Odysseus is reliant upon divine help to draw him back to where he belongs, to bring him home.

Emphasis is consistently placed upon the Father's agency in Soul's redemption because of his great mercy and pity for her. *Psalm* 103.1–5 (102.1–5 LXX) is drawn upon as a proof text for this notion, which praises God as forgiver, healer and ransom payer who saves the soul from death (134,16–25), and when the citation of *GJohn* 6.44 appears just a few lines later at 134,1–4 it continues this theme of God's decisive role in the believer's redemption. In addition to the Father's agency, Soul's own role in securing her salvation by ceasing fleshly pursuits and showing outward signs of penitence is prominent. In line with this interpretation, I argue that the word 'dead' (ⲙⲟⲟⲩⲧ) for the author of *ExegSoul* does not refer to the inevitable end result of mortality. Rather the author uses the term symbolically to describe the sinful, defiled state of the human soul prior to redemption through Christ. When the author speaks of the soul's salvation being 'the resurrection from the dead' what is being described is the transformed, newly purified soul, which is able to ascend to the Father being rid of polluting sin. The soul has been raised, or *resurrected*, from a spiritually dead condition to one of glory. The 'last day' which the Johannine Jesus marks out as the time when the believer will be raised is not for the author of *ExegSoul* a futuristic event of the Parousia. Rather, it is interpreted as the point at which the soul achieves its purified state and is *able* to be raised to heaven, following the believer's atoning behaviour and their union with the Saviour through ritual. This recalls the argument of *GPhilip* relating to what constitutes 'death', and also the importance the author of that text places on ritual union with Christ through participation in the sacraments:

> A gentile (i.e. a non-Christian) does not die, as he has never lived in order that he may die. He who has believed in the truth has found life, and is in danger of dying, because he is alive since Christ came.[38]

Similarly to *ExegSoul*, then, *GPhilip* interprets death as a state prior to having been fully joined with and redeemed by Christ. With this understanding of death, the

---

37. See the reconstruction notes in the critical edition of Bentley Layton, *Nag Hammadi Codex II, 2–7, together with XIII, 2* Brit. Lib. Or. 4926(1) and P. Oxy. 1, 654, 655* (NHS 20; Leiden: Brill, 2003), 166.

38. *GPhilip* 52,15–19. See Lundhaug, *Images of Rebirth*, 236.

notion of a resurrection in this life is entirely appropriate, and the eschatological component prominent in *GJohn* is absent.

The Exegesis on the Soul's *Egyptian Monastic Context*

By way of some concluding thoughts, I would like to point out that the degree to which we can consider *ExegSoul* a counter-narrative to the resurrection perspective that we find in *GJohn* requires that we take into account the former's reception in the fourth century, from when the manuscript itself originates. It is a well-argued position in recent studies of the Nag Hammadi codices that they were the products of Pachomian monastic scribal workshops, and were read as part of eclectic monastic libraries before becoming too controversial, possibly in the aftermath of Athanasius of Alexandria's Festal Letter of 367 CE condemning certain 'heretical' reading material.[39] One window into this connection is the apparent popularity of Origen among the monasteries of late-antique Egypt, identified by Epiphanius in his *Panarion* 64.4.1, and suggested by the echoes of Origenist ideology in some of the Nag Hammadi texts.[40] In addition, the Pachomian *Vitae* also show evidence of a redactive agenda that sought to show Pachomius as specifically anti-Origen, in a probable attempt to bring him more in line with Alexandrian 'orthodoxy' and suppress any suggestion of the movement being sympathetic to Origenist thought. The reality was probably very different, as has been highlighted in recent years by James Goehring, who emphasizes that the ideological outlook of early Egyptian monasticism was complex and varied, and transcended interpretative boundaries

---

39. On the connection between the Pachomian monks and the Nag Hammadi Codices, see Hugo Lundhaug and Lance Jenott, *The Monastic Origins of the Nag Hammadi Codices* (Studien und Texte zu Antike und Christentum 97; Tübingen, Mohr Siebeck, 2015); Kimberley A. Fowler, 'Reading Gospel of Thomas 100 in the Fourth Century: From Roman Imperialism to Pachomian Concern over Wealth', *Vigiliae Christianae* 72 (2018), 421–46; Kimberley A. Fowler, 'The Ascent of the Soul and the Pachomians: Interpreting the Exegesis on the Soul (NHC II.6) within a Fourth Century Monastic Context', *Gnosis* 2 (2017), 63–93; Eduard Iricinschi, 'The Teaching Hidden in Silence (NHC II 1,4): Questions, Answers and Secrets in a Fourth-Century Egyptian Book', in *Beyond the Gnostic Gospels: Studies Building on the Work of Elaine Pagels*, ed. Eduard Iricinschi, Lance Jenott, Nicola Denzey Lewis and Philippa Townsend (Studien und Texte zu Antike Christentum 82; Tübingen: Mohr Siebeck, 2013), 297–319.

40. See, for instance, Hugo Lundhaug, 'Begotten, Not Made, to Arise in This Flesh: The Post-Nicene Soteriology of the Gospel of Philip', in *Beyond the Gnostic Gospels: Studies Building on the Work of Elaine Pagels*, ed. Eduard Iricinschi, Lance Jenott, Nicola Denzey Lewis and Philippa Townsend (Studien und Texte zu Antike Christentum 82; Tübingen: Mohr Siebeck, 2013), 235–71; on the fall of the soul in Origen and *ExegSoul*, see Fowler, 'The Ascent of the Soul and the Pachomians', 85.

that modern categorization has frequently imposed, including 'Gnostic', 'orthodox', 'Origenist' and so forth.[41]

I have highlighted above that both *GJohn* and *ExegSoul* share an emphasis on redemption in the present, whereby the earthly body of the believer (and Christ for *GJohn*) is an important location for redemption. This is despite *GJohn* also making clear that a resurrection post-mortem is the reward for Christ's followers. When *ExegSoul* interprets *GJohn* 6.44 as part of its argument for redemption prior to death, therefore, it must be borne in mind that the author is not departing radically from the entire position of the fourth evangelist, but rather choosing to emphasize one aspect of the Gospel's resurrection theology over another. The 'realised eschatology' that *GJohn* implies elsewhere is essentially interpreted into *GJohn* 6.44 by the author of *ExegSoul*. When the penchant for Origenist ideas among monks in Upper Egypt came to be viewed as a problem, however, *ExegSoul*'s Origenist-like rejection of the flesh and emphasis on redemption in the here and now would not have fared well, and this text which did not specifically start out as a counter-narrative to the Johannine resurrection account could easily be viewed as just that. The fact that *GJohn* and *ExegSoul* share a type of 'realized eschatology' would become less important amidst the tense theological environment of the late-fourth-early-fifth century than the fact that *ExegSoul*'s view of the flesh and its relevance for resurrection is markedly negative, contrasting in that sense with *GJohn*'s perspective.

While bodily resurrection of believers at the end of time is what the Johannine narrative suggests when Jesus speaks of raising believers up on the last day in 6.44, this is not how the author of *ExegSoul* interprets or uses this biblical verse.

---

41. See James Goehring, 'Some Reflections on the Nag Hammadi Codices and the Study of Early Egyptian Monasticism', *Meddelanden från Collegium Patristicum Lundense* 25 (2010), 61–70. See also his *Ascetics, Society, and the Desert: Studies in Early Egyptian Monasticism* (Harrisburg, PA: Trinity Press International, 1999), 137–61. The Pachomians were of course not the only prominent monastic movement inhabiting the late-antique Egyptian desert. We similarly find an anti-Origenist agenda in Shenoute's writings, which might also be motivated by a desire to counter what were considered problematic monastic reading habits in this federation. See most notably Shenoute's *I am Amazed*, for which see the most recent critical edition of Hans-Joachim Cristea, *Schenute von Atripe. Contra Origenistas: Edition des koptischen Textes mit annotierter Übersetzung und Indizes einschließlich einer Übersetzung des 16. Osterfestbriefs des Theophilus in der Fassung des Hieronymus (ep. 96)* (Studien und Texte zu Antike und Christentum 60; Tübingen: Mohr Siebeck, 2011). For a discussion of Shenoute's anti-Origenism in relation to the Nag Hammadi Codices, see Hugo Lundhaug, 'Origenism in Fifth-Century Upper Egypt: Shenoute of Atripe and the Nag Hammadi Codices', in *Studia Patristica LXIV: Papers Presented at the Sixteenth International Conference on Patristic Studies held in Oxford 2011, vol. 12: Ascetica, Liturgica, Orientalia, Critica et Philologica*, ed. Markus Vinzent (Leuven: Peeters, 2013), 217–28. Lundhaug briefly considers the attitudes to the resurrection body in the *TrRes* and the *GPhilip* in connection with Origenist thought (at 225–26), but does not here discuss *ExegSoul*.

Rather, we have here a view of resurrection that sees it as the culmination of an earthly soteriological journey, involving penitence and the Father's mercy, and importantly, union with Christ. The focus of *ExegSoul*'s mythical narrative is the soul's return to its original state, before it was sullied with earthly sins, and the ultimate ascent of the soul to its heavenly home. It could of course be argued that this is something achieved at the moment of the believer's death, and that the apparent ritual practices described in the tractate are preparatory. Regardless, there is nothing futuristically eschatological in *ExegSoul*'s conception of resurrection. Indeed, that resurrection was understood by several early Christian teachers both inside and outside of the New Testament as a 'this worldly' affair is evident from the various examples we have noted, even though these representations are not identical, and in the cases of some of the Nag Hammadi examples are difficult to completely reconstruct.

It is not possible to say for certain whether the author of *ExegSoul* rejected completely the notion of some sort of resurrection for believers at the end times. While this is not the way the term is used in the narrative of Soul and her journey back to the Father, we do not find condemnation of other groups and their resurrection viewpoints in this text as we do in *GPhilip*, *TrRes* and *TestTruth*, for example. The style and tone of *ExegSoul* is different, offering an elaborately narrated message to its readers that they should strive to overcome fleshly desires and actively seek the Father's mercy. We have seen that *ExegSoul* picks up *GJohn* 6.44, as it does numerous other biblical texts, and repurposes its words, making good use of the ambiguity surrounding its language once it has been lifted from its Gospel setting. While John's Jesus speaks here of a resurrection for believers at the end of time, *ExegSoul* presents an alternative interpretation whereby an individual soul can be raised from its spiritually dead condition as soon as the believer undergoes the necessary procedure. It is strongly plausible, however, that the ideological difference between *ExegSoul*'s position on the resurrection and that of *GJohn* was seen to be greater in the climate of anti-Origenist debates which placed monastic readers of both these texts under increased pressure to align themselves with the emerging dominant position. In this environment, the particular aspects of *GJohn*'s resurrection theology which *ExegSoul* disagreed with were those which Alexandrian 'orthodoxy' sought to promote.

9

LOSING THE PLOT: IRENAEUS, BIBLICAL NARRATIVE, AND THE RULE OF TRUTH

Devin L. White

This essay asks whether Irenaeus's rule of truth contains within it an anti-Valentinian counter-narrative.[1] For the purposes of this exercise, 'counter-narrative' means one story that must be incompatible with another telling of the same story. Of course, not all variant tellings of the same stories are necessarily incompatible. Narratives can be voiced coherently from multiple points of view. Consider, for example, *Hamlet* and *Rosencrantz and Guildenstern Are Dead*. But many variances in narration do arise from more substantial disagreements. The situation described at the end of Matthew's gospel seems a better analogue for understanding Irenaeus and the Valentinians than Shakespeare and Stoppard on the melancholy Dane. There, as Matthew explains, the Apostles and the Sanhedrin provide competing narrations of Jesus's last days. Either he rose from the dead, or the disciples stole his body and claimed that he had (*GMt* 28.11–15).

Before proceeding to Irenaeus and the rule of truth, let me clarify what this definition does and does not entail. First, examining Irenaean and Valentinian counter-narratives is not another way of asking whether second-century Christians disagree on well-known points of doctrine. They obviously do. But Irenaeus's conflict with the Valentinians extends beyond propositional truth claims to include rival tellings of the stories central to early Christian life. Several questions naturally follow from the sort of counter-narratives reported in, for example, *GMatthew* 28 and *Against Heresies*. Which version of the story is correct? Does it matter which story comes first and which second?

These questions allow us to dispense with a second and third false assumption that might obscure an evaluation of Irenaean and Valentinian counter-narratives.

---

1. When this essay calls Irenaeus's opponents 'Valentinians', it follows Christoph Markschies's suggestion that the Valentinians functioned as something akin to a philosophical school. While this school traced its roots back to Valentinus, over successive generations its doctrines and emphases likely shifted. See Christoph Markschies, 'Valentinian Gnosticism: Toward the Anatomy of a School', in John B. Turner and Anne McGuire, *The Nag Hammadi Library after Fifty Years* (Leiden: Brill, 1997), 401–38.

In the evaluation of counter-narratives, as I define them, neither correctness nor chronological primacy is of particular significance. Regarding 'correctness' or its near synonym, 'truth', the following pages neither defend nor critique Irenaeus's statements about Valentinians, Valentinianism or Valentinian readings of scripture. Likewise, the temporal sequence in which the stories were told is equally irrelevant. Read against the definition of counter-narrative just given, both Matthew's and the Sanhedrin's stories are counter-narratives, their mutual exclusivity alone sufficing to set them in a dyadic, competitive relation. There is no narrative and counter-narrative, original and response. There is only counter-narrative and counter-narrative. So understood, my definition of counter-narrative is not compatible, for example, with Walter Bauer's classic definitions of orthodoxy and heresy, in which orthodoxy emerges as a response to prior heresy.[2]

With 'counter-narrative' defined and qualified, is it a useful concept for the historical study of Irenaeus's rule of truth? Though, as will become clear, attempts to define the rule of truth abound, the best explanations are often the vaguest. In barest grammatical terms, the relation of 'rule' and 'truth' is explanatory or appositive. That is, for Irenaeus, the truth is the rule and the rule is the truth. Whether all parties would agree on the content and structure of Irenaean truth is, of course, doubtful. For the purposes of this essay, the governing question is not whether we can exhaustively catalogue that truth, but whether Irenaeus presents at least some truth as a counter-narrative.

Clearly, throughout *Against Heresies* Irenaeus wields the rule as an anti-Valentinian cudgel. He is out to counter something. But it is less clear that Irenaeus presents the rule as one alternative, possibly narrative in form, to Valentinianism. I suggest that while Irenaeus does not describe the rule of truth entire as a narrative or metanarrative, he does see the biblical story, a single, scriptural plot, as one component of the rule. And, just as importantly, Irenaeus claims that he and the Valentinians provide irreconcilable accounts of that plot. It is here that the notion of counter-narrativity proves its value, since it allows us to underscore one source of real difference between Irenaeus and the Valentinians. Irenaeus accuses his opponents of failing to follow basic grammatical rules for construing textual meaning, rules he and other ancient elites learned during their secondary educations. Had they done so, he argues, their account of scripture's plot would have naturally aligned with the plot preserved in publicly available apostolic tradition. Though we possess no ancient Valentinian response to Irenaeus's critique, we might fairly ask whether all ancient Christians, from Paul to Origen and beyond, would have agreed that ancient grammar allowed its practitioner access to scriptural mysteries.

---

2. See Walter Bauer, *Orthodoxy and Heresy in Earliest Christianity* (Eng. tr.; Philadelphia, PA: Fortress, 1979).

Truth and its sources

Though Irenaeus appeals to the rule of truth throughout his surviving works, his concern for narrative truth is especially apparent in the first book of *Against Heresies*. From the very first line, Irenaeus's complaint against the Valentinians is clear. What they teach is simply not true. They reject the truth (*refutantes veritatem*) and offer outright lies (*verba falsa*) in its place.[3] The Valentinian system, Irenaeus claims, is so misguided that it recapitulates in itself all previous heresy.[4] To counter this heresy, Irenaeus himself appeals to Christian truth as the standard for judgement. For him, demonstrating the Valentinians's deviance from the truth, understood as a rule norming all Christian doctrine, is sufficient to prove their deficiency.[5]

But if we project ourselves into the second century, we might ask whether and on what grounds Irenaeus should express such confidence in his Great Church and its monopoly on the truth. What sets them apart from the Valentinians? Irenaeus, in reply, would point us to the same source to which he directed his first audience: the rule of faith or, in its more common Irenaean formulation, the 'rule of truth' (κανὼν τῆς ἀληθείας / *regula veritatis*).[6] While it is rhetorically expedient to appeal to a rule to which oneself as well as one's opponents must adhere, Irenaeus's appeals do raise the question of that rule's composition.

When it comes to the rule of truth, contemporary readers have to consider not only the rule's place in Irenaeus's critique of the Valentinians but also the many scholarly attempts to explain it. Though the rule of truth is the single dogmatic concept most closely associated with Irenaeus, a survey of modern Irenaean scholarship demonstrates a remarkable lack of agreement regarding the rule's form and constitution. For Frances Young, the rule is a theological abstract which focuses on 'key perspectives' or an 'assertion of ... doctrine'.[7] For Eric Osborn, who emphasizes the reasonableness of the rule, it is a theological

---

3. Unless otherwise noted, the Greek and Latin of Irenaeus, *Against Heresies* is taken from Adelin Rousseau and Louis Doutreleau, *Irénée de Lyon: Contre les Hérésies*, SC 100, 152-53, 210-11, 263-64, 293-94 (Paris: Cerf, 1965-82).

4. Cf. *Adv. Haer.* 4. Pr. 2. See too Ysabel de Andia, 'L'hérésie et sa réfutation selon Irénée de Lyon', *Augustinianum* 25 (1985), 613-24.

5. Cf., e.g., *Adv. Haer.* 1.22.1: 'If, therefore, we hold fast this Rule, we shall easily prove that they have strayed from the Truth, even though their statements are quite varied and numerous' (Unless otherwise noted, all translations of *Adv. Haer.* book 1 are taken from Dominic J. Unger and John J. Dillon, *St. Irenaeus of Lyons Against the Heresies*, ACW 55 [New York: Newman, 1992], here 81).

6. Cf. *Adv. Haer.* 1.10.1, 22.1; 3.4.1; *Demonstration* 6. For discussions of the rule of faith in writers other than Irenaeus, see esp. Heinz Ohme, *Kanon ekklesiastikos: Die Bedeutung des altkirchlichen Kanonbegriffs* (Berlin: de Gruyter, 1998).

7. Frances Young, *The Art of Performance: Towards a Theology of Holy Scripture* (London: Darton, Longman & Todd, 1990), 51, 52.

argument.[8] For John Behr, 'The "canon" of faith or truth is … not an arbitrary principle, or set of inherited doctrines, which must be maintained, but an attempt to articulate the hypothesis of the Christian faith, which is itself found in the coherence of the image of Christ portrayed in the Scriptures or the symphony produced by these same Scriptures in the coming of Christ.'[9] For Paul Blowers, the rule is nothing less than an early Christian metanarrative, a controlling story lending coherence to communal faith and practice.[10] If second-century Christianity was diverse, scholarly attempts to summarize Irenaeus's rule of truth seem at least equally varied. While distinct methodologies, audiences or theological commitments often lie at the root of such scholarly disagreements, in this case, its cause is, at least in part, Irenaeus's own imprecision.

Despite his frequent mention of 'truth', the 'body of truth' or the 'rule of truth', Irenaeus never reduces the rule to any single source, proposition or text. This haziness has led those scholars cited above and more to simplify or clarify the rule, reading it for example as a pre-credal creed.[11] These efforts regularly find their theses overturned by other literature reasserting the indistinctness of Irenaeus's appeals to the rule. As a result, the most defensible explanations of the rule's composition tend to be the most general. For example, in Valdemar Ammundsen's formulation, '*The Rule* is *The Truth* itself.'[12] As a formal definition, the value of Ammundsen's turn of phrase lies not least in its studied ambiguity. But appeals to abstract 'truth' are question-begging affairs. This is especially so in polemical texts like *Against Heresies*. How is Irenaeus's audience to know that he is telling the truth while the Valentinians 'just cannot distinguish what is false from what is true?'[13]

While 'the Truth' itself may remain elusive, it is clear that Irenaeus describes three primary loci where Christian truth may be apprehended.[14] It is received via baptism,[15] preserved in apostolic tradition[16] and presented in the reading of

8. Eric Osborn, 'Reason and the Rule of Faith in the Second Century AD', in *The Making of Orthodoxy: Essays in Honour of Henry Chadwick*, ed. Rowan Williams (Cambridge: Cambridge University Press, 1989), 40–61.

9. John Behr, *Irenaeus of Lyons: Identifying Christianity* (Oxford: Oxford University Press, 2013), 114.

10. Paul M. Blowers, 'The *Regula Fidei* and the Narrative Character of Early Christian Faith', *ProEccl* 6 (1997), 199–228.

11. For a discussion of such attempts, see J. N. D. Kelly, *Early Christian Creeds*, 3rd edn. (London: Longman, 1972), 76–82.

12. 'The Rule of Truth in Irenaeus', *JTS* 13 (1912), 574–80, 578. Emphasis Ammunden's. See too Damien van den Eynde, *Les Normes d'enseignement chrétien dans la littérature patristique des trois premiers siècles* (Paris: J. Ducolot, 1933), 283. Cf. *Adv. Haer.* 2.28.1 (*Habentes itaque regulam ipsam veritatem*).

13. *Adv. Haer.* 1.pr.1.

14. Bengt Hägglund, 'Die Bedeutung der 'regula fidei' als grundlage theologischer Aussagen', *ST* 12 (1958), 1–44, 4.

15. *Adv. Haer.* 1.9.4; *Demonstration* 7.

16. *Adv. Haer.* 3.1.1–2.

universally recognized scripture.[17] This diversity of sources for Irenaean truth leads Lewis Ayres to treat the rule, like Ammundsen, as 'not … a summary document but a collection of ways for speaking about the content of the Gospel', and 'a supple and complex language for identifying the standard for thought that the Church's inherited faith provided'.[18] For our purposes, however, we are not primarily interested in the array of ways in Irenaeus's church speaks about the truth but, more narrowly, in investigating whether 'narrative' might be one of a constellation of ways in which it speaks. We are led, then, to Irenaeus's account of scripture and its place in the rule.

Scripture's story

Like many ancient readers of the Bible, Irenaeus made use of the technical apparatus of ancient literary criticism.[19] Be that as it may, his grammatical and rhetorical abilities are only beginning to receive scholarly attention.[20] His philosophical acumen and that of his Valentinian opponents notwithstanding, Irenaeus's education was broader, his intellectual horizons shaped by intellectual traditions other than philosophy.[21] Recall Justin Martyr's description of the Pythagorean sage. That teacher's requirements for would-be students ought to remind us that even philosophers frequently passed through elementary and secondary stages of education, the so-called encyclical studies (ἐγκύκλιος παιδεία), before studying philosophy.[22] We should not, consequently, be surprised when Irenaeus deploys

---

17. *Adv. Haer.* 4.35.4.

18. Lewis Ayres, 'Irenaeus and the Rule of Truth', in *The Rise of the Christian Intellectual*, ed. H. Clifton Ward and Lewis Ayres (Berlin: de Gruyter, forthcoming).

19. See, e.g., Bernhard Neuschäfer, *Origenes als Philologe*, 2 vols (Basel: Friedrich Reinhardt, 1987); Ansgar Wucherpfennig, *Heracleon Philologus: Gnostische Johannesexegese im zweiten Jahrhundert*, WUNT 142 (Tübingen: Mohr Siebeck, 2002), 48–103.

20. See Lewis Ayres, 'Irenaeus vs. the Valentinians: Toward a Rethinking of Patristic Exegetical Origins', *JECS* 23 (2015), 153–87; Anthony Briggman, 'Literary and Rhetorical Theory in Irenaeus, Part 1', *VC* 69 (2015), 500–27; Anthony Briggman, 'Literary and Rhetorical Theory in Irenaeus, Part 2', *VC* 70 (2016), 31–50; David Jorgensen, *Treasure Hidden in a Field: Early Christian Reception of the Gospel of Matthew*, SBR 6 (Berlin: de Gruyter, 2016), 32–84.

21. See Anthony Briggman, 'Revisiting Irenaeus' Philosophical Acumen', *VC* 65 (2011), 115–24. For a summary of Irenaeus's educational background, see Jorgensen, *Treasure*, 46–53.

22. Justin, *Dial.* 3. Cf. Ps.-Plutarch, *Lib. ed.* 4b. On ancient tertiary education, see M. L. Clarke, *Higher Education in the Ancient World* (New York: Routledge, 2012); Raffaella Cribiore, *Gymnastics of the Mind* (Princeton, NJ: Princeton University Press, 2001), 220–44; Henri Marrou, *A History of Education in Antiquity*, trans. George Lamb (New York: Sheed and Ward, 1956), 284–91.

concepts derived from ancient literary culture, probably learned via his secondary education, to theological or polemical ends.[23]

One example of Irenaeus's use of technical grammatical categories is his frequent appeal to the concept of a plot summary (ὑπόθεσις / *argumentum*). In ancient schools, producing plot summaries was central to the study of the literature, including, for example, tragedians like Euripides, whose *Phoenician Women* was perhaps the most widely studied piece in its genre.[24] One of Irenaeus's contemporaries, Sextus Empiricus, defines ὑπόθεσις as follows:

> And for the sake of the sequence, I first need to state that the word 'hypothesis' is used in many different senses. Just now it will suffice to mention three. In one sense, it denotes the dramatic plot [ἡ δραματικὴ περιπέτεια]. Thus we say that there is both a tragic and a comic hypothesis and certain hypotheses of the tales from Euripides and Sophocles by Dicaearchus, calling hypothesis nothing other than the plot of the play [τὴν τοῦ δράματος περιπέτειαν].[25]

'Dicaearchus' is a name probably unfamiliar to most students of earliest Christianity, but he is known for having produced hypotheses of major literary works, plot summaries in the form of abbreviated narratives, that apparently circulated independently of the works they summarized.[26] The term ὑπόθεσις, it is true, was flexible. Beyond ancient literary culture, it could mean less a plot summary than a statement of fundamental facts, a summary of a text's (not necessarily narrative) contents, or presuppositions bearing on an ensuing argument.[27] It is generally agreed, however, that Irenaeus uses ὑπόθεσις in its proper literary-critical sense: that is, to reference a narrative summary of a well-known literary work, the equivalent of the plot (ἡ περιπέτεια).[28]

23. Cf. Irenaeus's list of *artes liberales* in *Adv. Haer.* 2.32.2.

24. See Raffaella Cribiore, 'The Grammarian's Choice: The Popularity of Euripides's *Phoenissae* in Hellenistic and Roman Education', in *Education in Greek and Roman Antiquity*, ed. Yun Lee Too (Leiden: Brill, 2001), 241–60; Günther Zuntz, *The Political Plays of Euripides* (Manchester: Manchester University Press, 1955), 129–52. On the ὑπόθεσις more generally, see Roos Meijering, *Literary and Rhetorical Theories in Greek Scholia* (Groningen: E. Forsten, 1987), 105–33.

25. *Math* 3.3 (trans. Gertjan Verhasselt, 'The Hypotheses of Euripides and Sophocles by "Dicaearchus"', *GRBS* 55 [2015], 608–36, 609).

26. On this narrative ὑπόθεσις, see esp. Monique van Rossum-Steenbeek, *Greek Readers' Digests? Studies on a Selection of Subliterary Papyri* (Brill: Leiden, 1998), esp. 1–31. See too, Meijering, *Literary and Rhetorical Theories*, 72–90.

27. For an alternate position, see John Behr, who, citing Aristotle's discussion of ὑπόθεσις in *Met.* 5.1.2 (1013a17), reads ὑπόθεσις in Irenaeus as the first line in a philosophical argument (*Irenaeus of Lyons*, 111–12).

28. See W. C. van Unnik, 'An Interesting Document of Second Century Theological Discussion (Irenaeus, *Adv. Haer.* 1.10.3)', in *Sparsa Collecta: The Collected Essays of W. C. Van Unnik. Part Four*, NovTSupp 156 (Brill: Leiden, 2014), 306–35, 315–16; Richard A.

Like any other literary activity, a plot summary could vary in quality. As a self-conscious example of the genre, consider one third-century text, *Bodleian Greek Inscription* 3019. The inscription, part of a third-century CE school book from Roman Egypt, offers a prose summary of the beginning of the Iliad:[29]

> I shall begin, Muse, holding fast to this hypothesis from you: for standing by me yourself, Mistress, telling of the anger of Achilles and the disasters which came to the Greeks as a result of it. For it was for this reason that many and numberless men suffered the end of their lives, with the result that on account of the number of dead they abrogated the rule of burial for some.... In order that I may accurately lay hold of the whole hypothesis of the matter tell me which of the gods first drove Agamemnon and Achilles to this quarrel from the start. The hypothesis of the quarrel of Agamemnon and Achilles was born from nothing other than Apollo himself.[30]

The unknown author, Teresa Morgan suggests, structures his summary around 'the impressively scientific but thoroughly unhomeric word *hypothesis*' which appears 'three times ... in order to stress that the order of events is being rationally explained'. The inclusion of the phrase, 'In order that I may accurately lay hold of the whole hypothesis' is there to demonstrate to the reader 'the completeness and accuracy of the paraphrase'.[31] In this case, the author has done little more than turn poetry to prose, but the exercise does reveal the intellectual concerns of those who summarized major literary works: completeness, accuracy, rational explanation. What better way to demonstrate one's mastery of the entire text? According to Quintilian, constructing a paraphrase forced students to read methodically, poring over every detail in order to discriminate between the essential and the inessential, and, as a result, gaining an appreciation of the literary work otherwise unattainable.[32]

Whatever the original intentions of Irenaeus's Valentinian rivals, Irenaeus treats their account of the biblical narrative as one plot summary gone awry, and, as will become clear, this elementary literary concept proves central to Irenaeus's rule of truth. Two of the best-known examples of Irenaeus's appeal to scripture's plot are his comparison of Valentinian exegesis to a Homeric cento and to a

---

Norris, 'Theology and Language in Irenaeus of Lyon', *ATR* 76 (1994), 285–95, 287–90; Robert M. Grant, *Irenaeus of Lyons* (New York: Routledge, 1997), 46–53; Briggman, 'Literary and Rhetorical Theory in Irenaeus, Part 1', 502–16; Lewis Ayres, 'Irenaeus and the "Rule of Truth"', forthcoming.

29. See P. J. Parsons, 'A School-Book from the Sayce Collection', *ZPE* 6 (1970), 133–49.

30. Trans. Teresa Morgan, *Literate Education in the Hellenistic and Roman Worlds* (Cambridge: Cambridge University Press, 1998), 206.

31. Morgan, *Literate Education*, 207.

32. Quintilian, *Institutio Oratoria* 10.5.8.

misconstructed, perhaps even vandalized, mosaic. We will consider each of these examples in turn.

Though few have survived antiquity, many literate individuals composed Homeric centos, poems in which lines taken from random portions of the Homeric corpus were reassembled to form a new poem.³³ At the end of his summary of Valentinian thought running from *Against Heresies* 1.1–8,³⁴ Irenaeus attacks their account of scripture's plot by comparing it to one of these centos:

> Their own hypothesis (ὑπόθεσιν / *argumentationem*) being fabricated, they then collect sayings and names scattered here and there and transfer them, as we have said before, from a natural to a non-natural sense. They (thus) act like those who propose whatever hypotheses (ὑποθέσεις / *controversias*) they chance upon, and then endeavor to deliver them from the poems of Homer, so that the ignorant believe that Homer composed the poems with that hypothesis, which in reality has only recently been constructed.… Who among the simple-minded would not be led away by these verses and believe that Homer composed them in accordance with that hypothesis? But the one who knows the Homeric writings, will recognize the verses but will not recognize the hypothesis.… Moreover, if he takes them and restores each one to its proper place, he will make (their) hypothesis disappear.… By restoring each one of the passages to its proper order and by adapting it to the body of truth, he will lay bare their fiction (πλάσμα / *figmentum*) and prove it (to be) without foundation.³⁵

Irenaeus's complaint against the offshoots of Valentinus's school, then, is expressed in the language of literary criticism. Unlike the author of *Bodleian Greek Inscription* 3019, they assume a plot completely unlike the plot of the work itself. As a result, when they cut and splice random pieces of scripture together, they treat these secondary creations as if they were the original.

In this instance, however, 'the original' is not Homer but scripture. Because of the deficiencies in their account of scripture's narrative, the Valentinians rearrange its contents, retaining its words, but losing the plot. Readers familiar with the original work, on the other hand, will recognize their work for what it is. As a cento, it reflects a certain use of original materials, yes, but one divorced from the structure of the original. Compared with a plot summary one might produce for a teacher, a cento is a different literary-critical exercise altogether, since its author works without the goal of reproducing (and so coming to appreciate) the plot of the original. In a school, under a watchful grammarian's gaze, this might be no

---

33. See, e.g., M. D. Usher, *Homeric Stitchings: The Homeric Centos of the Empress Eudocia* (New York: Rowman & Littlefield, 1998).

34. On the so-called *Grande Notice*, see François Sagnard, *La Gnose valentinienne et le Témoignage de Saint Irénée* (Paris: Vrin, 1947), 31–50.

35. *Adv. Haer.* 1.9.3–4 (trans. Briggman, 'Literary and Rhetorical Theory in Irenaeus, Part 1', 504).

great crime. But here, from Irenaeus's perspective, the minds of simpler folk who cannot read scripture for themselves are at stake.

Irenaeus sees the Valentinians's summary of scripture's plot as a sort of skeleton which they then attempt to flesh out with names and places gathered from the rest of scripture. But if they have missed the plot, it follows that their treatments of specific textual details are equally distorted.[36] This latter point leads to still another sense in which the accurate summary of scripture's plot is central to Irenaeus's argument, economy (οἰκονομία). Οἰκονομία entails that the treatment of discrete elements in the literary work accords with the intention of the whole, that is, its ὑπόθεσις.[37] We find exactly this literary logic undergirding Irenaeus's well-known metaphor of the mosaic:

> Such is their system (*illorum argumentum*) which neither the prophets preached, nor the Lord taught, nor the apostles handed down … They disregard the order and the connection of the scriptures and … they disjoint the members of the Truth. They transfer passages and rearrange them; and, making one thing out of another, they deceive many by the badly composed phantasy of the Lord's words that they adapt. By way of illustration, suppose someone would take the beautiful image of a king, carefully made out of precious stones by a skillful artist, and would destroy the features of the man on it and change around and rearrange the jewels, and made the form of a dog, or of a fox, out of them, and that a rather bad piece of work. Suppose he would then say with determination that this is the beautiful image of the king that the skilful artist had made, at the same time pointing to the jewels which had been beautifully fitted together by the first artist into the image of the king, but which had been badly changed by the second into the form of a dog.[38]

The Valentinians's summary is not a good one, Irenaeus argues, because it disregards scripture's proper order and the connection between the parts and the whole. To make this point, Irenaeus indicates that scripture should be read like any text in a grammarian's classroom. The lack of interest in scripture's proper plot, then, shows the Valentinians to be poor readers. When it comes to applying the authoritative narrative inherent in the rule of truth to Valentinian exegesis of scripture, Irenaeus's concern is recognizable among the canons of ancient literary criticism. He is concerned that no one violate the plot (λύειν τὴν ὑπόθεσιν).[39]

The two examples given above are certainly Irenaeus's best-known critiques of Valentinian biblical interpretation. But Irenaeus's polemical appeals to scripture's plot extend beyond these evocative, if general, examples. In *Against Heresies*

---

36. Cf., e.g., the critique of Valentinian numerology and etymology in *Adv. Haer.* 2.22.
37. Briggman, 'Literary and Rhetorical Theory in Irenaeus, Part 1', 517–23.
38. *Adv. Haer.* 1.8.1.
39. See René Nünlist, *The Ancient Critic at Work: Terms and Concepts of Literary Criticism in Greek Scholia* (Cambridge: Cambridge University Press, 2009), 67.

1.9.2–4, he applies the principle that an accurate account of individual passages of scripture depends upon an accurate plot summary to Valentinian exegesis of the Johannine prologue:

> Manifest, then, is the false fabrication of their exegesis. To be sure, John preached one God Almighty, and one Only-begotten Christ Jesus, through whom he says *all things were made*.… But these men speciously distort the exegesis, and they hold there is an Only-begotten by virtue of an emission, whom they call Beginning; but they hold that another became the Saviour; and still another became the Word of the Only-begotten Son; and another became Christ who was emitted for setting the Fullness right. They wrest each of the sayings from the Truth. They misuse the names and transfer them to their own system (*in suam argumentationem transtulerunt*), so that, according to them, John does not mention the Lord Jesus Christ in these passages. For if he did speak of Father, Grace, Only-begotten, Truth, Word, Life, Man, and Church, according to their own system, he spoke of the first Ogdoad, in which there was yet no Jesus or Christ, John's teacher. But the Apostle himself made it clear that he did not speak of their conjugal couples, but of our Lord Jesus Christ, whom he knew to be the Word of God. For, by way of resuming what he said in the beginning about the Word, he adds: *And the Word became flesh and dwelt among us*. Now, according to their system, the Word did not become flesh, since he never even went out of the Fullness; but the Saviour did [become flesh], the one who was made out of all [the Aeons], who was generated later than the Word.[40]

According to Irenaeus, the transfer of key terms from the Johannine prologue to their place in the Valentinian account of the creation narrative results in distorted interpretation of *GJohn*, and, for that matter, of Truth itself. Irenaeus is concerned that the Valentinians have confused the biblical characters, narrating the procession of the Word from the Pleroma while differentiating Saviour from Word.

Irenaeus continues his attack on Valentinian Christology in *Against Heresies* 1.9.3–4. Though he has so far emphasized the logical dependence of exegetical harmony (οἰκονομία) on scripture's plot summary (ὑπόθεσις), here he suggests that careful consideration of one passage, like the Johannine prologue, ought to make readers question whether their initial plot summary is sufficient. On one hand, 'Flesh … is the ancient handiwork made by God out of the earth as in Adam. But it is this which John points out that the Word of God truly became. So he [John] broke up their first and principal Ogdoad.… And with this broken up, their entire system falls through (*decidit illorum omnis argumentatio*) – this empty allusion for the defense of which they mistreat the Scripture.'[41]

We should read Irenaeus's account of the Valentinian plot summary with some caution. After all, it reflects his summary of their summary. But neither should we

---

40. *Adv. Haer.* 1.9.2.
41. *Adv. Haer.* 1.9.3–4.

write Irenaeus's paraphrase off as irredeemably tainted by his polemical attitude. The production of a plot summary was a common part of a grammatical education and so recognizable a literary form that he was likely familiar with it. It is hard not to sympathize with Irenaeus's opponents on this point, however.[42] Even if Irenaeus has accurately recounted something like a Valentinian summary of scripture's plot, should not the suitability of commonplace grammatical reading strategies to the study of scripture be open for debate? It is not clear that all Valentinians, even those with grammatical educations, thought such elementary reading strategies essential for biblical interpretation, nor, for that matter, did all early Christian exegetes, from Paul to Origen, share Irenaeus's reverence for the literal sense of the text on which the plot summary is based. For the task at hand, however, it is sufficient to note that Irenaeus charges the Valentinians with gross mischaracterization of the plot of scripture.

The plot of scripture and the rule of truth

But this raises a question in turn. If Irenaeus thinks his opponents have failed to summarize scripture's plot accurately, how might a more technically grounded plot summary read? Several paragraphs after his rebuttal of the Valentinian exegesis of the Johannine prologue, Irenaeus offers what is probably his clearest description of scripture's plot. In *Against Heresies* 1.10.1, quoted here in full, he writes,

> The Church, although dispersed throughout the whole world, even to the ends of the earth, has received from the apostles and their disciples the faith in one God, the Father Almighty, who made the heaven and the earth and the sea and all that are in them; and in one Christ Jesus, the Son of God, who was incarnated for our salvation; and in one Holy Spirit, who has proclaimed through the prophets the economies: the coming, the birth from the virgin, the passion, the resurrection from the dead, and the bodily ascension into the heavens of the beloved Christ Jesus, our Lord, and his coming from the heavens in the glory of the Father to recapitulate all things, and to raise up all flesh of the whole human race, in order that to Christ Jesus our Lord, and God, and Saviour, and King, according to the good pleasure of the invisible Father, every knee should bow, of those in heaven and on the earth and under the earth, and every tongue confess him, and that he should render a just judgment toward all, and, on the one hand, he would send to eternal fire the spiritual forces of evil, the angels who transgressed and became apostates, and the impious, unjust, lawless, and blasphemous among men, but, on the other hand, to the righteous, and holy, and those who have kept his commandments, and have persevered in his love – both those who did so

---

42. See Robert McLachlan Wilson, *Gnosis and the New Testament* (Philadelphia, PA: Fortress, 1968), 84; Elaine Pagels, 'Irenaeus, the "Canon of Truth", and the "Gospel of John": "Making a Difference" through Hermeneutics and Ritual', *VC* 56 (2002), 339–71, 351.

from the beginning, and those who did so after repentance – he would confer, graciously bestowing, life incorruptible, and lay up eternal glory.[43]

There are at least two noteworthy features in this passage. First, just like the author of *Bodleian Greek Inscription* 3019 who names Achilles and Agamemnon, Irenaeus begins by relating the *dramatis personae* of scripture. Literary plot summaries of this sort frequently begin by listing the main characters before summarizing, with few details, the story's main events.[44] Read against the Valentinian interpretation of the Johannine prologue described in *Against Heresies* 1.9.2–4, even this simple list of characters takes on a polemical edge. Then, beginning with the creation narrative, Irenaeus lists in turn the promise and accomplishment of salvation, the recapitulation of all things in Christ and the final judgement.

Not surprisingly, Irenaeus emphasizes the oneness of 'Christ Jesus, the Son of God'. On Irenaeus's analysis, moreover, Jesus's incarnation requires the actual assumption of flesh. Similarly, in Irenaeus's summary of scripture's plot there is only one creator, and people created by God will face a just judgement: that is, one not predetermined by their creation according to certain fixed anthropological categories.[45]

By now it should be clear that in *Against Heresies* we do find a clash of narratives. According to Irenaeus, he and the Valentinians summarize the plot of scripture differently. Moreover, this difference in plot summaries leads to still more conflict over scripture's meaning, since interpretation of individual passages presupposes, Irenaeus argues, some sense of the whole. Hence his complaints about Valentinian exegesis of the prologue to *GJohn*. What is less clear, however, is how Irenaeus relates a narrative summary of scripture's contents, like that which we find in *Against Heresies* 1.10.1, to the rule of truth itself. Should we read it as one more summary of the rule of truth, an analogue to *Against Heresies* 1.22.1, or is it something else entirely?

At this point, secondary scholarship on Irenaeus and the rule of truth could easily confuse readers new to the topic. While most scholars agree that Irenaeus describes his conflict with the Valentinians as a dispute over scripture's plot, especially the right way to discern that plot, here it fragments into at least two distinctive positions. At stake is the relationship between scripture's plot, as Irenaeus summarizes it, and the rule of truth.

First, Anthony Briggman offers a minimalist account. *Against Heresies* 1.10.1, he suggests, summarizes scripture's plot, but this summary is not coterminous with the rule of truth. Briggman rightly notes that *Against Heresies* 1.10.1 would have to be the only rule-summary in Irenaeus not to explicitly announce itself as

---

43. *Adv. Haer.* 1.10.1 (trans. Briggman, 'Literary and Rhetorical Theory in Irenaeus, Part 1', 506, lightly edited).

44. Zuntz, *The Political Plays of Euripides*, 135.

45. These are several of Irenaeus's key anti-Valentinian concerns, on which, see de Andia, 'L'hérésie et sa réfutation', 611.

such. Moreover, the very fulsomeness of the prose that (potentially) makes *Against Heresies* 1.10.1 such a valuable description of the rule of truth is itself a reason to treat it as a summary of scripture's hypothesis but not of the rule; no other statement of the rule's contents is so developed. Finally, Briggman notes that if we treat *Against Heresies* 1.10.1 as a description of scripture but not the rule, we can resolve a significant the debate between two parties, one who conceives of Irenaeus's rule as an identity-forming metanarrative, and one which does not.[46]

We should bracket, if only for the moment, Briggman's argument and its historical merits to consider the implicit debate he is trying to resolve. When searching for a foundational Christian narrative that might have been normative for second-century Christians, Irenaeus's rule of truth is apt to strike us as a promising candidate. We would not be the first. In fact, some recent scholarship on the rule of truth argues that the rule is best understood as the early church's identity-forming metanarrative.[47] Wayne Meeks offers an attenuated form of this argument, but Paul Blowers has offered a more rigorous and provocative articulation of the position.[48] Blowers concludes that Irenaeus's 'struggle with the Gnostics is not just a battle of straightforward or atomized doctrinal propositions, which presumably Irenaeus could have tendered in the debate. It is more fundamentally a contention of "our story versus theirs", a collision of metanarratives, one Christian and one (or more) not.'[49] Most importantly, Blowers claims, 'Thus when Irenaeus expounds the Rule of Faith for his friend Marcianus in his *Epideixis* … he does it literally by retelling the biblical story and indicating the underlying nexus between its constitutive elements as though he were unfolding the sequences of a drama.'[50]

Let us return, then, to the question of the rule of truth and its relation to scripture, as Briggman poses it. Can we say that *Against Heresies* 1.10.1 summarizes the plot of scripture but not as an expression of the rule of truth? If he is correct, it follows that the primary discrepancy between Blowers and other readers of the rule is resolved. Blowers has indeed isolated a story, if not a metanarrative, central to Irenaean thought, but Frances Young is equally correct to see something like a non-narrative theological abstract as the rule of truth itself. In this case, Irenaeus would be offering a counter-narrative to the Valentinian plot summary, but it would not fall under the aegis of the rule of truth.

---

46. Briggman, 'Literary and Rhetorical Theory in Irenaeus, Part 1', 506–9.

47. See, e.g., Ellen Davis and Richard B. Hays, ed., *The Art of Reading Scripture* (Grand Rapids, MI: Eerdmans, 2003), 1–2; Kevin J. Vanhoozer, *The Drama of Doctrine: A Canonical Linguistic Approach to Christian Theology* (Louisville, KY: Westminster John Knox, 2005), 204.

48. Wayne Meeks, *The Origins of Christian Morality: The First Two Centuries* (New Haven, CT: Yale, 1995), 210; Blowers, 'The *Regula Fidei*'.

49. Blowers, 'The *Regula Fidei*', 210–11.

50. Blowers, 'The *Regula Fidei*', 212. For a reply to Blowers's reading of the rule of truth in *Demonstration*, see Nathan MacDonald, 'Israel and the Old Testament Story in Irenaeus's Presentation of the Rule of Faith', *JTI* 9 (2009), 281–98.

This brings us to a second scholarly description of the relationship between the rule of truth and a summary of scripture's plot. Lewis Ayres finds Briggman's division of scripture's plot from the rule unnecessary, since Irenaeus clearly presents the words of scripture as the rule of truth:[51]

> But as we follow for our teacher the one and only true God, and possess his words as the rule of truth [*et regulam veritatis habentes eius sermones*], we do all speak alike with regard to the same things, knowing but one God, the Creator of this universe, who sent the prophets, who led forth the people from the land of Egypt, who in these last times manifested his own Son, that he might put the unbelievers to confusion, and search out the fruit of righteousness.[52]

But Ayres's rejoinder, rather than settling the matter, raises afresh the problem of the relationship between a text and its summary. Briggman, after all, could gladly concede Ayres's point. *Against Heresies* 4.35.4 does claim that scripture's words are the rule of truth. *Against Heresies* 1.10.1, on the other hand, does not offer scripture's words but a secondary summary of its narrative arc. It is not immediately obvious that such a plot summary should bear the same authority as scripture itself.

To adjudicate between Briggman and Ayres, it may help to reconsider Irenaeus's description of scripture's plot summary as an example of apostolic tradition. Before the summary of the biblical plot in *Against Heresies* 1.10.1, Irenaeus claims that the church has 'received this faith from the apostles and their disciples' (*ab apostolis et discipulis eorum accepit eam fidem*). In other words, Irenaeus's plot summary is not his alone. It belongs to publicly available apostolic tradition. It follows that even if Irenaeus would agree that a plot summary does not bear the authority of an original – a plausible but uncertain point – in this case, because the biblical plot (ὑπόθεσις) resides in apostolic tradition, it is nonetheless to be identified as the rule of truth itself. Here we see the complexity of Irenaeus's notions of truth and the rule of truth. On the one hand, he is disputing the right interpretation of scripture, one of the sources of truth. But, on the other hand, scripture's plot, properly narrated, resides in apostolic tradition, another source of truth. For Irenaeus, truth is singular, though its sources are plural.

If *Against Heresies* 1.10.1 offers a critical statement of the contents of the rule of truth, and if that statement outlines the biblical ὑπόθεσις, what can we say about the Irenaean and Valentinian counter-narratives? First, and perhaps most importantly, Irenaeus presents his and the Valentinians' respective summaries of scripture's plot as differing not in kind but in quality. Imagine some third party seeking to adjudicate between Irenaeus and a Valentinian like Ptolemy. She might suggest setting each party's plot summary alongside the other and then appeal

---

51. Ayres, 'Irenaeus and the Rule of Truth', forthcoming; similarly, Jorgensen, *Treasure*, 43–44.

52. *Adv. Haer.* 4.35.4. See Ayres, 'Irenaeus and the "Rule of Truth"', forthcoming.

to the rule of truth to determine which (if any) plot summary is true and which false. This, after all, would seem to hold with the basic notion of a 'rule', a *regula*, a κανών, and not merely a ὑπόθεσις, a plot summary. In philosophical usage, a rule is a metaphorical ruler or plumb line, the means for determining whether another line of argument is actually straight or just straight enough to deceive the naked eye. Origen gives a good example of such an understanding of rule: 'For how can those who are turned aside receive that which is straight? It is as if you put a perfectly straight ruler against a curved line; the crookedness of the thing will indeed be patently shown by the ruler, but it is not the ruler that made the line go crooked.'[53]

Plausible as this third party's suggestion might seem, here we would do well to remember that in *Against Heresies* the Latin *regula* can translate both the Greek ὑπόθεσις and κανών.[54] That is, where Irenaeus accuses the Valentinians of producing a faulty or misleading plot summary, he sees his own plot summary not as a competing version of the same literary exercise but as an essential component of the very ruler used to judge their summary. His plot summary is more than just another attempt at the truth. It is the truth. Consequently, if Irenaeus's scriptural narrative stood on its own, there would be no external means of verifying whether he or the Valentinians had produced a 'straighter' account of the biblical plot. To Irenaeus's mind, his plot summary is not just another putatively straight line waiting to have its slant verified. It is rather the edge of the ruler that verifies other lines.

Conclusion

Irenaeus's rule of truth, then, contains within it a narrative. This narrative is both like and unlike other rival narratives. On one hand, Irenaeus suggests both he and the Valentinians are practising the same literary-critical exercise, producing their own summaries of scripture's plot. On the other hand, by virtue of its truth, as witnessed by the apostles and their disciples, Irenaeus places his account of the biblical plot over and apart from his opponents'. When he summarizes the plot of scripture in *Against Heresies* 1.10.1, Irenaeus thinks he is offering more than a plausible alternative to the Valentinians's own summary. As the rule of truth itself, Irenaeus's narrative summary is meant to serve as a defeater in their argument.

So understanding Irenaeus's narrative implies that Blowers and Meeks, in their attempts to portray the rule of truth as a metanarrative, have overread the evidence. There is indeed a powerful narrative internal to the rule, the plot of scripture, but it does not follow that all apostolic tradition, all early baptismal

---

53. *Comm. Cant.* 2.2 (trans. R. P. Lawson, *The Song of Songs, Commentary and Homilies*, ACW 26 [New York: Paulist, 1957], 109).

54. Bruno Reynders, *Lexique comparé du texte grec et des versions latine, arménienne et syriaque de l' "Adversus Haereses" de Saint Irénée* (Louvain: Durbecq, 1954), 2:278.

liturgy or, for that matter, every example of scriptural truth is reducible to a category like 'metanarrative'. Rather, in the rule of truth we have a collection of ways for speaking about the truth, no one more important than the next. This is not to lessen the importance of narrative but to elucidate its proper role as one of Irenaeus's most important modes of discourse in his dispute with the Valentinians.

Finally, one function of examining Irenaeus's counter-narrative is to shed additional light on the nature of early Christian exegetical practice, specifically second-century appropriations of ancient grammar. Irenaeus's insistence on the importance of a proper, grammatically sound plot summary notwithstanding, it is not clear that his Valentinian opponents shared, or should have shared, his conviction. To be sure, the Valentinian exegetes we can still read were critically sophisticated by ancient standards, but if Irenaeus's critique raises any single question it is not whether ancient Christians interpreted biblical texts using common technical methods but rather how they decided which bits of ancient grammar were relevant to their exegetical enterprise.

BIBLIOGRAPHY

Alexander, Philip, 'Jewish Elements in Gnosticism and Magic c. CE 70—c. 270', in *The Cambridge History of Judaism*, vol. 3, ed. William Horbury, W. D. Davies and John Study. Cambridge: Cambridge University Press, 1999, 1052-78.

Ammundsen, Valdemar, 'The Rule of Truth in Irenaeus', *JTS* 13 (1912), 574-80.

Anatolios, Khaled, *Athanasius: The Coherence of His Thought*. London: Routledge, 1998.

Andrews, Molly, 'Counter-Narratives and the Power to Oppose', in *Considering Counter-Narratives: Narrating, Resisting, Making Sense*, ed. Molly Andrews and Michael G. W. Bamberg. Amsterdam: John Benjamins, 2004, 1-6.

Arthur, Rose Horman, *The Wisdom Goddess: Feminine Motifs in Eight Nag Hammadi Documents*. Lanham, MD: University Press of America, 1984.

Ashton, John, *Understanding the Fourth Gospel*. Oxford: Clarendon Press, 1991.

Attridge, Harold W. (ed.), *Nag Hammadi Codex I (The Jung Codex), Introductions, Translations, Texts, Indices*, NHC 22. Leiden: Brill, 1985.

Ayres, Lewis, 'Irenaeus vs. the Valentinians: Toward a Rethinking of Patristic Exegetical Origins', *JECS* 23 (2015), 153-87.

Ayres, Lewis, 'Irenaeus and the Rule of Truth', in *The Rise of the Christian Intellectual*, ed. H. Clifton Ward and Lewis Ayres. Berlin: de Gruyter, forthcoming.

Bamberg, Michael, 'Considering Counter Narratives', in *Considering Counter-Narratives: Narrating, Resisting, Making Sense*, ed. Molly Andrews and Michael G. W. Bamberg. Amsterdam: John Benjamins, 2004, 351-71.

Bar-Kochva, Bezalel, *The Image of the Jews in Greek Literature: The Hellenistic Period*. Berkeley: University of California Press, 2010.

Barc, Bernard, and Michel Roberge, *L'Hypostase des archontes: Traité gnostique sur l'origine de l'homme, du monde et des archontes (NH II,4), suivi de Noréa (NH IX,27,11-29,5)*, Bibliothèque Copte de Nag Hammadi. Textes, 5. Leuven: Peeters, 1980.

Barc, Bernard, and Wolf-Peter Funk, *Le livre des secrets de Jean, Recension brève (NH III,1 et BG,2)*. Bibliothèque Copte de Nag Hammadi. Textes, 35. Leuven: Peeters, 2012.

Barclay, John M. G., *Against Apion: Translation and Commentary*. Leiden: Brill, 2007.

Barnes, Timothy David, *Tertullian: A Historical and Literary Study*, rev. edn Oxford: Clarendon Press, 1985.

Bauer, Walter, *Orthodoxy and Heresy in Earliest Christianity*. Philadelphia, PA: Fortress, 1979.

BeDuhn, Jason D., *The First New Testament: Marcion's Scriptural Canon*. Salem, OR: Polebridge, 2013.

Behr, John, *Irenaeus of Lyons: Identifying Christianity*. Oxford: Oxford University Press, 2013.

Bergermann, M., and Ch.-F. Collatz (ed.), *Epiphanius I: Ancoratus und Panarion Haer. 1-33*, GCS NF 10/1-2. Berlin: de Gruyter, 2013.

Bianchi, Ugo, 'Der demiurgische Trickster und die Religionsethnologie', in *Selected Essays on Gnosticism, Dualism, and Mysteriosophy*. Leiden: Brill, 1978, 335-43.

Blowers, Paul M., 'The Regula Fidei and the Narrative Character of Early Christian Faith', *ProEccl* 6 (1997), 199–228.
Bonnet, Maximilian, *Acta Apostolorum Apocrypha II,1*, repr. New York: Georg Olms, 1990.
Brakke, David, 'Self-Differentiation among Christian Groups: The Gnostics and Their Opponents', in *The Cambridge History of Christianity*, ed. M. Mitchell and F. Young. Cambridge: Cambridge University Press, 2006, 245–60.
Brakke, David, *The Gnostics: Myth, Ritual, and Diversity in Early Christianity*. Cambridge, MA: Harvard University Press, 2010.
Brakke, David, 'A New Fragment of Athanasius's Thirty-Ninth Festal Letter: Heresy, Apocrypha, and the Canon', *HTR* 103 (2010), 47–66.
Brankaer, Johanna, and Hans-Gebhard Bethge, *Codex Tchacos: Texte und Analysen*, TU 161. Berlin: de Gruyter, 2007.
Briggman, Anthony, 'Revisiting Irenaeus' Philosophical Acumen', *VC* 65 (2011), 115–24.
Briggman, Anthony, 'Literary and Rhetorical Theory in Irenaeus, Part 1', *VC* 69 (2015), 500–27.
Briggman, Anthony, 'Literary and Rhetorical Theory in Irenaeus, Part 2', *VC* 70 (2016), 31–50.
van den Broek, R., *Gnostic Religion in Antiquity*. Cambridge: Cambridge University Press, 2013.
Bruce, F. F., *The Epistle to the Galatians: A Commentary on the Greek Text*, NIGNT. Grand Rapids, MI: Eerdmans, 1982.
Buell, Denise K., *Why This New Race: Ethnic Reasoning in Early Christianity*. New York: Columbia University Press, 2005.
Bullard, Roger Aubrey, *The Hypostasis of the Archons: The Coptic Text with Translation and Commentary*, PTS 10. Berlin: de Gruyter, 1970.
Bury, R. G. (trans.), *Plato: Timaeus, Critias, Cleitophon, Menexenus, Epistles*, LCL 234. Cambridge, MA: Harvard University Press, 1929.
Cahana, Jonathan, 'Gnosticism and Radical Feminism: From Pathologizing Submersion to Salvaging Re-emergence', in *Submerged Literature in Ancient Greek Culture: The Comparative Perspective*, ed. Andrea Ercolani and Manuela Giordano. Berlin: de Gruyter, 2016, 183–200.
Cahana, Jonathan, 'Salvific Dissolution: The Mystery of the Betrayal between the New Testament and the Gospel of Judas', *NTS* 63 (2017), 111–24.
Cahana-Blum, Jonathan, *Wrestling with Archons: Gnosticism as a Critical Theory of Culture*. Lanham, MD: Lexington Books, 2018.
Cameron, Ron (ed.), *The Other Gospels: Non-Canonical Gospel Texts*. Guildford: Lutterworth Press, 1983.
Chapman, David W., *Ancient Jewish and Christian Perceptions of Crucifixion*, WUNT II 244. Tübingen: Mohr Siebeck, 2008.
Clarke, M. L., *Higher Education in the Ancient World*. New York: Routledge, 2012.
Cobb, L. Stephanie, *Divine Deliverance: Pain and Painlessness in Early Christian Martyr Texts*. Oakland: University of California Press, 2016.
Connolly, R. Hugh, *Didascalia Apostolorum: The Syriac Version Translated and Accompanied by the Verona Latin Fragments*. Oxford: Clarendon Press, 1969.
Coquin, René-Georges, 'Les lettres festales d'Athanase (CPG 2102). Un nouveau complément: le manuscript IFAO 25', *Orientalia Lovaniensia Periodica* 15 (1984), 133–58.
Creech, David, *The Use of Scripture in the Apocryphon of John: A Diachronic Analysis of the Variant Versions*, WUNT II 441. Tübingen: Mohr Siebeck, 2017.

Cribiore, Raffaella, *Gymnastics of the Mind*. Princeton, NJ: Princeton University Press, 2001.
Cribiore, Raffaella, 'The Grammarian's Choice: The Popularity of Euripides's Phoenissae in Hellenistic and Roman Education', in *Education in Greek and Roman Antiquity*, ed. Yun Lee Too. Leiden: Brill, 2001, 241–60.
Cristea, Hans-Joachim, *Schenute von Atripe: Contra Origenistas. Edition des koptischen Textes mit annotierter Übersetzung und Indizes einschließlich einer Übersetzung des 16. Osterfestbriefs des Theophilus in der Fassung des Hieronymus (ep. 96)*, STAC 60. Tübingen: Mohr Siebeck, 2011.
Davis, Ellen, and Richard B. Hays (ed.), *The Art of Reading Scripture*. Grand Rapids, MI: Eerdmans, 2003.
de Andia, Ysabel, 'L'hérésie et sa réfutation selon Irénée de Lyon', *Augustinianum* 25 (1985), 613–24.
de Boer, Esther, 'A Stoic Reading of the Gospel of Mary: The Meaning of "Matter" and "Nature" in the Gospel of Mary 7.1–8.11', in *Stoicism in Early Christianity*, ed. Tuomas Rasimus, Ismo Dunderberg and Troels Engberg-Pedersen. Grand Rapids, MI: Baker, 2010, 199–219.
DeConick, A. D., *The Gnostic New Age: How a Countercultural Spirituality Revolutionized Religion from Antiquity to Today*. New York: Columbia University Press, 2016.
Dekkers, D. Eligius, and Iohannes Fraipont (ed.), *Sancti Aurelii Augustini Enarrationes in Psalmos CI-CL*, CCL 40. Turnhout: Brepols, 1956.
Denzey Lewis, Nicola, *Introduction to 'Gnosticism': Ancient Voices, Christian Worlds*. Oxford: Oxford University Press, 2013.
Denzey Lewis, Nicola, and Justine Ariel Blount, 'Rethinking the Origins of the Nag Hammadi Codices', *JBL* 133 (2014), 399–419.
Droge, Arthur, 'Homeric Exegesis among the Gnostics', in *Historia, Theologica, Gnostica, Biblica et Apocrypha: Papers Presented to the Tenth International Conference on Patristic Studies Held in Oxford 1987*, ed. Elizabeth A. Livingstone. Leuven: Peeters, 1989, 313–21.
Dubois, Jean-Daniel, 'Le docétisme des christologies gnostiques revisité', *NTS* 63 (2017), 279–304.
Dunderberg, Ismo, *Beyond Gnosticism: Myth, Lifestyle, and Society in the School of Valentinus*. New York: Columbia University Press, 2008.
Dunderberg, Ismo, 'The Eucharist in the Gospels of John, Philip, and Judas', *Early Christianity* 7 (2016), 484–507.
Dunn, Geoffrey D., 'Tertullian's Scriptural Exegesis in de praescriptione haereticorum', *JECS* 14 (2006), 141–55.
Edwards, Mark J., 'The Epistle to Rheginus: Valentinianism in the Fourth Century', *NovT* 37 (1995), 76–91.
Ehrman, Bart D., *The Lost Gospel of Judas Iscariot: A New Look at Betrayer and Betrayed*. Oxford: Oxford University Press, 2006.
Elliott, J. K., *The Apocryphal New Testament*. Oxford: Clarendon Press, 1993.
Endsjø, Dag Øistein, *Greek Resurrection Beliefs and the Success of Christianity*. New York: Palgrave Macmillan, 2009.
Engel, Amir, *Gershom Scholem: An Intellectual Biography*. Chicago, IL: University of Chicago Press, 2017.
Evans, Ernest (ed.), *Tertullian Adversus Marcionem*, 2 vols. Oxford: Oxford University Press, 1972.

van den Eynde, Damien, *Les Normes d'enseignement chrétien dans la littérature patristique des trois premiers siècles.* Paris: J. Ducolot, 1933.
Fallon, F. T., 'The Law in Philo and Ptolemy: A Note on the Letter to Flora', *VC* 30 (1976), 45–51.
Feine, P., *Das gesetzesfreie Evangelium des Paulus.* Leipzig: J. C. Hinrichs, 1899.
Fine, M., and A. Harris (ed.), 'Under the Covers: Theorising the Politics of Counter Stories', *International Journal of Critical Psychology* 4 (2001).
Foerster, W., 'Die Grundzüge der Ptolemaeischen Gnosis', *NTS* 6 (1959–60), 16–31.
Foerster, W., *Die Gnosis. Band I: Zeugnisse der Kirchenväter.* Zürich-Stuttgart: Artemis, 1969, repr. 1997.
Foerster, W., *Gnosis: A Selection of Gnostic Texts, I. Patristic Evidence, English Translation*, ed. R. McL. Wilson. Oxford: Clarendon Press, 1972.
Fossum, Jarl, 'Origin of the Gnostic Concept of the Demiurge', *Ephemerides Theologicae Lovanienses* 61 (1985), 142–52.
Foster, Paul, 'Polymorphic Christology: Its Origins and Development in Early Christianity', *JTS* 58 (2007), 66–99.
Fowler, H. N. (trans.), *Plato: Euthyphro, Apology, Crito, Phaedo, Phaedrus*, LCL 36. Cambridge, MA: Harvard University Press, 1914.
Fowler, Kimberley A., 'The Ascent of the Soul and the Pachomians: Interpreting the Exegesis on the Soul (NHC II,6) within a Fourth-Century Monastic Context', *Gnosis* 2 (2017), 63–93.
Fowler, Kimberley A., 'Reading Gospel of Thomas 100 in the Fourth Century: From Roman Imperialism to Pachomian Concern over Wealth', VC 72 (2018), 421–46.
Gallagher, Edmon L., and John D. Meade, *The Biblical Canon Lists from Early Christianity: Texts and Analysis.* Oxford: Oxford University Press, 2017.
Gilhus, Ingvild Sælid, 'The Gnostic Demiurge – an Agnostic Trickster', *Religion* 14 (1984), 301–11.
Gilhus, Ingvild Sælid, *The Nature of the Archons: A Study in the Soteriology of a Treatise from Nag Hammadi (CGII, 4).* Wiesbaden: O. Harrassowitz, 1985.
Goehring, James, *Ascetics, Society, and the Desert: Studies in Early Egyptian Monasticism.* Harrisburg, PA: Trinity Press International, 1999.
Goehring, James, 'Some Reflections on the Nag Hammadi Codices and the Study of Early Egyptian Monasticism', *Meddelanden från Collegium Patristicum Lundense* 25 (2010), 61–70.
Gonzalez, Eliezer, 'Anthropologies of Continuity: The Body and Soul in Tertullian, Perpetua, and Early Christianity', *JECS* 21.4 (2013), 479–502.
Goodacre, Mark, 'Fatigue in the Synoptics', *NTS* 44 (1998), 45–58.
Goodacre, Mark, *Thomas and the Gospels: The Making of an Apocryphal Text.* London: SPCK, 2012.
Goodacre, Mark, 'How Reliable Is the Story of the Nag Hammadi Discovery?', *JSNT* 35 (2013), 303–22.
Grant, Robert M., *Irenaeus of Lyons.* New York: Routledge, 1997, 46–53.
Hägglund, Bengt, 'Die Bedeutung der "regula fidei" als grundlage theologischer Aussagen', *ST* 12 (1958), 1–44.
Hardy, Edward Rochie (ed.), *Christology of the Later Fathers*, Library of Christian Classics 3. London: SCM Press, 1954.
von Harnack, Adolf, *Der kirchengeschichtliche Ertrag der exegetischen Arbeiten des Origenes*, 2 vols. Leipzig: Hinrichs, 1918–19.

von Harnack, Adolf, *Marcion: Das Evangelium vom fremden Gott*. Leipzig: Hinrichs, 1924²; Eng. tr. *The Gospel of the Alien God*, trans. John E. Steely and Lyle D. Bierma. Durham, NC: Labyrinth, 1990; Eugene, OR: Wipf & Stock, 1990.

Hartenstein, Judith, *Die zweite Lehre: Erscheinungen des Auferstandenen als Rahmenerzählungen frühchristlicher Dialoge*, TU 146. Berlin: de Gruyter, 2000.

Head, Raymond, 'The Hymn of Jesus: Holst's Gnostic Exploration of Time and Space', *Tempo* 208 (July 1999), 7–13.

Heil, John P., *Blood and Water: The Death and Resurrection of Jesus in John 18–21*, CBQMS 27. Washington, DC: Catholic Biblical Association, 1995.

Heimola, Minna, *Christian Identity in the Gospel of Philip*, Publications of the Finnish Exegetical Society 201. Helsinki: Finnish Exegetical Society, 2011.

Hengel, M., *Crucifixion in the Ancient World and the Folly of the Message of the Cross*. Philadelphia, PA: Fortress, 1989.

Holl, K., *Epiphanius, Band I: Ancoratus und Panarion Haer. 1–33*, GCS. Berlin: Akademie Verlag, 1915.

Holl, K., *Epiphanius, Band II: Ancoratus und Panarion Haer. 34–64*, rev. Jürgen Dummer, GCS. Berlin: Akademie Verlag, 1985.

Holsinger Friesen, Thomas, *Irenaeus and Genesis: A Study in Competition in Early Christian Hermeneutics*. Winona Lake, IN: Eisenbraun, 2009.

Hooker, Morna, *From Adam to Christ: Essays on Paul*. Cambridge: Cambridge University Press, 1990.

Horsley, R. A. (ed.), *Hidden Transcripts and the Arts of Resistance: Applying the Work of James C. Scott to Jesus and Paul*, Semeia Studies 48. Atlanta, GA: SBL, 2004.

Horsley, R. A. (ed.), *Oral Performance, Popular Tradition, and Hidden Transcript in Q*, Semeia Studies 60. Atlanta, GA: SBL, 2006.

Hultgren, A. J., 'Paul's Pre-Christian Persecutions of the Church: Their Purpose, Locale, and Nature', *JBL* 95 (1976), 97–111.

Hyvärinen, Matti, 'Analyzing Narratives and Story-Telling', in *The SAGE Handbook of Social Research Methods*, ed. Pertti Alasuutari, Leonrad Bickman and Julia Brannen. Thousand Oaks, CA: Sage, 2008, 447–60.

Iricinschi, Eduard, 'The Teaching Hidden in Silence (NHC II 1,4): Questions, Answers and Secrets in a Fourth-Century Egyptian Book', in *Beyond the Gnostic Gospels: Studies Building on the Work of Elaine Pagels*, ed. Eduard Iricinschi, Lance Jenott, Nicola Denzey Lewis and Philippa Townsend, STAC 82. Tübingen: Mohr Siebeck, 2013, 297–319.

Jacobi, Christine, '"Dies ist die geistige Auferstehung": Paulusrezeption im Rheginusbrief und im Philippusevangelium', in *Receptions of Paul in Early Christianity: The Person of Paul and His Writings through the Eyes of His Early Interpreters*, ed. Jens Schröter, Simon Butticaz and Andreas Dettwiler, BZNW 234. Berlin: de Gruyter, 2018, 355–75.

Jacobs, A. S., *Epiphanius of Cyprus: A Cultural Biography of Late Antiquity*. Oakland: University of California Press, 2016.

Jenott, Lance, *The Gospel of Judas: Coptic Text, Translation, and Historical Interpretation of 'the Betrayer's Gospel'*, STAC 64. Tübingen: Mohr Siebeck, 2011.

Jeremias, Gert, *Der Lehrer der Gerechtigkeit*. Göttingen: Vandenhoeck & Ruprecht, 1963.

Jonas, Hans, *The Gnostic Religion: The Message of the Alien God and the Beginnings of Christianity*. Boston, MA: Beacon, 1963.

Jorgensen, David, *Treasure Hidden in a Field: Early Christian Reception of the Gospel of Matthew*, SBR 6. Berlin: de Gruyter, 2016.

Junod, Eric, and Jean-Daniel Kaestli (ed.), *Acta Iohannis*, 2 vols, CCSA. Turnhout: Brepols, 1983.

Kaiser, Ursula Ulrike, *Die Hypostase der Archonten (Nag-Hammadi-Codex II,4)*. Berlin: de Gruyter, 2006.

Kasser, Rodolphe, 'L'Eksêgêsis etbe tpsukhê [NH II, 6]: Histoire de l'âme puis exégèse parénétique de ce mythe gnostique', *Apocrypha* 8 (1997), 71–80.

Kasser, Rodolphe, G. Wurst, M. Meyer and F. Gaudard (ed.), *The Gospel of Judas, together with the Letter from Peter to Philip, James, and a Book of Allogenes from Codex Tchacos: Critical Edition*. Washington, DC: National Geographic, 2007.

Kelly, J. N. D., *Early Christian Creeds*, 3rd edn. London: Longman, 1972, 76–82.

Kim, R. Young, *Epiphanius of Cyprus: Imagining the Orthodox World*. Ann Arbor: University of Michigan Press, 2015.

Kim, Seyoon, *The Origin of Paul's Gospel*, WUNT II 4. Tübingen: Mohr Siebeck, 1981.

King, Karen L., 'Ridicule and Rape, Rule and Rebellion: The Hypostasis of the Archons', in *Gnosticism and the Early Christian World in Honor of James M. Robinson*, ed. James E. Goehring. Sonoma, CA: Polebridge Press, 1990, 3–24.

King, Karen L., 'Why All the Controversy? Mary in the Gospel of Mary', in *Which Mary? The Marys of Early Christian Tradition*, ed. F. Stanley Jones, SBL Symposium Series 19. Atlanta, GA: Society of Biblical Literature, 2002, 53–74.

King, Karen L., *The Gospel of Mary of Magdala: Jesus and the First Woman Apostle*. Santa Rosa, CA: Polebridge Press, 2003.

King, Karen L., *What Is Gnosticism?*, Cambridge, MA.: Harvard University Press, 2003.

King, Karen L., *The Secret Revelation of John*, Cambridge, MA: Harvard University Press, 2006.

King, Karen L., 'Christians Who Sacrifice and Those Who Do Not?: Discursive Practices, Polemics, and Ritualizing', in *'One Who Sows Bountifully': Essays in Honor of Stanley K. Stowers*, ed. Caroline E. Johnson Hodge, Saul M. Olyan, Daniel C. Ullucci and Emma Wasserman. Providence, RI: Brown University Press, 2013, 307–18.

Koester, Craig R., and Reimund Bieringer (ed.), *The Resurrection of Jesus in the Gospel of John*, WUNT I 222. Tübingen: Mohr Siebeck, 2008.

Koetschau, P. (ed.), *Origenes Werke 2*, GCS 3. Leipzig: Hinrichs, 1899.

Kraus, Thomas J., Michael J. Kruger, and Tobias Nicklas, *Gospel Fragments*, Oxford Early Christian Gospel Texts. Oxford: Oxford University Press, 2009.

Krause, Martin, 'Die Sakramente in der "Exegese über die Seele"', in *Les textes de Nag Hammadi: Colloque du Centre d'Histoire des Religions (Strasbourg, 23–25 octobre 1974)*, ed. Jacques-É. Ménard. Leiden: Brill, 1975, 47–60.

Krosney, H., M. Meyer and G. Wurst, 'Preliminary Report on New Fragments of Codex Tchacos', *Early Christianity* 1 (2010), 282–94.

Kroymann, A., and E. Evans (ed.), *Quinti Septimi Florentis Tertulliani Opera Pars II Opera Montanistica*, CCSL 2.2. Turnhout: Brepols, 1954.

Kugel, James L., *Traditions of the Bible*, Cambridge, MA: Harvard University Press, 1998.

Kuhn, Heinz-Wolfgang, 'The Impact of Selected Qumran Texts on the Understanding of Pauline Theology', in *The Bible and the Dead Sea Scrolls Volume Three: The Scrolls and Christian Origins*, ed. James H. Charlesworth. Waco, TX: Baylor University Press, 2006, 153–86.

Labib, Pahor, *Coptic Gnostic Papyri in the Coptic Museum at Cairo*. Cairo: Government Press, 1956.

Lahe, J., *Gnosis und Judentum: Alttestamentliche und jüdische Motive in der gnostischen Literatur und das Ursprungsproblem der Gnosis*, NHMS 75. Leiden: Brill, 2012.

Lampe, P., *Die stadtrömische Christen in den ersten Jahrhunderten*, WUNT II 18. Tübingen: Mohr Siebeck, 1989².

Lawson, R. P., *The Song of Songs, Commentary and Homilies*, ACW 26. New York: Paulist, 1957.

Layton, Bentley (ed.), 'The Hypostasis of the Archons or the Reality of the Rulers', *HTR* 67 (1974), 351–94.

Layton, Bentley (ed.), 'The Hypostasis of the Archons (Conclusion)', *HTR* 69 (1976), 31–101.

Layton, Bentley (ed.), *The Gnostic Scriptures: A New Translation*. New York: Doubleday, 1987.

Layton, Bentley (ed.), *Nag Hammadi Codex II, 2–7, together with XIII, 2* Brit. Lib. Or. 4926(1) and P. Oxy. 1, 654, 655: Volume One: Gospel According to Thomas, Gospel According to Philip, Hypostasis of the Archons, and Indexes*, NHS 20. Leiden: Brill, 1989¹, 2003².

Layton, Bentley (ed.), 'The Soul as a Dirty Garment (Nag Hammadi Codex II, Tractate 6, 131:27–34)', *Muséon* 91 (1989), 155–69.

Le Boulluec, A., *La notion d'hérésie dans la littérature grecque (IIe-IIIe siècles)*, 2 vols. Paris: Études augustiniennes, 1985.

Lefort, L.-Th. (ed.), *S. Athanase Lettres Festale et Pastorales en Copte*, CSCO 150–151. Louvain: L. Durbecq, 1955.

Lehtipuu, Outi, *Debates over the Resurrection of the Dead: Constructing Early Christian Identity*, Oxford Early Christian Studies. Oxford: Oxford University Press, 2015.

Lieu, Judith, *Marcion and the Making of a Heretic: God and Scripture in the Second Century*. Cambridge: Cambridge University Press, 2015.

Lincoln, Andrew T., '"I Am the Resurrection and the Life": The Resurrection Message of the Fourth Gospel', in *Life in the Face of Death: The Resurrection Message of the New Testament*, ed. Richard N. Longenecker. Grand Rapids, MI: Eerdmans, 1998, 122–44.

Lindars, Barnabas, *New Testament Apologetic: The Doctrinal Significance of the Old Testament Quotations*. London: SCM Press, 1973.

Litwa, M. David (ed.), *Refutation of All Heresies*, WGRW 40. Atlanta, GA: SBL Press, 2016, 539–63.

Logan, A. H. B., *Gnostic Truth and Christian Heresy: A Study in the History of Gnosticism*. Edinburgh: T&T Clark, 1996.

Löhr, W. A., 'La doctrine de Dieu dans la Lettre à Flora de Ptolémée', *RHPhR* 75 (1995), 177–91.

Löhr, W. A., 'Die Auslegung des Gesetzes bei Markion, den Gnostikern und den Manichäern', in *Stimuli: Exegese und ihre Hermeneutik in Antike und Christentum. FS E. Dassmann*, ed. G. Schöllgen and C. Scholten, JbAC Ergänzungsband 23. Münster: Aschendorff, 1996, 77–95.

Löhr, W. A., 'Ptolemäus, Gnostiker', in *Theologische Realenzyklopädie* 27 (1997), 699–702.

Löhr, W. A., 'Did Marcion Distinguish between a Just God and a Good God?', in *Marcion und seine kirchengeschichtliche Wirkung: Marcion and His Impact on Church History, Vorträge der Internationalen Fachkonferenz zu Marcion, gehalten vom 15.-18. August 2001 in Mainz*, ed. Gerhard May and Katharina Greschat. Berlin: de Gruyter, 2002, 131–46.

Lohse, B., 'Meliton von Sardes und der Brief des Ptolemäus an Flora', in *Der Ruf Jesu und die Antwort der Gemeinde: FS Joachim Jeremias*, ed. E. Lohse, Christoph Burchard and Berndt Schaller. Göttingen: Vandenhoeck & Ruprecht, 1970.

Longenecker, Richard N., *Galatians*, WBC 41. Columbia: Word, 1990.

Lüdemann, G., 'Zur Geschichte des ältesten Christentums in Rom, I. Valentin und Marcion; II. Ptolemäus und Justin', *ZNW* 70 (1979), 86–114.
Lührmann, Dieter, *Die apokryph gewordenen Evangelien: Studien zu Neuen Texten und zu Neuen Fragen*, NovTSupp 112. Leiden: Brill, 2004.
Lundhaug, Hugo, '"These Are the Symbols and Likenesses of the Resurrection": Conceptualizations of Death and Transformation in the Treatise on the Resurrection (NHC I,4)', in *Metamorphoses: Resurrection, Taxonomies and Transformative Practices in Early Christianity*, ed. Turid Karlsen Seim and Jorunn Økland, Ekstasis 1. Berlin: de Gruyter, 2009, 187–205.
Lundhaug, Hugo, *Images of Rebirth: Cognitive Poetics and Transformational Soteriology in the Gospel of Philip and the Exegesis on the Soul*, NHMS 73. Leiden: Brill, 2010.
Lundhaug, Hugo, 'Begotten, Not Made, to Arise in This Flesh: The Post-Nicene Soteriology of the Gospel of Philip', in *Beyond the Gnostic Gospels: Studies Building on the Work of Elaine Pagels*, ed. Eduard Iricinschi, Lance Jenott, Nicola Denzey Lewis and Philippa Townsend, STAC 82. Tübingen: Mohr Siebeck, 2013, 235–71.
Lundhaug, Hugo, 'Origenism in Fifth-Century Upper Egypt: Shenoute of Atripe and the Nag Hammadi Codices', in *Studia Patristica LXIV: Papers Presented at the Sixteenth International Conference on Patristic Studies held in Oxford 2011, vol. 12: Ascetica, Liturgica, Orientalia, Critica et Philologica*, ed. Markus Vinzent. Leuven: Peeters, 2013, 217–28.
Lundhaug, Hugo, and Lance Jenott, *The Monastic Origins of the Nag Hammadi Codices*, STAC 97. Tübingen, Mohr Siebeck, 2015.
Luttikhuizen, Gerard P., *Gnostic Revisions of Genesis Stories and Early Jesus Traditions*, NHMS 58. Leiden: Brill, 2006.
MacDonald, Nathan, 'Israel and the Old Testament Story in Irenaeus's Presentation of the Rule of Faith', *JTI* 9 (2009), 281–98.
Mansfeld, Jaap, 'Bad World and Demiurge: A "Gnostic" Motif from Parmenides and Empedocles to Lucretius and Philo', in *Studies in Gnosticism and Hellenistic Religions, Festschrift for Gilles Quispel*, ed. R. van den Broek and M. J. Vermaseren, ÉPRO 91. Leiden: Brill, 1981, 261–314.
Marjanen, Antti, 'The Mother of Jesus or the Magdalene? The Identity of Mary in the So-Called Gnostic Christian Texts', in *Which Mary? The Marys of Early Christian Tradition*, ed. F. Stanley Jones, SBL Symposium Series 19. Atlanta, GA: Society of Biblical Literature, 2002, 31–42.
Markschies, Christoph, *Valentinus Gnosticus? Untersuchungen zur valentinianischen Gnosis mit einem Kommentar zu den Fragmenten Valentins*, WUNT 65. Tübingen: Mohr Siebeck, 1992.
Markschies, Christoph, 'Valentinian Gnosticism: Toward the Anatomy of a School', in *The Nag Hammadi Library after Fifty Years*, ed. John B. Turner and Anne McGuire. Leiden: Brill, 1997, 401–38.
Markschies, Christoph, 'New Research on Ptolemaeus Gnosticus', *ZAC* 4 (2000), 225–54.
Marrou, Henri, *A History of Education in Antiquity*, trans. George Lamb. New York: Sheed and Ward, 1956, 284–91.
Martínez, Florentino García, 'Galatians 3.10–14 in the Light of Qumran', in *The Dead Sea Scrolls and Pauline Literature*, ed. Jean-Sébastian Rey. Leiden: Brill, 2014, 51–67.
May, Gerhard, *Schöpfung aus dem Nichts: Die Entstehung der Lehre von der creatio ex nihilo*, Arbeiten zur Kirchengeschichte 48. Berlin: de Gruyter, 1978.
May, Gerhard, 'Marcion in Contemporary Views', in *Markion: Gesammelte Aufsätze*, ed. Katharina Greschat and Martin Meiser. Mainz: Philipp von Zabern, 2005, 13–34.

McGlothlin, Thomas D., *Resurrection as Salvation: Development and Conflict in Pre-Nicene Paulinism*. Cambridge: Cambridge University Press, 2018.
McGowan, Andrew, 'Tertullian and the "Heretical" Origins of the "Orthodox" Trinity', *JECS* 14 (2006), 437–57.
McGuire, Anne, 'Virginity and Subversion: Norea against the Powers in the Hypostasis of the Archons', in *Images of the Feminine in Gnosticism*, ed. Karen L. King. Pennsylvania, PA: Trinity Press International, 1988, 239–59.
McGuire, Anne, 'Gnosis and Nag Hammadi', in *The Routledge Companion to Early Christian Thought*, ed. D. Jeffrey Bingham. London: Routledge, 2010, 204–27.
Meeks, Wayne, *The Origins of Christian Morality: The First Two Centuries*. New Haven, CT: Yale University Press, 1995.
Meijering, Roos, *Literary and Rhetorical Theories in Greek Scholia*. Groningen: E. Forsten, 1987, 105–33.
Meyer, Marvin (ed.), *The Nag Hammadi Scriptures*. New York: HarperCollins, 2007.
Meyer, Marvin, 'Interpreting Judas: Ten Passages in the Gospel of Judas', in *The Gospel of Judas in Context*, ed. M. Scopello. Leiden: Brill, 2008, 41–55.
Miles, Jack, *God: A Biography*. London: Simon & Schuster, 1995.
Moreschini, Claudio, and Enrico Norelli, *Early Christian Greek and Latin Literature: A Literary History*, trans. Matthew J. O'Connell, 2 vols. Peabody, MA: Hendrickson, 2005.
Morgan, Teresa, *Literate Education in the Hellenistic and Roman Worlds*. Cambridge: Cambridge University Press, 1998.
Mutua, Kagendo, 'Counternarrative', in *The SAGE Encyclopedia of Qualitative Research Methods*, ed. Lisa M. Given. Thousand Oaks, CA: Sage, 2008.
Nel, Marius J., 'He Who Laughs Last: Jesus and Laughter in the Synoptic and Gnostic Traditions', *HTS Teologiese Studies/Theological Studies* 70 (2014), 1–8.
Neuschäfer, Bernhard, *Origenes als Philologe*, 2 vols. Basel: Friedrich Reinhardt, 1987.
Nickelsburg, George W., *Resurrection, Immortality, and Eternal Life in Intertestamental Judaism and Early Christianity*. Cambridge, MA: Harvard University Press, 2006.
Nienhuis, David R., *Not by Paul Alone: The Formation of the Catholic Epistles Collection and the Christian Canon*. Waco, TX: Baylor University Press, 2007.
Norden, E., *Die antike Kunstprosa vom VI. Jh. v. Chr. bis in die Zeit der Renaissance*, 2 vols. Leipzig: Teubner, 1909; Stuttgart: Teubner, 1983.
Norris, Richard A., 'Theology and Language in Irenaeus of Lyon', *ATR* 76 (1994), 285–95.
Nünlist, René, *The Ancient Critic at Work: Terms and Concepts of Literary Criticism in Greek Scholia*. Cambridge: Cambridge University Press, 2009.
O'Brien, Kelli S., 'The Curse of the Law (Galatians 3.13): Crucifixion, Persecution, and Deuteronomy 21.22–23', *JSNT* 29 (2006), 55–76.
Ohme, Heinz, *Kanon ekklesiastikos: Die Bedeutung des altkirchlichen Kanonbegriffs*. Berlin: de Gruyter, 1998.
Osborn, Eric, 'Reason and the Rule of Faith in the Second Century AD', in *The Making of Orthodoxy: Essays in Honour of Henry Chadwick*, ed. Rowan Williams. Cambridge: Cambridge University Press, 1989, 40–61.
Paffenroth, Kim, *Judas: Images of the Lost Disciple*. Louisville, KY: Westminster John Knox, 2001.
Pagels, Elaine, 'The Demiurge and His Archons: A Gnostic View of the Bishops and Presbyters?', *HTR* 69 (1976), 301–24.
Pagels, Elaine, *The Gnostic Gospels*. New York: Random House, 1979.
Pagels, Elaine, 'Irenaeus, the "Canon of Truth", and the Gospel of John: "Making a Difference" through Hermeneutics and Ritual', *VC* 56 (2002), 339–71.

Pagels, Elaine H., and Karen L. King, *Reading Judas: The Gospel of Judas and the Shaping of Christianity*. New York: Viking, 2007.
Painchaud, Louis, 'Polemical Aspects of the Gospel of Judas', in *The Gospel of Judas in Context*, ed. Madeleine Scopello. Leiden: Brill, 2008, 171–86.
Parkhouse, Sarah, 'Matter and the Soul: The Bipartite Eschatology of the Gospel of Mary', in *Connecting Gospels: Beyond the Canonical/Non-Canonical Divide*, ed. Francis Watson and Sarah Parkhouse. Oxford: Oxford University Press, 2018, 216–32.
Parkhouse, Sarah, *Eschatology and the Saviour: The Gospel of Mary among Early Christian Dialogue Gospels*, SNTSMS 176. Cambridge: Cambridge University Press, 2019.
Parsons, P. J., 'A School-Book from the Sayce Collection', *ZPE* 6 (1970), 133–49.
Pate, C. Marvin, *Reverse of the Curse: Paul, Wisdom, and the Law*, WUNT I 114. Tübingen: Mohr Siebeck, 2000.
Pearson, Birger A., *Gnosticism and Christianity in Roman and Coptic Egypt*. London: T&T Clark, 2004.
Pearson, Birger A., 'Use, Authority and Exegesis of Mikra in Gnostic Literature', in *Mikra: Text, Translation, Reading and Interpretation of the Hebrew Bible in Ancient Judaism and Early Christianity*, ed. Martin Jan Mulder and Harry Sysling. Peabody, MA: Hendrickson, 2004, 635–52.
Pearson, Birger A., 'Gnosticism as a Religion', in *Was There a Gnostic Religion?*, ed. Antti Marjanen. Helsinki: Finnish Exegetical Society, 2005, 81–101.
Pearson, Birger A., *Ancient Gnosticism: Traditions and Literature*. Minneapolis, MN: Fortress, 2007.
Pearson, Birger, and Søren Giverson (ed.), *Nag Hammadi Codices IX and X*, NHS 15. Leiden: Brill, 1981.
Peel, Malcolm L., 'The Treatise on the Resurrection (I,4)', in *The Nag Hammadi Library in English*, ed. James M. Robinson. Leiden: Brill, 1996^4, 52–57.
Pelikan, Jaroslav, 'The Eschatology of Tertullian', *Church History* 21.2 (1952), 108–22.
Perkins, Pheme, *The Gnostic Dialogue: The Early Church and the Crisis of Gnosticism*. New York: Paulist Press, 1980.
Pétrement, Simone, *A Separate God: The Christian Origins of Gnosticism*, trans. Carol Harrison. San Francisco, CA: Harper & Row, 1990.
Pourkier, A., *L'hérésiologie chez Épiphane de Salamine*, Christianisme antique 4. Paris: Beauchesne, 1992.
Pretty, Robert A., *Adamantius: Dialogue on the True Faith in God, De Recta in Deum Fide*, ed. Garry W. Trompf. Leuven: Peeters, 1997.
Quispel, Gilles, *Ptolémée, Lettre à Flora: Analyse, texte critique, traduction, commentaire et index*, SC 24. Paris: Cerf, 1949–66.
Quispel, Gilles, 'The Origins of the Gnostic Demiurge', in *Gnostic Studies*, Vol. 1, Publications de l'Institut historique et archéologique néerlandais de Stamboul, 34. Istanbul: Dutch Historical and Archaeological Institute, 1974, 213–20.
Rasimus, Tuomas, *Paradise Reconsidered in Gnostic Mythmaking: Rethinking Sethianism in Light of the Ophite Evidence*, NHMS 68. Leiden: Brill, 2009.
Reynders, Bruno, *Lexique comparé du texte Grec et des versions latine, arménienne et syriaque de l' "Adversus Haereses" de Saint Irénée*. Louvain: Durbecq, 1954.
Robinson, James M. (ed.), *The Facsimile Edition of the Nag Hammadi Codices: Codex II*. Leiden: Brill, 1974.
Robinson, James M. (ed.), *The Nag Hammadi Library in English*. Leiden: Brill, 1984^2, 1996^4.

Robinson, James M. 'The Discovery of the Nag Hammadi Codices', *Journal of Coptic Studies* 11 (2009), 1–21.
Robinson Jr., William C., 'The Exegesis on the Soul', *NovT* 12 (1979), 112–17.
van Rossum-Steenbeek, Monique, *Greek Readers' Digests? Studies on a Selection of Subliterary Papyri*. Leiden: Brill, 1998.
Roszak, T., *The Making of a Counter Culture*. Berkeley, CA: UCA Press, 1968.
Roth, Dieter T., *The Text of Marcion's Gospel*, NTTSD 49. Leiden: Brill, 2015.
Roth, Dieter T., 'Evil in Marcion's Conception of the Old Testament God', in *Evil in Second Temple Judaism and Early Christianity*, ed. Chris Keith and Loren T. Stuckenbruck, WUNT II 417. Tübingen: Mohr Siebeck, 2016, 340–56.
Rousseau, Adelin, and Louis Doutreleau (ed.), *Irenée de Lyon, Contre les Hérésies*, 10 vols, SC. Paris, Cerf, 1965–92.
Runia, David, *Creation of the Cosmos according to Moses*. Atlanta, GA: SBL Press, 2005.
Sagnard, F.-M.-M., *La Gnose valentinienne et le témoignage de saint Irénée*, Études de philosophie historique 36. Paris: Vrin, 1947.
van de Sande Bakhuyzen, W. H., *Der Dialog des Adamantius*, GCS 4. Leipzig: Hinrichs, 1901.
Saxon, Deborah Niederer, *The Care of the Self in Early Christian Texts*. Cham: Palgrave Macmillan, 2017.
Schaberg, Jane, *The Resurrection of Mary Magdalene: Legends, Apocrypha, and the Christian Testament*. London: Bloomsbury, 2004.
Schäfer, Peter, *Judeophobia: Attitudes toward the Jews in the Ancient World*. Cambridge, MA: Harvard University Press, 1997.
Scheck, Thomas P., *Jerome's Commentaries on Galatians, Titus, and Philemon*. Notre Dame, IN: University of Notre Dame Press, 2010.
Schenke, H.-M., 'Das sethianische System nach Nag-Hammadi-Handschriften', in *Studia Coptica*, ed. P. Nagel. Berlin: Akademie Verlag, 1974, 165–74.
Schenke, H.-M., 'The Phenomenon and Significance of Gnostic Sethianism', in *The Rediscovery of Gnosticism: Proceedings of the International Conference on Gnosticism at Yale, New Haven, Connecticut, March 28–31, 1978, vol. 2: Sethian Gnosticism*, ed. Bentley Layton. Leiden: Brill, 1981, 588–616.
Scherbenske, Eric W., 'Marcion's Antitheses and the Isagogic Genre', *VC* 64 (2010), 255–79.
Schmid, Herbert, *Die Eucharistie ist Jesus: Anfänge einer Theorie des Sakraments im koptischen Philippusevangelium (NHC II,3)*, VCSupp 88. Leiden: Brill, 2007.
Schmid, Herbert, 'Ist der Soter in Ptolemäus' Epistula ad Floram der Demiurg? Zu einer These von Christoph Markschies', *ZAC* 15 (2011), 249–71.
Schmid, Ulrich, *Marcion und sein Apostolos: Rekonstruktion und historische Einordnung der Marcionitischen Paulusbriefausgabe*. Berlin: de Gruyter, 1995.
Schneiders, Sandra M., *Jesus Risen in Our Midst: Essays on the Resurrection of Jesus in the Fourth Gospel*. Collegeville, MN: Liturgical Press, 2013.
Scholem, Gershom, 'Redemption through Sin', in *The Messianic Idea in Judaism and Other Essays on Jewish Spirituality*. New York: Schocken Books, 1971.
Scopello, Madeleine, 'Jewish and Greek Heroines in the Nag Hammadi Library', in *Images of the Feminine in Gnosticism*, ed. Karen L. King. Harrisburg, PA: Trinity Press International, 2000, 71–90.
Seifrid, Mark A., *Justification by Faith: The Origin and Development of a Central Pauline Theme*, NovTSupp 68. Leiden: Brill, 1992.

Shoemaker, Stephen J., 'Rethinking the "Gnostic Mary": Mary of Nazareth and Mary of Magdala in Early Christian Tradition', *JECS* 9 (2001), 555–95.

Smit Sibinga, Joost, *The Old Testament Text of Justin Martyr*. Leiden: Brill, 1963.

Smith, Richard, 'Sex Education in Gnostic Schools', in *Images of the Feminine in Gnosticism*, ed. Karen L. King. Harrisburg, PA: Trinity Press International, 2000, 354–55.

Stroumsa, Guy, *Another Seed: Studies in Gnostic Mythology*. Leiden: Brill, 1984.

Thomassen, Einar, 'The Platonic and Gnostic "Demiurge"', in *Apocryphon Severini presented to Søren Giversen*, ed. Per Bilde, Helge Kjaer Nielsen and Jorgen Podemann Sorensen. Aarhus: Aarhus University Press, 1993, 227–44.

Thomassen, Einar, *The Spiritual Seed: The Church of the 'Valentinians'*, NHMS 60. Leiden: Brill, 2006.

Thomson, R. W., *Athanasius, Contra Gentes and De Incarnatione*, Oxford Early Christian Texts. Oxford: Oxford University Press, 1971.

Tränkle, Hermann (ed.), *Q.S.F. Tertulliani Adversus Iudaeos mit Einleitung und kritischem Kommentar*. Wiesbaden: Franz Steiner, 1964.

Tsutsui, Kenji, *Die Auseinandersetzung mit den Markioniten im Adamantios-Dialog: Ein Kommentar zu den Büchern I-II*. Berlin: de Gruyter, 2004.

Tuckett, Christopher M., *The Gospel of Mary*. Oxford: Oxford University Press, 2007.

Unger, Dominic J., and John J. Dillon, *St. Irenaeus of Lyons against the Heresies*, ACW 55. New York: Newman, 1992.

van Unnik, W. C., 'Der Fluch der Gekreuzigten: Deuteronomium 21,23 in der Deutung Justinus des Märtyrers', in *Theologia Crucis–Signum Crucis, FS E. Dinkler*, ed. C. Andresen and G. Klein, Tübingen: Mohr Siebeck, 1979, 483–99.

van Unnik, W. C., 'An Interesting Document of Second Century Theological Discussion (Irenaeus, Adv. Haer. 1.10.3)', in *Sparsa Collecta: The Collected Essays of W.C. Van Unnik. Part Four*, NovTSupp 156. Brill: Leiden, 2014, 306–35.

Usher, M. D., *Homeric Stitchings: The Homeric Centos of the Empress Eudocia*. New York: Rowman & Littlefield, 1998.

Vanhoozer, Kevin J., *The Drama of Doctrine: A Canonical Linguistic Approach to Christian Theology*. Louisville, KY: Westminster John Knox, 2005.

Verhasselt, Gertjan, 'The Hypotheses of Euripides and Sophocles by "Dicaearchus"', *GRBS* 55 (2015), 608–36.

Verheyden, J., 'Epiphanius of Salamis on Beasts and Heretics: Some Introductory Comments', in *Heretics and Heresies in the Ancient Church and in Eastern Christianity*, ed. J. Verheyden and H. Teule, Eastern Christian Studies 10. Leuven: Peeters, 2011, 143–73.

Vinzent, Markus, *Marcion and the Dating of the Synoptic Gospels*. Leuven: Peeters, 2014.

Wace, Henry (ed.), *St. Athanasius: Select Works and Letters*, NPNF 4, repr. Grand Rapids, MI: Eerdmans, 1975.

Waldstein, Michael, 'Das Apocryphon des Johannes', in *Nag Hammadi Deutsch. Band 1: NHC I,1-V,1*, ed. Hans-Martin Schenke, Hans-Gebhard Bethge and Ursula Ulrike Kaiser. Berlin: de Gruyter, 2001, 95–150.

Waldstein, Michael, and Frederik Wisse, *The Apocryphon of John: Synopsis of Nag Hammadi Codices II,1: II,1; and IV,1 with BG 8502,2*, NHMS 33. Leiden: Brill, 1995.

Wanke, D., 'Irenäus und die Häretiker in Rom: Thesen zur geschichtlichen Situation von Adversus haereses', *ZAC* 3 (1999), 202–40.

Watson, Francis, and Sarah Parkhouse (ed.), *Connecting Gospels: Beyond the Canonical/Non-Canonical Divide*. Oxford: Oxford University Press, 2018.

Wevers, John William (ed.), *Genesis, Septuaginta: Vetus Testamentum Graecum Auctoritate Academiae Scientiarum Gottingensis editum*. Göttingen: Vandenhoeck & Ruprecht, 1974.
Williams, Francis E., *Mental Perception: A Commentary on NHC VI.4, The Concept of Our Great Power*. Leiden: Brill, 2001.
Williams, Frank, *The Panarion of Epiphanius of Salamis, Book I (Sects 1–46)*, NHS 35. Leiden: Brill, 1987[1], NHMS 63, 2009[2].
Williams, Michael Allen, 'Realized Eschatology in the Gospel of Philip', *ResQ* 14 (1971), 1–17.
Williams, Michael Allen, 'The Demonizing of the Demiurge: The Innovation of Gnostic Myth', in *Innovations in Religious Traditions*, ed. Michael A. Williams, C. Cox and Martin S. Jaffe. Berlin: de Gruyter, 1992, 73–107.
Williams, Michael Allen, *Rethinking 'Gnosticism': An Argument for Dismantling a Dubious Category*. Princeton, NJ: Princeton University Press, 1996.
Wilson, Robert McL., *Gnosis and the New Testament*. Philadelphia, PA: Fortress, 1968.
Wilson, Robert McL., 'Old Testament Exegesis in the Gnostic Exegesis on the Soul', in *Essays on the Nag Hammadi Texts in Honour of Pahor Labib*, ed. Martin Krause. Leiden: Brill, 1975, 217–24.
Wisse, Frederik, 'On Exegeting "The Exegesis on the Soul"', in *Les textes de Nag Hammadi: Colloque du Centre d'Histoire des Religions (Strasbourg, 23–25 octobre 1974)*, ed. Jacques-É. Ménard. Leiden: Brill, 1975, 68–81.
Wucherpfennig, Ansgar, *Heracleon Philologus: Gnostische Johannesexegese im zweiten Jahrhundert*, WUNT I 142. Tübingen: Mohr Siebeck, 2002.
Yinger, J. Milton, *Countercultures: The Promise and the Peril of a World Turned Upside Down*. New York: Free Press, 1982.
Young, Frances, *The Art of Performance: Towards a Theology of Holy Scripture*. London: Darton, Longman & Todd, 1990.
Zuntz, Günther, *The Political Plays of Euripides*. Manchester: Manchester University Press, 1955.

AUTHOR INDEX

Alexander, P. 35, 35 n.10
Ammundsen, V. 156, 156 n.12, 157
Anatolios, K. 2 n.1
Andrews, M. 7 n.1, 122 nn. 4, 5
Arthur, R. H. 142 n.23
Ashton, J. 46 n.1
Attridge, H. W. 25 n.62
Ayres, L. 157, 157 n.18, 157 n.20, 158 n.28, 166 nn.51, 52

Bamberg, M. 121 n.1, 122 n.5
Bar-Kochva, B. 19 n.31
Barc, B. 27 n.66, 33 n.3, 39 n.1, 48 n.5
Barclay, J. M. G. 19 n.31
Barnes, T. D. 79 n.5
Bauer, W. 154, 154 n.2
BeDuhn, J. D. 20 n.35, 20 n.37, 21 n.41, 46 n.2, 58 n.32
Behr, J. 156, 156 n.9, 158 n.27
Bergermann, M. 98 n.7, 103 n.21
Bethge, H.-G. 49 n.10, 55 n.25
Bianchi, U. 14, 14 n.5
Bieringer, R. 139 n.13
Blount, J. A. 4 n.4,
Blowers, P. M. 156, 156 n.10, 165, 165 nn.48, 49, 50, 167
Bonnet, M. 52 n.18
Brakke, D. 3 n.2, 96 n.2
Brankaer, J. 55 n.25
Briggman, A. 157 nn.20, 21, 158 n.28, 160 n.35, 161 n.37, 164, 164 n.43, 165, 165 n.46, 166
van den Broek, R. 14 n.7, 99 n.11, 119 n.69
Bruce, F. F. 16 n.14
Buell, D. K. 123 n.11
Bullard, R. A. 32 n.3, 39 n.1
Bury, R. G. 90 n.30

Cahana-Blum, J. v, vii, 8, 63, 64 n.4, 65 n.5, 70 n.20, 71 n.22, 73 n.26
Cameron, R. 50 n.16

Chapman, D. W. 16 n.18
Clarke, M. L. 157 n.22
Cobb, L. S. 122 n.2, 122 n.6
Collatz, Ch.-F. 98 n.7, 103 n.21
Connolly, R. H. 17 n.19
Coquin, R.-G. 3 n.2
Creech, D. 31 n.2
Cribiore, R. 157 n.22, 158 n.24
Cristea, H.-J. 150 n.41

Davis, E. 165 n.47
de Andia, Y. 155 n.4, 164 n.45
de Boer, E. 90 n.29
DeConick, A. D. 95 n.1
Dekkers, D. E. 17 n.20
Denzey Lewis, N. 4 n.4, 31 n.1, 149 nn.39, 40
Dillon, J. J. 155 n.5
Doutreleau, L. 48 n.6, 63 n.1, 155 n.3
Droge, A. 145 n.30
Dubois, J.-D. 53 n.20
Dunderberg, I. 69 n.17, 90 n.29, 100 n.13, 101 nn.18, 19, 138 n.10, 139 n.12, 140 n.17
Dunn, G. D. 79 n.5, 85 n.17, 85 n.18, 88 n.26

Edwards, M. J. 128 n.32
Ehrman, B. D. 69 n.17
Elliott, J. K. 17 n.19, 46 n.2, 50 n.16
Endsjø, D. Ø. 122, 123, 123 nn.7, 8
Engel, A. 71 n.22
Evans, E. 59 n.33
van den Eynde, D. 156 n.12

Fallon, F. T. 109 n.37
Feine, P. D. 16 n.17
Fine, M. 93 n.36
Foerster, W. 98 nn.7, 8, 100 n.12
Fossum, J. 14, 14 n.6
Foster, P. 53 n.21

Fowler, K. A. vi, vii, 9, 133, 141 n.20, 149 nn.39, 40
Fraipont, I. 17 n.20
Funk, W.-P. 27 n.66, 48 n.5

Gallagher, E. L. 3 n.2
Gaudard, F. 64 n.3
Gilhus, I. S. 14, 14 n.5, 31 n.1
Goehring, J. 28 n.71, 149, 150 n.41
Gonzalez, E. 93 n.35
Goodacre, M. v, vii, 4 n.4, 6, 7, 31
Grant, R. M. 158 n.28

Hägglund, B. 156 n.14
Hardy, E. R. 2 n.1
von Harnack, A. 46 n.2, 20, 20 n.36, 21 n.41
Harris, A. 93 n. 36
Hartenstein, J. 49 n.10, 79 n.3, 83 n.12, 84, 84 nn.13, 14
Hays, R. B. 165 n.47
Head, R. 54 n.22
Heil, J. P. 139 n.13
Heimola, M. 130 n.45, 137 n.8
Hengel, M. 18 nn.24, 25
Holl, K. 59 n.33, 103 n.21, 104 n.23
Holsinger Friesen, T. 48 n.7
Hooker, M. 19 n.32
Horsley, R. A. 96 n.3
Hultgren, A. J. 16 n.17
Hyvärinen, M. 122 n.4

Iricinschi, E. 149 nn.39, 40

Jacobi, C. 125 n.19, 130 n.43
Jenott, L. 4 n.5, 64 n.4, 149 nn.39, 40
Jonas, H. 70, 70 nn.18, 19, 20, 71, 71 n.22, 72 n.25
Jorgensen, D. 157 nn.20, 21, 166 n.51
Junod, E. 52 n.18, 52 n.19, 54 n.23, 55 n.24

Kaestli, J.-D. 52 n.18
Kaiser, U. U. 28 n.71, 49 n.10
Kasser, R. 64 n.3, 67 n.9, 133 n.2
Kelly, J. N. D. 156 n.11
Kim, R. Y. 98 n.6
Kim, S. 16 n.17
King, K. L. 28 n.71, 43 n.18, 46 n.2, 64 n.4, 69 n.16, 79, 79 n.4, 80, 80 n.6, 83 n.12, 88 n.24, 89 n.27, 93, 93 n.37, 106 n.29, 133 n.3, 137 n.9
Koester, C. R. 139 n.13
Koetschau, P. 18 n.29
Kraus, T. J. 50 n.16
Krause, M. 142 n.22, 144, 144 n.27, 145 n.29
Krosney, H. 64 n.3, 67 n.9
Kroymann, A. 23 n.53
Kruger, M. J. 50 n.16
Kugel, J. L. 18 n.24
Kuhn, H.-W. 16 n.18

Labib, P. 32 n.3, 144 n.27
Lahe, J. 99 n.11, 106 n.29
Lampe, P. 101 n.18, 103 n.20
Lawson, R.P. 167 n.53
Layton, B. 32 nn.3, 4, 5, 6, 33 nn.1, 2, 33, 33 n.7, 35 n.10, 38, 38 n.12, 39 n.1, 42 n.16, 44 n.19, 98 nn.7, 8, 100 n.12, 128 n.33, 144, 145 n.29, 148 n.37
Le Boulluec, A. 112 n.43, 115 n.55
Lefort, L.-Th. 3 n.2
Lehtipuu, O. vi, vii, 8, 9, 91 n.33, 92 n.34, 121, 123 n.8, 125 n.20, 126 nn.23, 24, 127 n.27, 131 n.47, 136 n.4, 138, 138 n.11, 141, 141 n.19, 142, 142 n.21, 147 n.31
Lieu, J. 15 n.12, 18 n.27, 20 nn.35, 36, 21 n.39, 59 n.34
Lincoln, A. T. 139 nn.13, 14, 140, 140 nn.15, 16, 141 n.18
Lindars, B. 16 n.18
Litwa, M. D. v, vii, 6, 13, 14 n.8
Logan, A. H. B. 99 n.11
Löhr, W. A. 18 n.27, 98 n.7, 99 n.11, 100 n.13, 101 n.19, 104 n.22, 105 nn.24, 25, 112 n.46, 113 nn.47, 48, 116 n.61, 117 n.62, 119 n.67
Lohse, B. 113 n.49
Longenecker, R. N. 17 n.22, 139 n.13
Lüdemann, G. 105 n.25, 120 n.70
Lührmann, D. 84 n.13
Lundhaug, H. 4 n.5, 126 n.25, 128 n.35, 136 n.4, 137, 137 n.8, 142 nn.22, 23, 143, 143 nn.24, 25, 144, 144 n.26, 145 n.29, 148 n.38, 149 nn.39, 40, 150 n.41
Luttikhuizen, G. P. 26 n.63, 26 n.64, 42 n.16

Author Index

MacDonald, N. 165 n.50
Mansfeld, J. 14, 14 n.7
Marjanen, A. 18 n.29, 83 n. 12
Markschies, C. 99 n.11, 100 n.13, 101 nn.18, 19, 104 n.22, 105 nn.24, 25, 26, 107 n.30, 108 nn.34, 35, 110 n.41, 116 n.58, 119 n.68, 153 n.1
Marrou, H. 157 n.22
Martínez, F. G. 16 n.18
May, G. 18 n.27, 20 n.35, 100 n.13
McGlothlin, T. D. 136 n.4
McGuire, A. 32 n.6, 35 n.9, 43 n.18, 153 n.1
Meade, J. D. 3 n.2
Meeks, W. 165, 165 n.48, 167
Meijering, R. 158 n.24, 158 n.26
Meyer, M. 46 n.2, 64 n.3, 66, 66 n.8
Miles, J. 18
Moreschini, C. 23 n.52
Morgan, T. 159, 159 nn.30, 31
Mutua, K. 122 n.3

Nel, M. J. 75 n.30
Neuschäfer, B. 157 n.19
Nickelsburg, G.W. 123 n.7
Nicklas, T. 50 n.16
Nienhuis, D. R. 57 n.28
Norden, E. 103 n.20
Norelli, E. 23 n.52
Norris, R. A. 158 n.28
Nünlist, R. 161 n.39

O'Brien, K. S. 16 n.18
Ohme, H. 155 n.6
Osborn, E. 80 n.8, 88, 88 n.26, 155, 156 n.8

Paffenroth, K. 67 n.11
Pagels, E. 14, 14 n.4, 64 n.4, 69 n.16, 79 n.3, 149 nn.39, 40, 163 n.42
Painchaud, L. 64 n.4
Parkhouse, S. iii, iv, v, vii, 1, 5 n.7, 7, 8, 39 n.1, 77, 82 n.11, 84 n.15, 88 n.25, 89 n.28
Parsons, P. J. 159 n.29
Pearson, B. A. 18 n.29, 37 n.11, 49 n.13, 100 n.13, 145 n.30
Peel, M. L. 125 n.18
Pelikan, J. 87, 87 n.23
Perkins, P. 79 n.3

Pétrement, S. 15 n.12, 105 n.25
Pourkier, A. 98 n.8
Pretty, R. A. 21 n.43

Quispel, G. 13, 14 n.3, 14 n.7, 98 n.7, 101 n.16, 101 n.19, 103 n.20, 104 n.23, 105 nn.24, 25, 26, 107 n.31, 108 n.33, 109 n.36, 109 n.38, 110 nn.40, 41, 42, 112 nn.43, 44, 45, 113 nn.47, 48, 114 n.50, 114 nn.52, 53, 115 n.54, 55, 56, 116 nn.60, 61, 117 nn.62, 63, 64

Rasimus, T. 28 n. 72, 90 n.29
Reynders, B. 167 n.54
Roberge, M. 32 n.3, 39 n.1
Robinson, J. M. 4 n.4, 28 n.71, 32 n.3, 125 n.18
Robinson Jr., W. C. 144, 144 n.28
van Rossum-Steenbeek, M. 158 n.26
Roszak, T. 95 n.1
Roth, D. T. 20 n.36, 27 n.68, 59 n.33, 60 n.35, 61 nn. 37, 38, 39, 40, 41
Rousseau, A. 155 n.3, 18 n.29, 48 n.6, 63 n.1
Runia, D. 19 n.33

Sagnard, F.-M.-M. 160 n.34, 100 n.13, 101 n.17, 103 n.20, 106 n.27, 110 n.39, 112 nn.43, 44, 114 n.50, 116 n.57, 116 n.61, 117 nn.64, 65, 119 n.66
van de Sande Bakhuyzen, W. H. 21 n.43
Saxon, D. N. 64 nn.4, 5
Schaberg, J. 79 n.3
Schäfer, P. 19 n.30
Scheck, T. P. 16 nn.14, 15
Schenke, H.-M. 32, 32 n.6, 49 n.10
Scherbenske, E. W. 20 n.36
Schmid, H. 108 n. 35, 129 n.40, 130 n.43
Schmid, U. 20 n.37
Schneiders, S. M. 139 n.13
Scholem, G. 63, 64 n.2, 71, 71 n.22, 72 nn.23, 25
Scopello, M. 64 n.4, 66 n.8, 133, 133 n.3
Seifrid, M. A. 16 n.17, 17 n.22
Shoemaker, S. J. 83 n.12
Smit Sibinga, J. 23 n.48
Smith, R. 142 n.23
Stroumsa, G. 15 n.11, 28 n.71

Thomassen, E. 14, 14 n.9, 99 n.11, 100 nn.13, 14, 136 n.4, 138 n.10
Thomson, R. W. 2 n.1
Tränkle, H. 23 n.52
Tsutsui, K. 26 n.65, 27 n.68
Tuckett, C. M. 79 n.3, 84 n. 13, 86 nn.20, 21, 87 n.22, 89 n.24

Unger, D. J. 165 n.5
van Unnik, W. C. 23 n.51, 158 n.28
Usher, M. D. 160 n.33

Vanhoozer, K. J. 165 n.47
Verhasselt, G. 158 n.25
Verheyden, J. v, vii, 7, 8, 95, 99 n.9
Vinzent, M. 58 n.32, 150 n.41

Waldstein, M. 47 n. 3, 49 n.10
Wanke, D. 100 n.12

Watson, F. iii, iv, v, vii, 1, 7, 39 n.1, 45, 82 n.11
Wevers, J. W. 15 n.13
Williams, F. E. 25 n.62, 66 n.7
Williams, F. 24 n.56, 24 n.57, 59 n.33, 98 n.7
Williams, M. A. 13 n.1, 14, 15, 15 nn.10, 11, 18 n.28, 49 n.14, 99 n. 11, 103 n.21, 107 nn.30, 31, 112 n.44, 136 n.5, 137 n.9
Wilson, R. M. 98 n.7, 144, 144 n.27, 145 n.29, 163 n.42
Wisse, F. 47 n.3, 142 n.23, 144, 145 n.29
Wucherpfennig, A. 157 n.19
Wurst, G. 64 n.3

Yinger, J. M. 95 n.1
Young, F. 77 n.1, 96 n.2, 155, 155 n.7, 165

Zuntz, G. 158 n.24, 164 n.44

SUBJECT INDEX

Acts of John
    and incompatibility between the God of the Hebrew Bible and Jesus 46, 46 n.2, 52, 52 n.18, 53–5, 62
    and the law 6
    and 'polymorphic Christology' 53 n.1
    and resurrection 131
Adam
    and antithesis with Christ 2–3, 5
    and *Apocalypse of Adam* 73 n.27
    and *ApocrJn* 47–8
    and divine curse 6, 13, 26, 26 n.65, 27, 27 n.66, 28, 28 n.72, 29, 31
    and *HypArch* 6, 35–8, 38 n.13, 39–42, 44
aeon(s)
    and Epiphanius 100
    in *GJudas* 69
    and Ptolemaeans 99 n.10
    in *The Concept of Our Great Power* 66
    in *TrRes* 126, 126 n.22
angel(s)
    and 'angel marriages' 47
    and *Apocalypse of Adam* 73 n.27
    and expulsion of rebel angels 10 n.9
    and *GJudas* 63, 68, 70, 73
    and *HypArch* 27 n.66
Apocalypse (see also *1ApocJas*)
    Apocalypse of Adam 73 n.27
    Apocalypse of Peter 6, 25
    Apocalypse of John 47
Apocryphon of James
    and God's curse 25
Apocryphon of John
    and divine curse 6, 25 n.60, 27
    and *GJudas* 72 n.24
    and *HypArch* 31, 32
    and incompatibility between the God of the Hebrew Bible and Jesus 7, 46–7, 47 n.4, 48, 48 n.5, 49–51, 58, 61–2
    and the law 6

apostles
    in *Adv. Haer.* 74 n.28
    and fleshly resurrection 92
    and *GMary* 79, 83–5, 92
    ignorance of male apostles 81, 83, 93
    and Tertullian 81, 83, 85, 91 n.33, 92–3
archons
    as the devil 45
    and the divine curse 25
    in *GJudas* 8, 65–6, 66 n.7, 70
    in *HypArch* 34, 42
Athanasius
    as formulator of 'orthodoxy' 2–6
    Thirty-Ninth Festal Letter 3, 3 n.2, 149
authority
    of *ApocrJn* 48
    apostolic 108, 123, 125, 127, 130–1, 161, 163, 166–7
    in *GMary* 78–9, 81, 83–5, 85 n.16, 92–3
    of husbands/men 44, 144
    and 'proto-orthodoxy' 77 n.1
    and Ptolemy 104, 112, 114, 118, 120
    scriptural 52, 104, 130, 145, 166

body
    and the divine curse 19 n.34
    in *GMary* 81, 90–1
    in *GPhil* 130
    and Ptolemy 108, 114
    and resurrection 8–9, 122–3, 123 n.8, 124, 126–7, 127 n.27, 130, 132–3, 135–6, 140–2, 144, 150, 150 n.41, 153
    in *TrRes* 126–7

Christology
    docetic 52–3
    polymorphic 53, 53 n.21
Clement of Alexandria 50 n.16, 57 n.30, 116–17

and orthodoxy 77, 77 n.1, 112 n.44
and Valentinians 124, 124 n.12
crucifixion 18
  in *AcJohn* 55
  and the divine curse 21 n.43, 25, 25 n.61, 28
  in *GJudas* 65, 67, 67 n.11, 70, 74
  and negative demiurgy 15 n.12
  as proof of opposition between the God of Israel and Jesus 54
  and resurrection 132, 139
codex
  Berlin (BG) 5, 77–8, 82–4, 86, 90–1
  Tchacos (CT) 5, 26 n.63, 46 n.2, 55 n. 25, 56, 56 n. 26, 57, 57 n.27, 58, 58 n.31, 64 n.3
Colossians
  and *HypArch* 32
1 Corinthians
  and divine curse 14, 17 n.21, 25, 29
  and *ExegSoul* 144, 144 n.26
  and Ptolemy 114–15
  and resurrection 127 n.26, 130 n.41, 130 n.44, 136–6, 138
2 Corinthians
  and *ExegSoul* 144 n.26
  and resurrection 127 n.26, 128 n.31
  and Tertullian 87
counter-narratives 5, 8–9
  definition 95–97, 121–2, 132, 154
  and heterodoxy and orthodoxy 79–81, 92–3
  and Irenaeus's rule of truth 153–4, 165, 168
  in *Letter to Flora* 103–4, 107 n.30, 109, 116, 120
  and 'negative demiurgy' 13
  and resurrection 124, 127, 129–30, 132, 134–5, 149–50
curse (*see also* crucifixion *and* negative demiurgy)
  definition 17
  as divine action 6, 13, 16, 19, 25–6
  in early Patristic thought 22–4
  and Eden 26 n.65, 27–8, 28 n.72
  and *HypArch* 37–8, 44
  and Jesus 13, 15–16, 19, 29, 29 n.29
  and Marcion 20–1, 21 n.41, 42, 22
  and Philo of Alexandria 19, 19 n.34

death 1–3, 8, 52
  in *ExegSoul* 134, 144, 148, 150–1
  in *GJohn* 139–41, 148, 150
  in *GMary* 89
  in *GPhilip* 128–9, 136–7, 137 n.8, 148
  of James 58
  of Jesus 22, 25, 26 n.64
  penalty 60
  in *Rom* 138
  in Tertullian, *Res.* 90
  in *TrRes* 124–8, 135
demiurge 14
  in *Letter to Flora* 108, 112 n.43, 113 n.48, 116–18
  and 'negative demiurgy' 6, 13–5, 15 n.12, 29
Deuteronomy, Book of
  and divine curse 17, 17 n.19, 17 nn.22–3, 18, 19 n.34, 20–4
  and *HypArch* 34
  and Marcion 60
disciples 7–8, 25, 45, 153
  in *1ApocJames* 56
  in *Adv. Haer.* 163, 166–7
  in *AcJohn* 52, 54–5
  in *ApocrJn* 50–1
  in *GJudas* 63–5, 67, 67 n.11, 68–9, 72–5, 75 n.30
  in *GMarcion* 61
  in *GMary* 82–5
  in *GMatthew* 56
  in *GThomas* 57

Ephesians
  and divine curse 28
  and *ExegSoul* 144 n.26
  and *HypArch* 32–3
  and Ptolemy 115
  and *TrRes* 125 n.21
Epiphanius 7, 24, 59 n.33, 61 n.41, 98, 98 nn.6, 7, 8, 99–103, 118, 149
  Panarion 21 n. 41, 24 n.56–7, 28 n.72, 59 n.33, 98, 98 nn.6–7, 99, 124 n.13 149
  and Ptolemy/*Letter to Flora* 98–103, 118
eschatology 6
  in *ExegSoul* 9, 134, 136 n.5, 141, 150
  synoptic 87

Eve 6, 13
  in *Apocalypse of Adam* 73 n.27
  in *ApocrJn* 47–8
  and the divine curse 26–7, 27 n.66, 28, 28 nn.71, 72
  in *HypArch* 35, 38–42, 44
  and Tertullian 85 n.16
evil
  and creator god 6, 13, 14 n.8, 19–20, 27
  and cursing 17, 27
  in *GMary* 82
  and God in *GJudas* 8, 64, 67 n.11
  in *HypArch* 37, 40
  in *Letter to Flora* 108–10, 112–14, 117
Exegesis on the Soul
  and *GJohn* 134, 141–2, 144–50
  and resurrection 6, 9–10, 128, 133–5, 137–51

female
  authority in *GMary* 78, 84, 85 n.16
  Barbelo 49
  gender of the soul in *ExegSoul* 133, 142, 142 n.23, 143
  principle in *HypArch* 28 n.72, 38, 41
First Apocalypse of James
  and divine curse 26
  and incompatibility between the God of the Hebrew Bible and Jesus 7, 46, 55–7, 62

Galatians
  and divine curse 6, 13, 15, 15 n.12, 16, 16 n.14, 17 n.21, 19–22, 24, 26
Genesis, Book of
  and *ApocrJn* 47–9, 51, 62
  and divine curse 13, 15, 26–9
  and *ExegSoul* 144, 144 n.26
  and *HypArch* 6–7, 31, 33, 35–44
  and the rule of truth 10
gnostic/Gnosticism 10, 14–15, 26, 32, 38, 49
  and crucifixion 65
  and *ExegSoul* 133, 150
  and *GJudas* 66, 71, 72 nn.24, 25, 73 n.27, 75 n.30
  and *GMary* 79
  and *Letter to Flora* 98 n.8, 100 n.13, 105, 109 nn.36, 38, 110 n.41
  and 'libertinism' 70, 70 n.20

Hebrews
  and divine curse 19
heterodoxy 7–8, 77–9, 84, 89, 92–3
Hosea, Book of
  and *ExegSoul* 144
Hypostasis of the Archons
  and *Col* and *Eph* 33
  and divine curse 27 n.67, 27 n.69, 28, 28 n.72
  and *Isa* 34
  and *Gen* 5–7, 31, 35–44
  and Seth 32

Irenaeus 9–10, 28, 48–9, 63, 73–4, 77, 77 n.1, 98 n.8, 100 n.12, 102, 117 n.64, 119 n.66, 123
  Adv. Haer. 18 n.29, 26 n.63, 26 n.65, 28 n.73, 48 nn.6–9, 63 n.1, 73 n.27, 74 n.28, 105 n.24, 110 n.40, 119, 123 n.10, 136 n.6, 137, 154–5, 162–7
  and literary criticism 157–63
  and rule of truth 153–6, 163–7
Israel
  God of 34, 46, 51, 54, 56–9, 72
Isaiah, Book of
  and *ExegSoul* 144
  and *HypArch* 34
  and Marcion 27 n.68, 60
Immortality 2, 122–3, 135, 138–9, 141

1 John
  and *Gen* 48
John, Gospel of
  and *ExegSoul* 134, 141–2, 144–50
  and *GMary* 81, 83, 85–6, 88, 91
  and incompatibility between the God of the Hebrew Bible and Jesus 45, 46 n.1
  and Ptolemy 108, 118
  and resurrection 9, 129–31, 134, 138–42, 144–51
  and 'rule of truth' 162, 163 n.42, 164
Judas, Gospel of
  and counter-narrative to sacrifice 69, 69 n.17
  and disciples 64
  and Irenaeus 63
  and salvation 64–7
  and salvific sin 71–4

Justin Martyr 23–24, 77 n.1 101 n.18, 105 n.25, 109 n.37, 112 n.43, 115 n.55, 120 n.70, 157
  Dialogue with Trypho 16, 16 n.16, 22, 22 n.45, 22 n.47, 23 n.49, 23 n.51, 110 n.40, 127–28, 157 n.22
  First Apology 22 n.44

law
  in *AcJohn* 54–5
  in *Adv. Marc.* 59–60
  and the divine curse 26
  in *GMarcion* 61
  God's 2, 6, 53
  and grace 45
  in *GJudas* 72
  and Moses 7, 45, 110
  and Ptolemy 10, 110–13
Leviticus, Book of
  and divine curse 17 n.23
Luke, Gospel of
  and *ApocrJn* 50
  and *ExegSoul* 144 n.26, 147
  and *GMary* 84, 87 n.22
  and Marcion 58 n.32, 59 n.3, 60–1

male
  adulterer in *ExegSoul* 143
  authority (of apostles/disciples) 79, 81–5, 93
  genitalia 142, 142 n.23
  saviour in *ExegSoul* 133
Marcionite Gospel
  and *GLuke* 61
  and incompatibility between the God of the Hebrew Bible and Jesus 59, 61–2
  and Tertullian 59, 59 n.33
Mark, Gospel of Mark
  and *GMary* 84, 87
Matthew, Gospel of
  and *ExegSoul* 144 n.26
  and *GJudas* 73 n.27
  and *GMary* 84, 86–8
  and *1ApocJames* 56
  and Marcionite Gospel 61
  and Ptolemy 102
Mary
  in *GMary* 77–9, 81–5, 88–9
  Magdalene 81, 83, 83 n.12
  Virgin 57 n. 29
Mary, Gospel of (see also soul)
  and *GJohn* 81, 83, 85–6, 88, 91
  and *GJudas* 65
  and intentional heterodoxy 7–8, 77–8, 79 n.3, 80–93
Monastic 3–4
  and Nag Hammadi codices 134–5
  Pachomian monks 149
Moses 5
  in *1ApocJas* 57
  in *ApocrJn* 47, 47 n.4, 48 n.5, 49, 51
  in *GMarcion* 59–60
  as 'lawgiver' 6–7, 45–7, 62
  in *Letter to Flora* 102, 109–16

Nag Hammadi Codices 4 n.4, 5 n.6, 9, 25 n.62, 28 n.71, 31, 33 n.1, 37, 41 n.15, 46 n.2, 48, 77, 128, 133, 145 n.29, 148 n.37, 149
  and Pachomian monks 8–10, 149, 150 n.41
  and resurrection 121, 124, 127, 134–5, 137
Numbers, Book of
  and divine curse 17 n.20

Old Testament/Hebrew Bible
  and the divine curse 16–18, 24
  in *ExegSoul* 147
  and *GJudas* 65
  and *GMary* 86
  in *HypArch* 34, 34 n.8, 35, 39
  and Nag Hammadi 5
  in opposition to Jesus Christ 45
Origen 123, 134, 149, 154, 163, 167
  Contra Celsum 28 n. 72, 57 n. 30, 123, 123 n.9
  and divine curse 17 n.23, 21 nn.41–2, 26 n.65, 27 n.68, 28 n. 72
  and *ExegSoul* 149 n.40
  and resurrection 134
orthodoxy
  'Alexandrian' 149, 151
  and Christologies 53
  and 'counter-narrative' 6, 8–9, 154
  and *ExegSoul* 134, 150
  and *Gen* 31
  and *GJudas* 67 n.11

Subject Index 191

and *GMary* 78–80, 80 n.7, 83–4, 85 n.19, 86–8, 91–3
and *HypArch* 32
lack of in early Christianity 77, 77 n.1
and Ptolemy 106

Paul, Apostle 2, 5–6
and the divine curse 13, 15–17, 19, 24–5
and *GJudas* 74
and Irenaeus 154, 163
and Ptolemy 114–15, 115 nn.55, 56, 116, 117 n.64, 120, 124
and resurrection 125–6, 130, 135, 138
and rule of truth 156
in Tertullian 89, 91 n.33
1 Peter
and divine curse 19
Peter, Apostle 5
in *Apocalypse of Peter* 6, 25
in *Apocryphon of James* 25
in *GMary* 7–8, 77–9, 81–4
in *GMatt* 56
Philip, Gospel of
and Origen 150 n. 41
and resurrection 8, 121, 124, 128–32, 135–8, 145, 148, 151
Philo of Alexandria
and the divine curse 26 n.65
and evil 19, 19 nn.33, 34
and the law 109 n.37
and the soul 142 n.22
Plato 14, 89–91
Phaedo 90
Republic 19
Timaeus 90, 90 n.30
Ptolemy 7, 98 n.8, 99–120, 124
Letter to Flora 6–7, 10, 95, 98, 103

Refutatio omnium haeresium (*Philosophoumena*) 14 n.8, 27 n.68, 28 n.72
resurrection (*see also* body, eschatology, *ExegSoul, GJohn, GPhilip*, Paul, soul, *TrRes*)
in *1ApocJas* 56
bodily 3, 122, 123 n.7, 132, 135, 150, 150 n.41
of flesh 122, 126–7, 129–30, 132, 134, 137, 141

in *GJudas* 67
in *GMary* 92–3, 93 n.35
and immortality 123
and 'orthodoxy' 79, 87, 89–91, 91 n.33, 124
and sacraments 137
Revelation
and *ApocrJn* 47
Romans
and divine curse 17 n.21
and *GJudas* 74, 74 n.29
and Ptolemy 115
and resurrection 125 n.21, 127 n.26, 135, 138
rule of faith
in Irenaeus 5–6, 155, 155 n.6
in Tertullian 79–81, 81 n.9, 85–7, 89, 91
rule of truth (*see also* Irenaeus) 9, 80 n.8
as anti-Valentinian 'counter-narrative' 153–6, 159, 161, 167–8
and the plot of scripture 163–7

scripture (*see also* authority and *rule of truth*) 8
Christian 28
in *ExegSoul* 134, 144–5
in *GMary* 85–9
Jewish 15, 46, 61
and Marcion 60
and theodicy 18 n.28
and Tertullian 85, 85 n.19, 86, 88–92
Seth
in *ApocrJn* 47
Second Treatise of Great Seth 5–6, 25, 28
in *HypArch* 32, 32 n.6
sin
in *ExegSoul* 142, 147–8
in *GJudas* 71, 72 n.24, 74, 74 n.29
in *GMary* 88 n.24
in *HypArch* 34
and the law 115
soul
in *ExegSoul* 9, 134, 141–2, 144, 146–8, 149 n.40, 151
in *GMary* 8, 78–9, 81–2, 88, 88 n.24, 89–90, 90 n.29, 91–2
in *HypArch* 44
and Philo of Alexandria 19 n.33, 142 n.22

and Ptolemy 114
and immortality/resurrection 122–3, 130, 147
in *TrRes* 127, 127 n.27
spirit
  ExegSoul 144
  in *TrRes* 127, 127 n.27, 130, 135–6
synoptic gospels (*see also* GMatthew, GMark, GLuke) 52–3, 55, 73 n.27, 86–7

Tertullian 21, 23, 23 n.52–5, 59–60, 77, 80, 80 n.7, 81, 85 nn.16, 17, 18, 19, 87–92, 99 n.11, 115 n.52, 137
  Adversus Marcionem 18 n.27, 21 n.38, 21 nn.42–3, 27 n.68, 59, 59 n.33, 60
  and *GJohn* 88, 91
  and *GMary* 81 n.9, 83–5, 87–92
  Prescription against Heretics 81, 83–5, 87, 89, 91–2
  On the Resurrection 87, 90–1, 91 n.33, 137
1 Thessalonians
  and *ExegSoul* 144 n.26

and *HypArch* 33
and resurrection 87
Thomas, apostle 5
  GThomas 31–2, 51, 57
2 Timothy
  and Ptolemy 118
  and resurrection 138
  and *TrRes* 128 n.31
Treatise on the Resurrection
  and resurrection 8–9, 121, 124–8, 130–2, 135, 137, 145, 147 n.31, 150 n.41, 151
  and Tertullian 92 n.34
Trimorphic Protennoia
  and divine curse 25, 25 n.61

Valentinian/Valentinus (*see also* rule of truth *and* Irenaeus 8–10, 14, 136 n.6
  and *ExegSoul* 137 n.6, 138 n.10
  and Ptolemy 99 n.11, 100 n.13, 108, 112 n.43, 113 n.47, 124
  and the rule of truth 153–5, 157, 159–61, 161 n.36, 162–4, 164 n.45, 165–6, 168

www.ingramcontent.com/pod-product-compliance
Lightning Source LLC
Chambersburg PA
CBHW070638300426
44111CB00013B/2151